PUBLIC IDENTITY

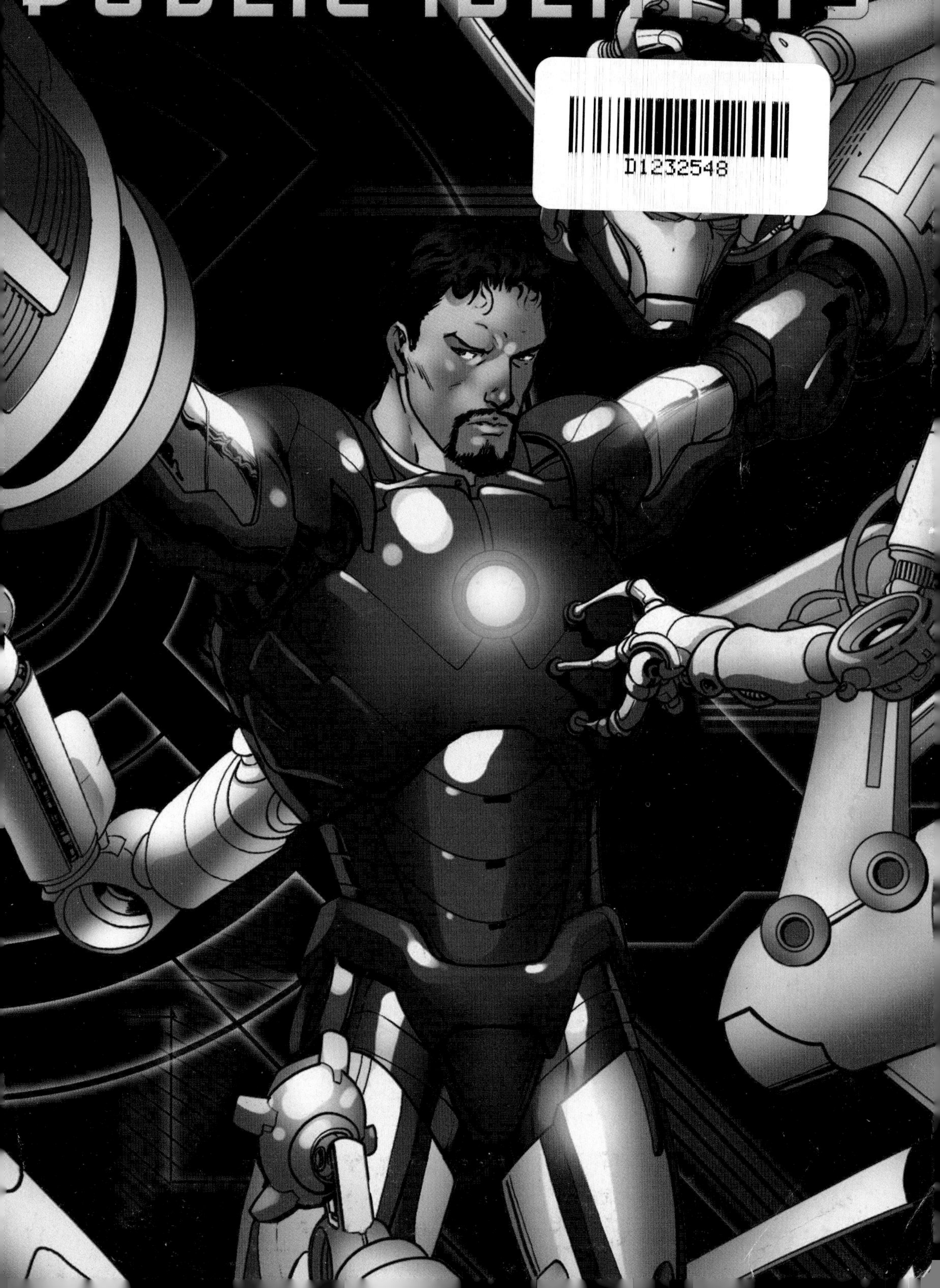

PUBLIC IDENTITY

PLOT: **JOE CASEY & JUSTIN THEROUX**
SCRIPT: **JOE CASEY**
PENCILS: **BARRY KITSON & RON LIM**
INKERS: **BARRY KITSON** WITH TOM PALMER, VICTOR OLAZABA, STEFANO GAUDIANO & MATTHEW SOUTHWORTH
COLORS: **MATT MILLA**
LETTERS: **VC'S CLAYTON COWLES**
COVER ART: **ADI GRANOV**

IRON MAN 2: AGENTS OF S.H.I.E.L.D.
WRITER: **JOE CASEY**
COVER ART: **SALVADOR LARROCA**

"WHO MADE WHO"
ARTIST: **TIM GREEN II**
COLORS: **JUAN DOE**
LETTERS: **VC'S JOE CARAMAGNA**

"JUST OFF THE FARM"
ARTIST: **FELIX RUIZ**
COLORS: **IAN HANNIN**
LETTERS: **VC'S CLAYTON COWLES**

"PROXIMITY"
ARTIST: **MATT CAMP**
COLORS: **IAN HANNIN**
LETTERS: **VC'S CLAYTON COWLES**

ASSISTANT EDITOR: **ALEJANDRO ARBONA**
EDITOR: **RALPH MACCHIO**
SPECIAL THANKS TO BRAD WINDERBAUM, JEREMY LATCHAM & WILL PILGRIM

COLLECTION EDITOR: **JENNIFER GRÜNWALD**
EDITORIAL ASSISTANTS: **JAMES EMMETT & JOE HOCHSTEIN**
ASSISTANT EDITORS: **ALEX STARBUCK & NELSON RIBEIRO**
EDITOR, SPECIAL PROJECTS: **MARK D. BEAZLEY**
SENIOR EDITOR, SPECIAL PROJECTS: **JEFF YOUNGQUIST**
SENIOR VICE PRESIDENT OF SALES: **DAVID GABRIEL**

EDITOR IN CHIEF: **JOE QUESADA**
PUBLISHER: **DAN BUCKLEY**
EXECUTIVE PRODUCER: **ALAN FINE**

MARVEL STUDIOS

IRON MAN 2

WITHDRAWN

PUBLIC IDENTITY

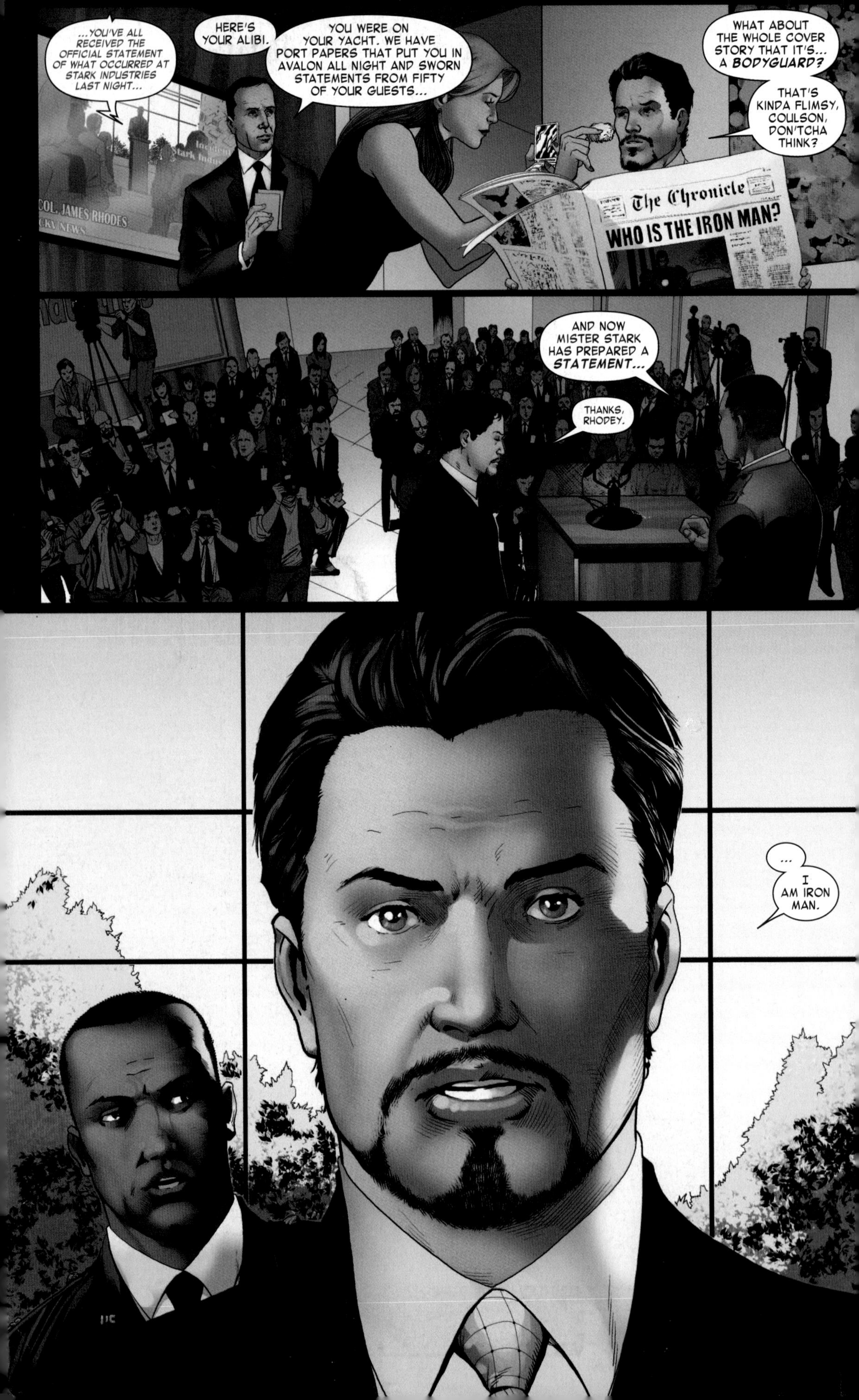
...YOU'VE ALL RECEIVED THE OFFICIAL STATEMENT OF WHAT OCCURRED AT STARK INDUSTRIES LAST NIGHT...
COL. JAMES RHODES
HERE'S YOUR ALIBI.
YOU WERE ON YOUR YACHT. WE HAVE PORT PAPERS THAT PUT YOU IN AVALON ALL NIGHT AND SWORN STATEMENTS FROM FIFTY OF YOUR GUESTS...
WHAT ABOUT THE WHOLE COVER STORY THAT IT'S... A BODYGUARD?
THAT'S KINDA FLIMSY, COULSON, DON'TCHA THINK?
The Chronicle
WHO IS THE IRON MAN?
AND NOW MISTER STARK HAS PREPARED A STATEMENT...
THANKS, RHODEY.
... I AM IRON MAN.

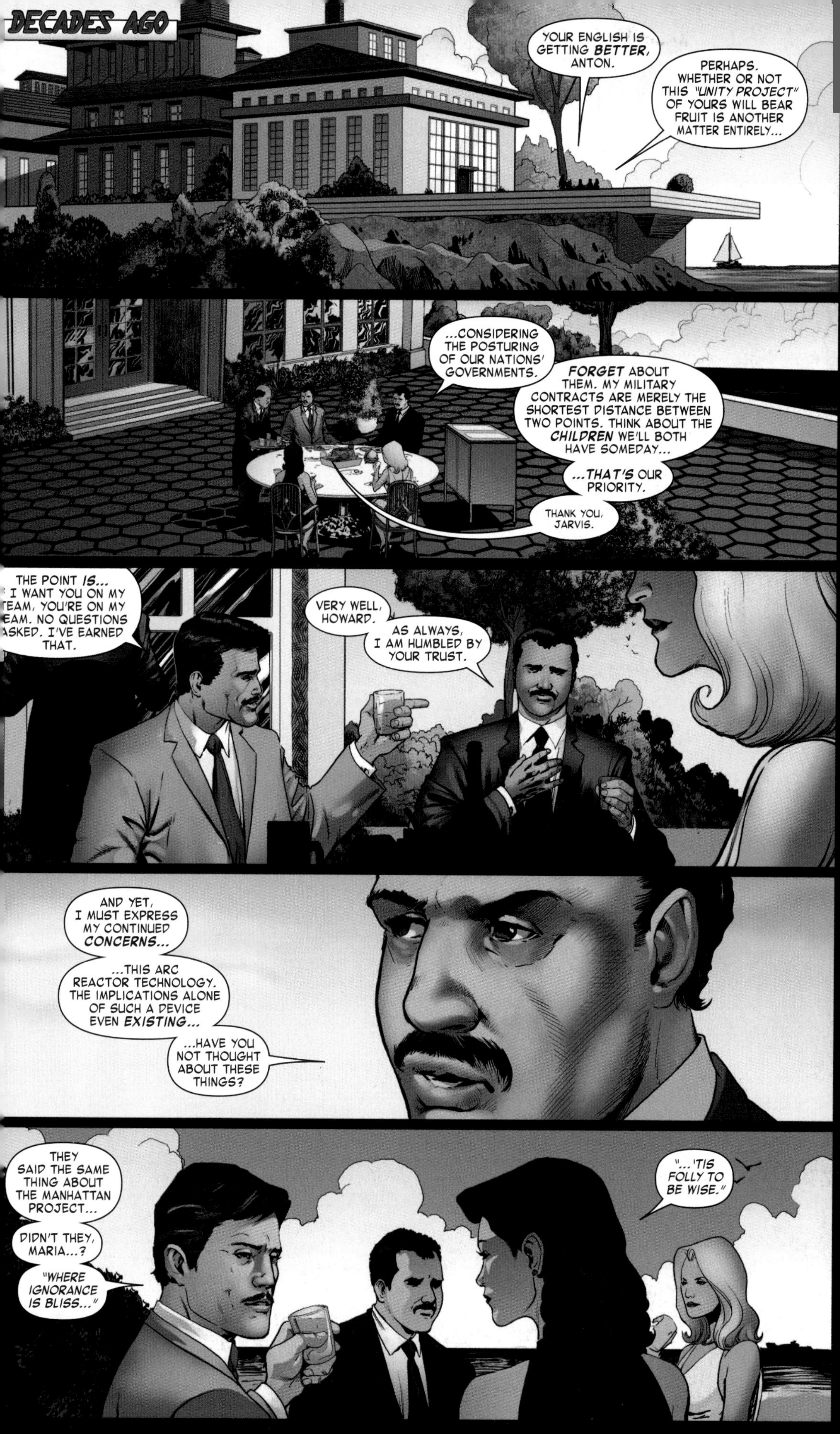
DECADES AGO
YOUR ENGLISH IS GETTING BETTER, ANTON.
PERHAPS. WHETHER OR NOT THIS "UNITY PROJECT" OF YOURS WILL BEAR FRUIT IS ANOTHER MATTER ENTIRELY...
...CONSIDERING THE POSTURING OF OUR NATIONS' GOVERNMENTS.
FORGET ABOUT THEM. MY MILITARY CONTRACTS ARE MERELY THE SHORTEST DISTANCE BETWEEN TWO POINTS. THINK ABOUT THE CHILDREN WE'LL BOTH HAVE SOMEDAY...
...THAT'S OUR PRIORITY.
THANK YOU, JARVIS.
THE POINT IS... I WANT YOU ON MY TEAM, YOU'RE ON MY EAM. NO QUESTIONS ASKED. I'VE EARNED THAT.
VERY WELL, HOWARD.
AS ALWAYS, I AM HUMBLED BY YOUR TRUST.
AND YET, I MUST EXPRESS MY CONTINUED CONCERNS...
...THIS ARC REACTOR TECHNOLOGY. THE IMPLICATIONS ALONE OF SUCH A DEVICE EVEN EXISTING...
...HAVE YOU NOT THOUGHT ABOUT THESE THINGS?
THEY SAID THE SAME THING ABOUT THE MANHATTAN PROJECT...
DIDN'T THEY, MARIA...?
"WHERE IGNORANCE IS BLISS..."
"...'TIS FOLLY TO BE WISE."

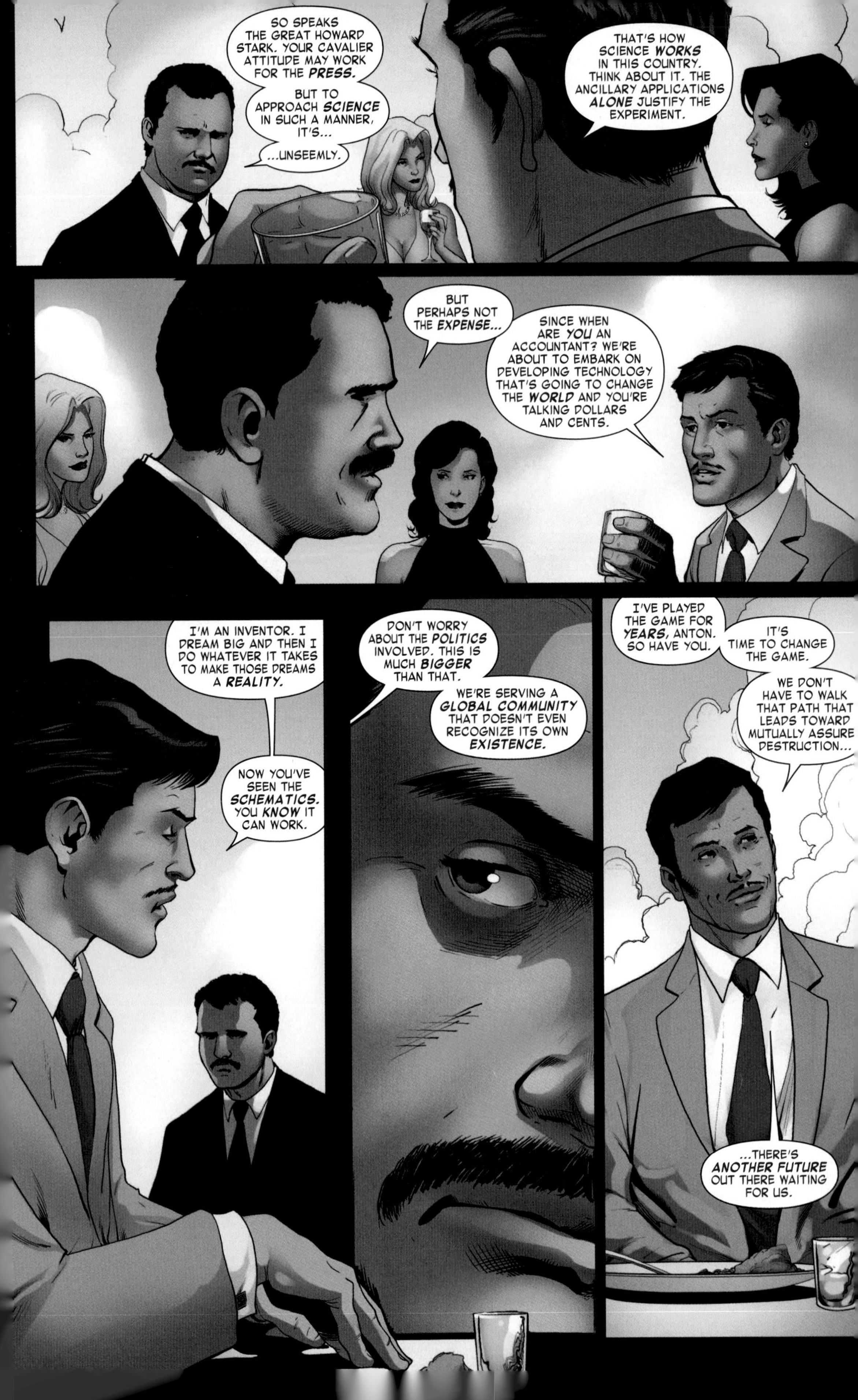
SO SPEAKS THE GREAT HOWARD STARK. YOUR CAVALIER ATTITUDE MAY WORK FOR THE PRESS.
BUT TO APPROACH SCIENCE IN SUCH A MANNER, IT'S...
...UNSEEMLY.
THAT'S HOW SCIENCE WORKS IN THIS COUNTRY. THINK ABOUT IT. THE ANCILLARY APPLICATIONS ALONE JUSTIFY THE EXPERIMENT.
BUT PERHAPS NOT THE EXPENSE...
SINCE WHEN ARE YOU AN ACCOUNTANT? WE'RE ABOUT TO EMBARK ON DEVELOPING TECHNOLOGY THAT'S GOING TO CHANGE THE WORLD AND YOU'RE TALKING DOLLARS AND CENTS.
I'M AN INVENTOR. I DREAM BIG AND THEN I DO WHATEVER IT TAKES TO MAKE THOSE DREAMS A REALITY.
NOW YOU'VE SEEN THE SCHEMATICS. YOU KNOW IT CAN WORK.
DON'T WORRY ABOUT THE POLITICS INVOLVED. THIS IS MUCH BIGGER THAN THAT.
WE'RE SERVING A GLOBAL COMMUNITY THAT DOESN'T EVEN RECOGNIZE ITS OWN EXISTENCE.
I'VE PLAYED THE GAME FOR YEARS, ANTON. SO HAVE YOU.
IT'S TIME TO CHANGE THE GAME.
WE DON'T HAVE TO WALK THAT PATH THAT LEADS TOWARD MUTUALLY ASSURE DESTRUCTION...
...THERE'S ANOTHER FUTURE OUT THERE WAITING FOR US.

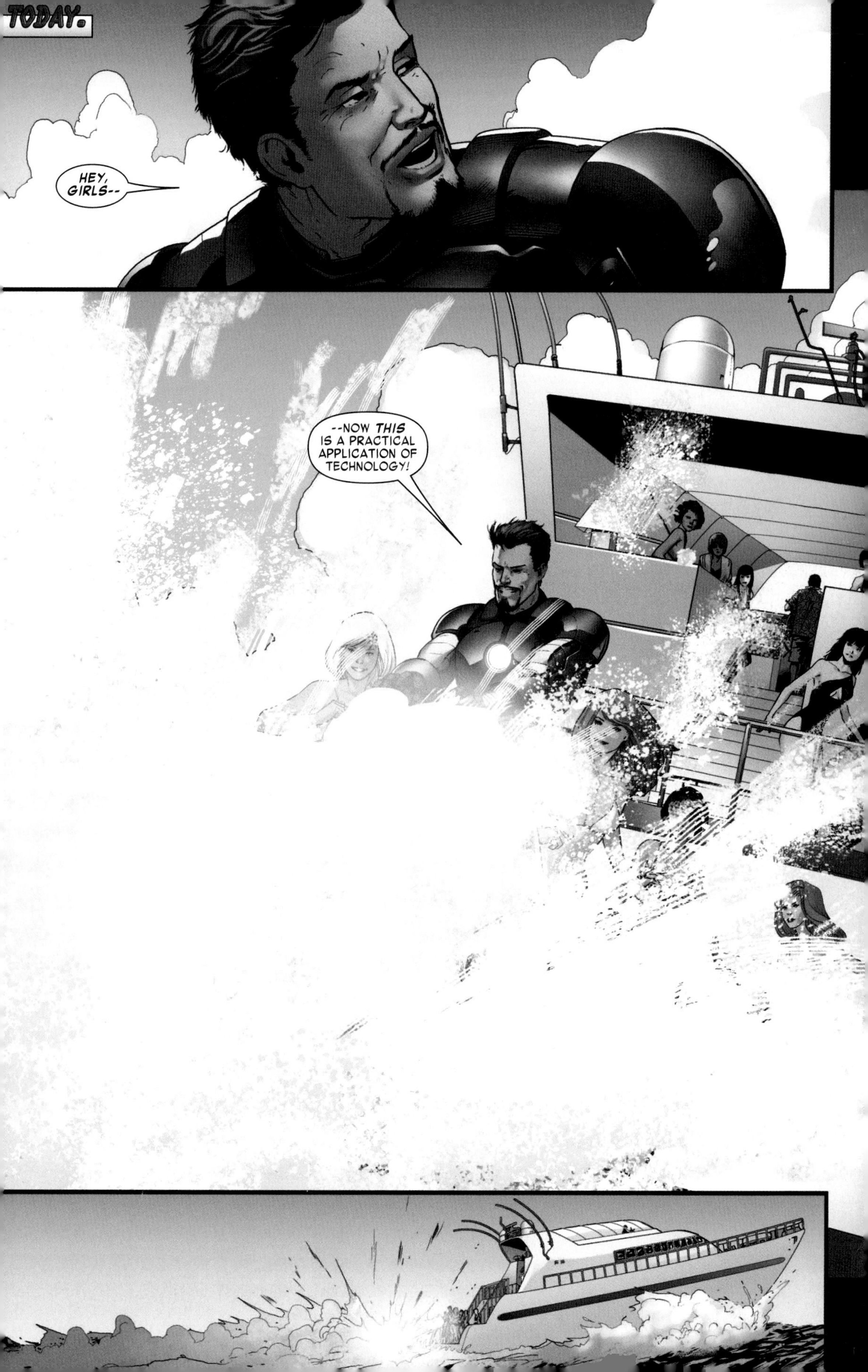
TODAY.
HEY, GIRLS--
--NOW THIS IS A PRACTICAL APPLICATION OF TECHNOLOGY!

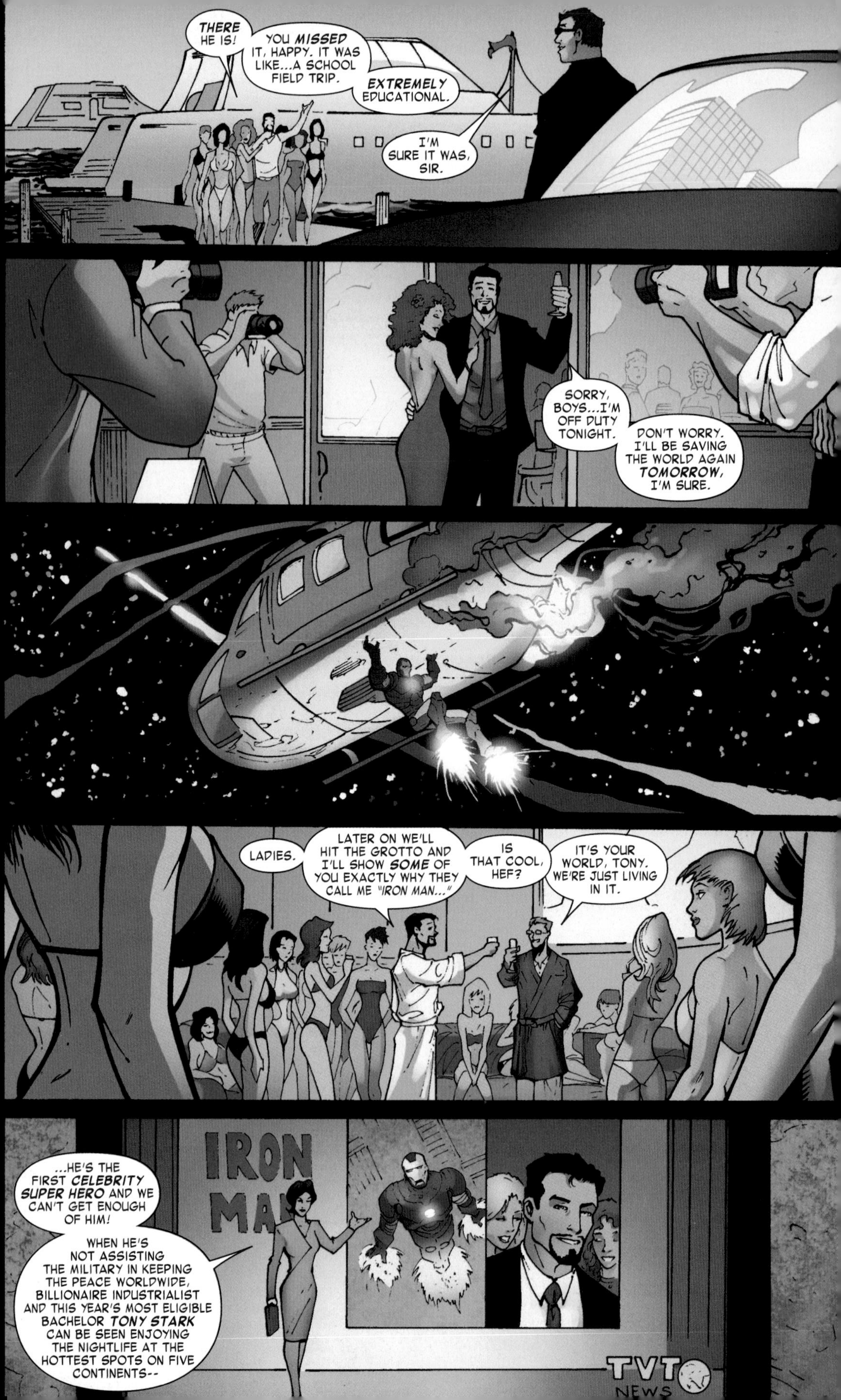
THERE HE IS!
YOU MISSED IT, HAPPY. IT WAS LIKE...A SCHOOL FIELD TRIP.
EXTREMELY EDUCATIONAL.
I'M SURE IT WAS, SIR.
SORRY, BOYS...I'M OFF DUTY TONIGHT.
DON'T WORRY. I'LL BE SAVING THE WORLD AGAIN TOMORROW, I'M SURE.
LADIES.
LATER ON WE'LL HIT THE GROTTO AND I'LL SHOW SOME OF YOU EXACTLY WHY THEY CALL ME "IRON MAN..."
IS THAT COOL, HEF?
IT'S YOUR WORLD, TONY. WE'RE JUST LIVING IN IT.
IRON MA
...HE'S THE FIRST CELEBRITY SUPER HERO AND WE CAN'T GET ENOUGH OF HIM!
WHEN HE'S NOT ASSISTING THE MILITARY IN KEEPING THE PEACE WORLDWIDE, BILLIONAIRE INDUSTRIALIST AND THIS YEAR'S MOST ELIGIBLE BACHELOR TONY STARK CAN BE SEEN ENJOYING THE NIGHTLIFE AT THE HOTTEST SPOTS ON FIVE CONTINENTS--
TVT NEWS

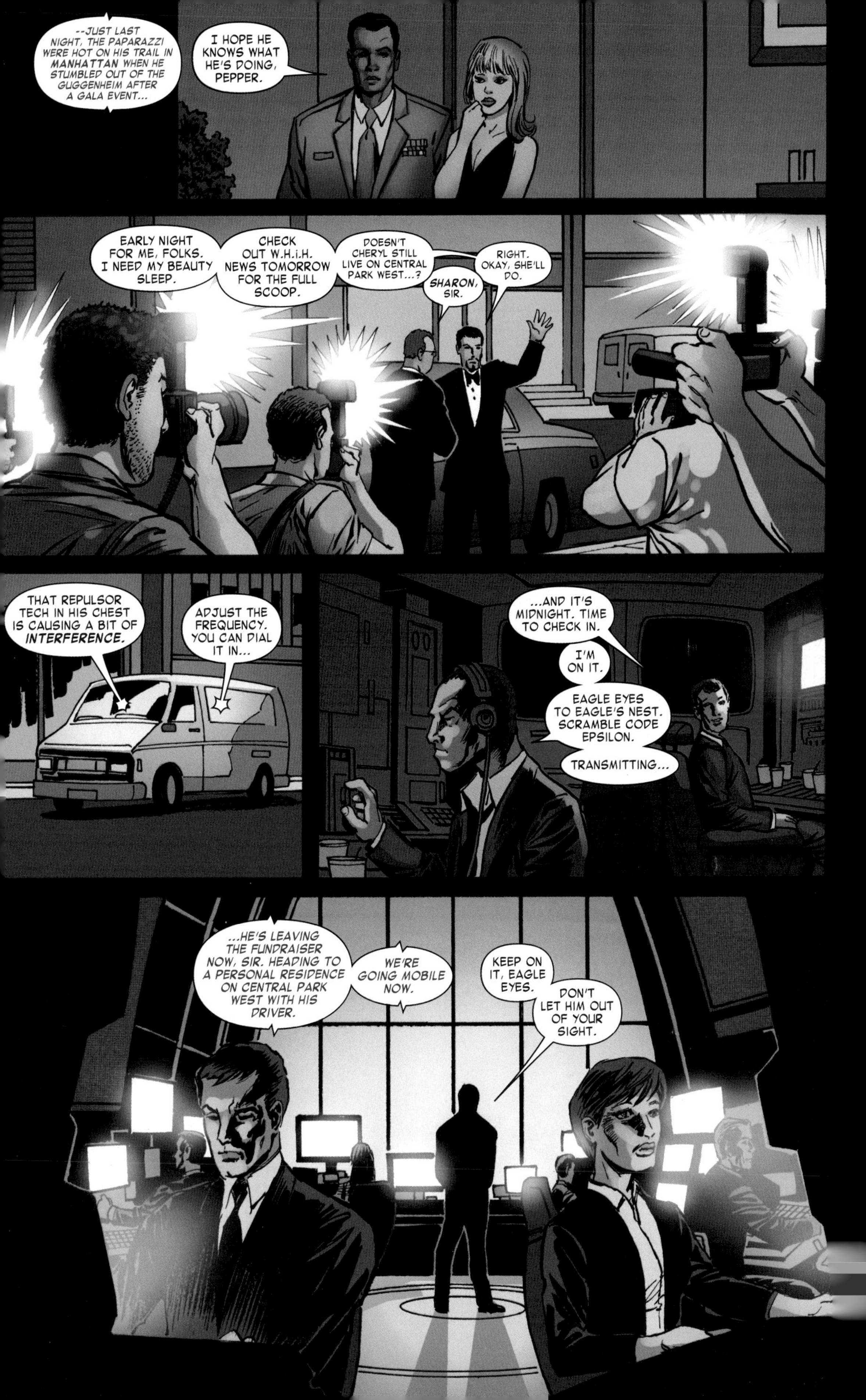
--JUST LAST NIGHT, THE PAPARAZZI WERE HOT ON HIS TRAIL IN MANHATTAN WHEN HE STUMBLED OUT OF THE GUGGENHEIM AFTER A GALA EVENT...
I HOPE HE KNOWS WHAT HE'S DOING, PEPPER.
EARLY NIGHT FOR ME, FOLKS. I NEED MY BEAUTY SLEEP.
CHECK OUT W.H.i.H. NEWS TOMORROW FOR THE FULL SCOOP.
DOESN'T CHERYL STILL LIVE ON CENTRAL PARK WEST...?
SHARON, SIR.
RIGHT. OKAY, SHE'LL DO.
THAT REPULSOR TECH IN HIS CHEST IS CAUSING A BIT OF INTERFERENCE.
ADJUST THE FREQUENCY. YOU CAN DIAL IT IN...
...AND IT'S MIDNIGHT. TIME TO CHECK IN.
I'M ON IT.
EAGLE EYES TO EAGLE'S NEST. SCRAMBLE CODE EPSILON.
TRANSMITTING...
...HE'S LEAVING THE FUNDRAISER NOW, SIR. HEADING TO A PERSONAL RESIDENCE ON CENTRAL PARK WEST WITH HIS DRIVER.
WE'RE GOING MOBILE NOW.
KEEP ON IT, EAGLE EYES.
DON'T LET HIM OUT OF YOUR SIGHT.

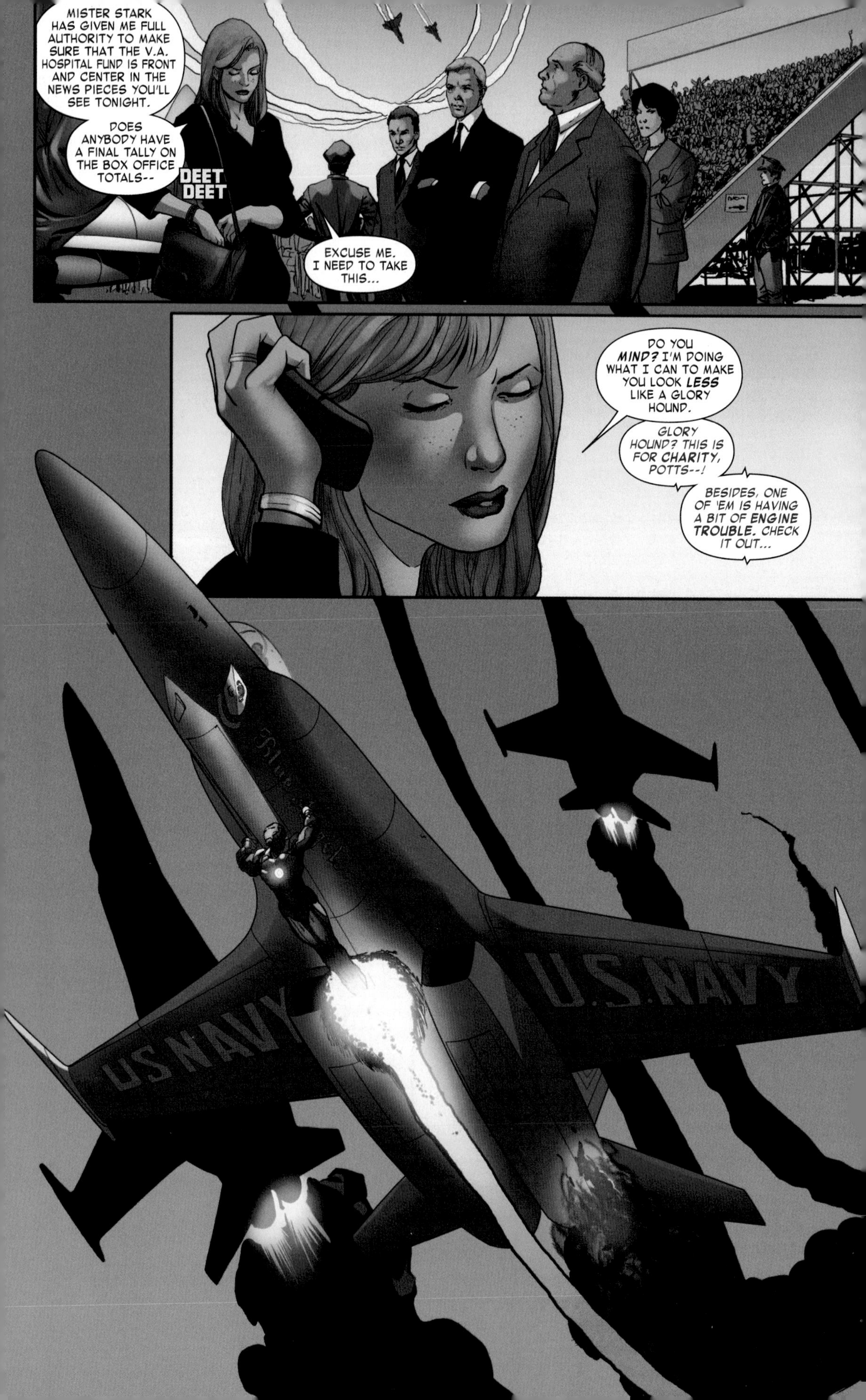
MISTER STARK HAS GIVEN ME FULL AUTHORITY TO MAKE SURE THAT THE V.A. HOSPITAL FUND IS FRONT AND CENTER IN THE NEWS PIECES YOU'LL SEE TONIGHT.
DOES ANYBODY HAVE A FINAL TALLY ON THE BOX OFFICE TOTALS--
DEET DEET
EXCUSE ME. I NEED TO TAKE THIS...
DO YOU MIND? I'M DOING WHAT I CAN TO MAKE YOU LOOK LESS LIKE A GLORY HOUND.
GLORY HOUND? THIS IS FOR CHARITY, POTTS--!
BESIDES, ONE OF 'EM IS HAVING A BIT OF ENGINE TROUBLE. CHECK IT OUT...
U.S. NAVY
U.S. NAVY

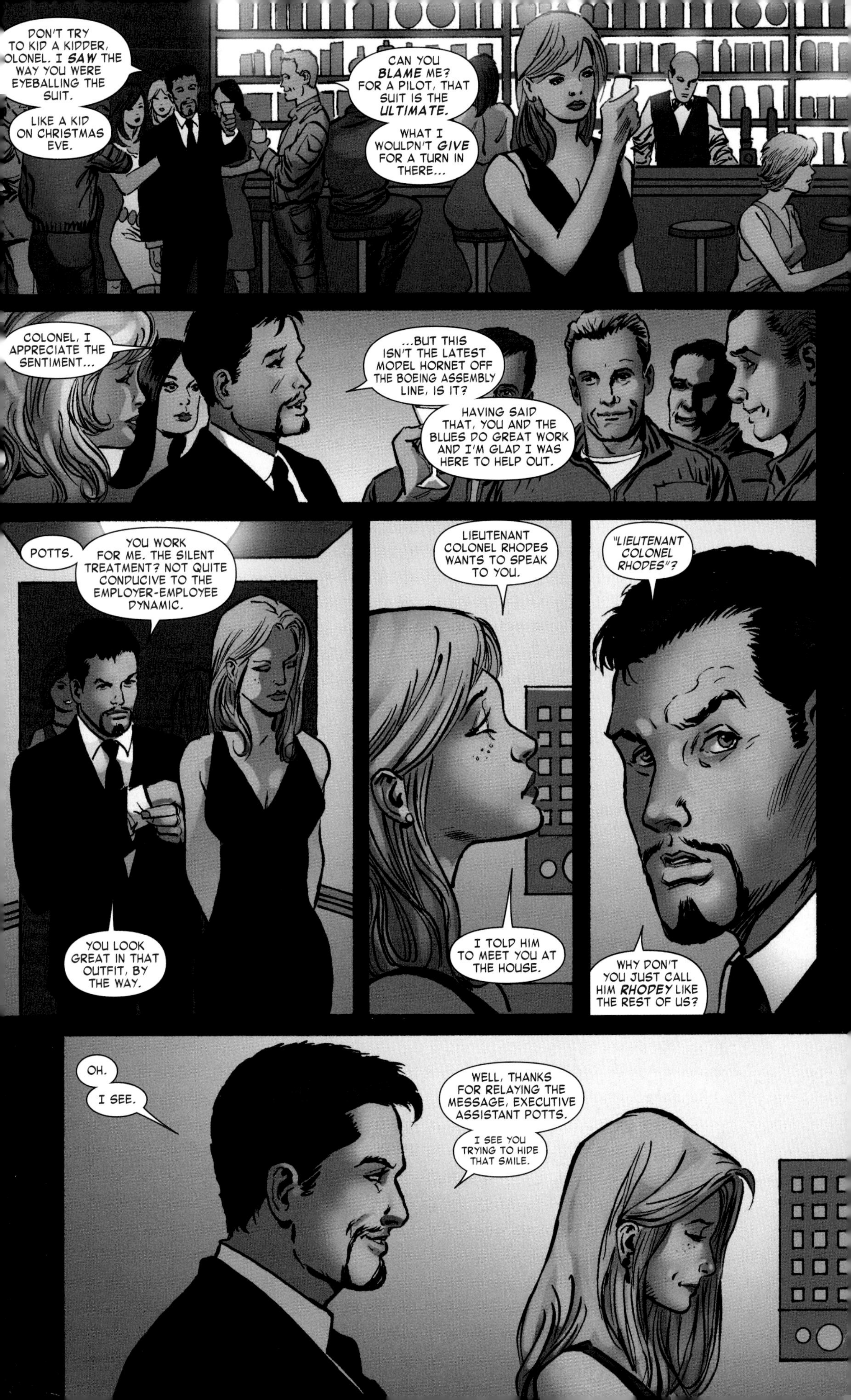
DON'T TRY TO KID A KIDDER, COLONEL. I SAW THE WAY YOU WERE EYEBALLING THE SUIT.
LIKE A KID ON CHRISTMAS EVE.
CAN YOU BLAME ME? FOR A PILOT, THAT SUIT IS THE ULTIMATE.
WHAT I WOULDN'T GIVE FOR A TURN IN THERE...
COLONEL, I APPRECIATE THE SENTIMENT...
...BUT THIS ISN'T THE LATEST MODEL HORNET OFF THE BOEING ASSEMBLY LINE, IS IT?
HAVING SAID THAT, YOU AND THE BLUES DO GREAT WORK AND I'M GLAD I WAS HERE TO HELP OUT.
POTTS.
YOU WORK FOR ME. THE SILENT TREATMENT? NOT QUITE CONDUCIVE TO THE EMPLOYER-EMPLOYEE DYNAMIC.
YOU LOOK GREAT IN THAT OUTFIT, BY THE WAY.
LIEUTENANT COLONEL RHODES WANTS TO SPEAK TO YOU.
I TOLD HIM TO MEET YOU AT THE HOUSE.
"LIEUTENANT COLONEL RHODES"?
WHY DON'T YOU JUST CALL HIM RHODEY LIKE THE REST OF US?
OH.
I SEE.
WELL, THANKS FOR RELAYING THE MESSAGE, EXECUTIVE ASSISTANT POTTS.
I SEE YOU TRYING TO HIDE THAT SMILE.

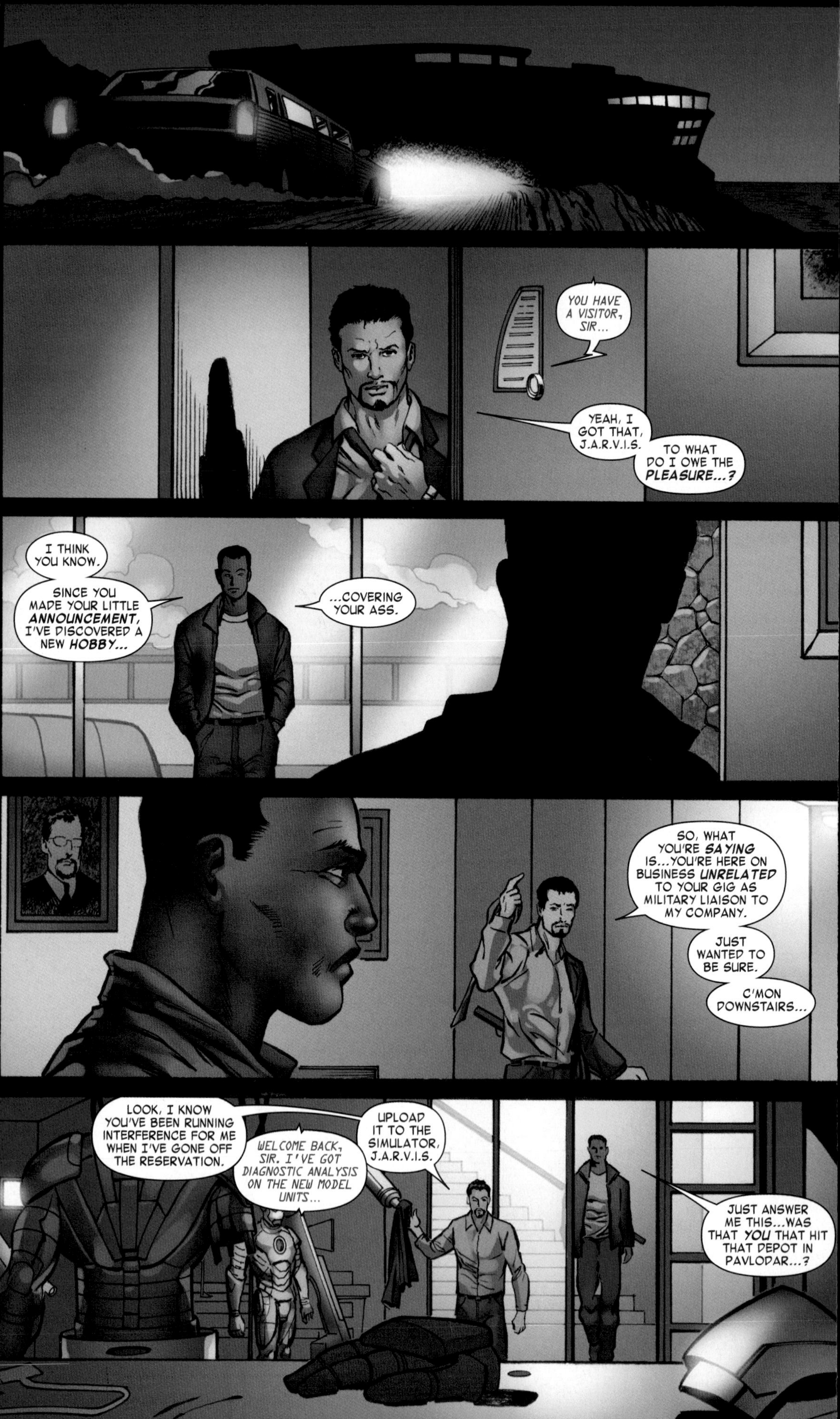

YOU HAVE A VISITOR, SIR...
YEAH, I GOT THAT, J.A.R.V.I.S.
TO WHAT DO I OWE THE PLEASURE...?
I THINK YOU KNOW.
SINCE YOU MADE YOUR LITTLE ANNOUNCEMENT, I'VE DISCOVERED A NEW HOBBY...
...COVERING YOUR ASS.
SO, WHAT YOU'RE SAYING IS...YOU'RE HERE ON BUSINESS UNRELATED TO YOUR GIG AS MILITARY LIAISON TO MY COMPANY.
JUST WANTED TO BE SURE.
C'MON DOWNSTAIRS...
LOOK, I KNOW YOU'VE BEEN RUNNING INTERFERENCE FOR ME WHEN I'VE GONE OFF THE RESERVATION.
WELCOME BACK, SIR. I'VE GOT DIAGNOSTIC ANALYSIS ON THE NEW MODEL UNITS...
UPLOAD IT TO THE SIMULATOR, J.A.R.V.I.S.
JUST ANSWER ME THIS...WAS THAT YOU THAT HIT THAT DEPOT IN PAVLODAR...?

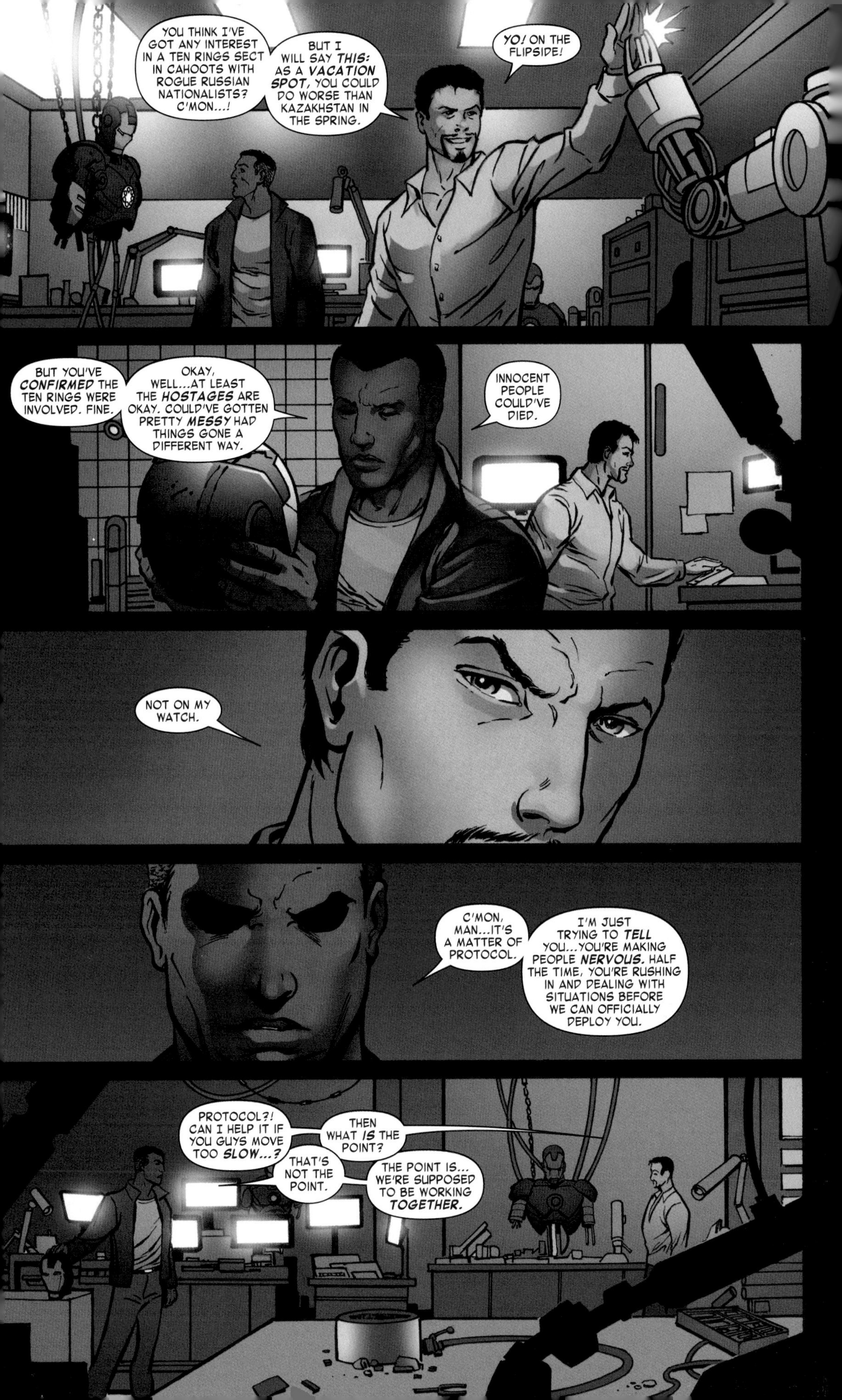

YOU THINK I'VE GOT ANY INTEREST IN A TEN RINGS SECT IN CAHOOTS WITH ROGUE RUSSIAN NATIONALISTS? C'MON...!
BUT I WILL SAY THIS: AS A VACATION SPOT, YOU COULD DO WORSE THAN KAZAKHSTAN IN THE SPRING.
YO! ON THE FLIPSIDE!
BUT YOU'VE CONFIRMED THE TEN RINGS WERE INVOLVED. FINE.
OKAY, WELL...AT LEAST THE HOSTAGES ARE OKAY. COULD'VE GOTTEN PRETTY MESSY HAD THINGS GONE A DIFFERENT WAY.
INNOCENT PEOPLE COULD'VE DIED.
NOT ON MY WATCH.
C'MON, MAN...IT'S A MATTER OF PROTOCOL.
I'M JUST TRYING TO TELL YOU...YOU'RE MAKING PEOPLE NERVOUS. HALF THE TIME, YOU'RE RUSHING IN AND DEALING WITH SITUATIONS BEFORE WE CAN OFFICIALLY DEPLOY YOU.
PROTOCOL?! CAN I HELP IT IF YOU GUYS MOVE TOO SLOW...?
THEN WHAT IS THE POINT?
THAT'S NOT THE POINT.
THE POINT IS... WE'RE SUPPOSED TO BE WORKING TOGETHER.

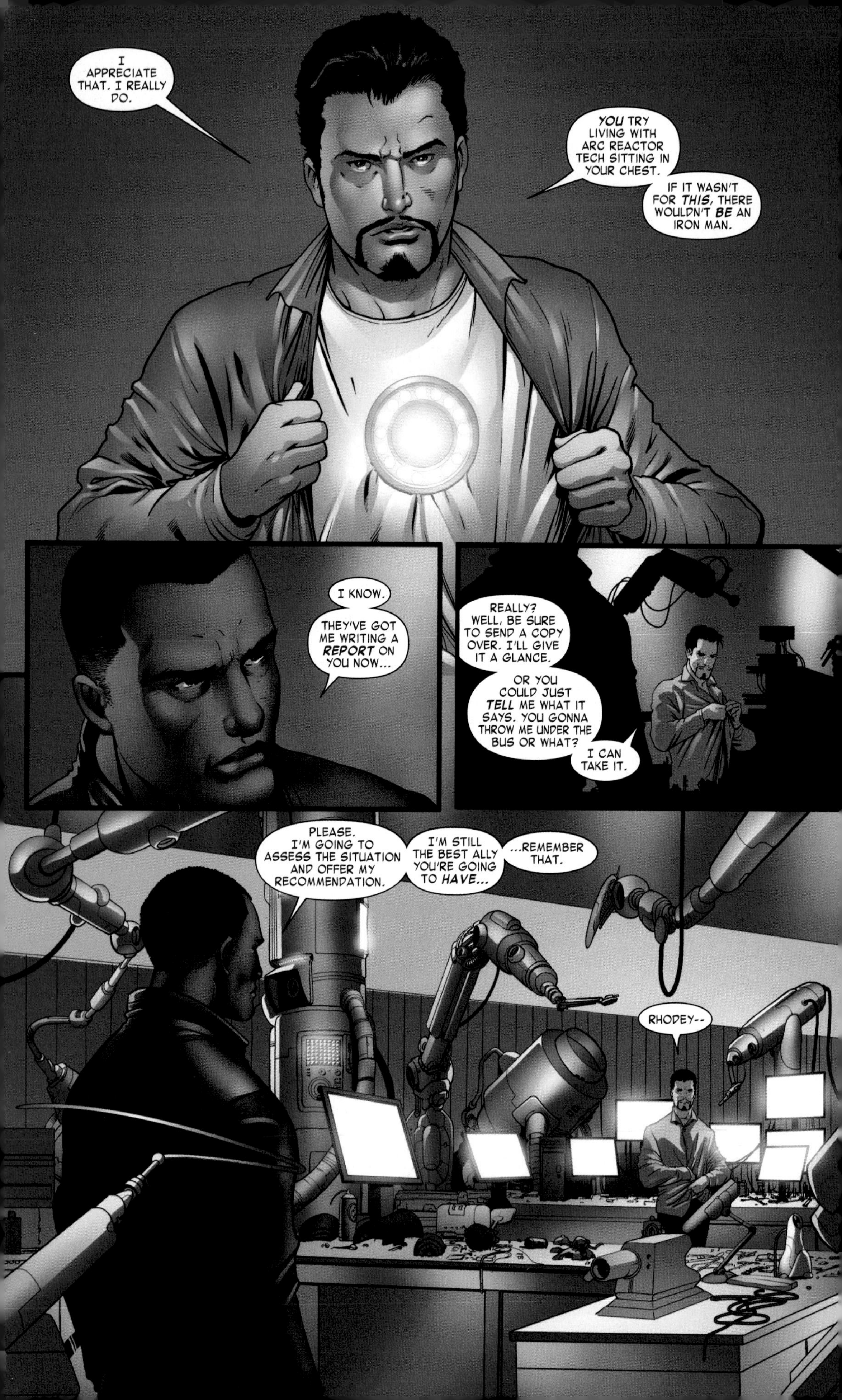

I APPRECIATE THAT. I REALLY DO.
YOU TRY LIVING WITH ARC REACTOR TECH SITTING IN YOUR CHEST.
IF IT WASN'T FOR THIS, THERE WOULDN'T BE AN IRON MAN.
I KNOW.
THEY'VE GOT ME WRITING A REPORT ON YOU NOW...
REALLY? WELL, BE SURE TO SEND A COPY OVER. I'LL GIVE IT A GLANCE.
OR YOU COULD JUST TELL ME WHAT IT SAYS. YOU GONNA THROW ME UNDER THE BUS OR WHAT?
I CAN TAKE IT.
PLEASE. I'M GOING TO ASSESS THE SITUATION AND OFFER MY RECOMMENDATION.
I'M STILL THE BEST ALLY YOU'RE GOING TO HAVE...
...REMEMBER THAT.
RHODEY--

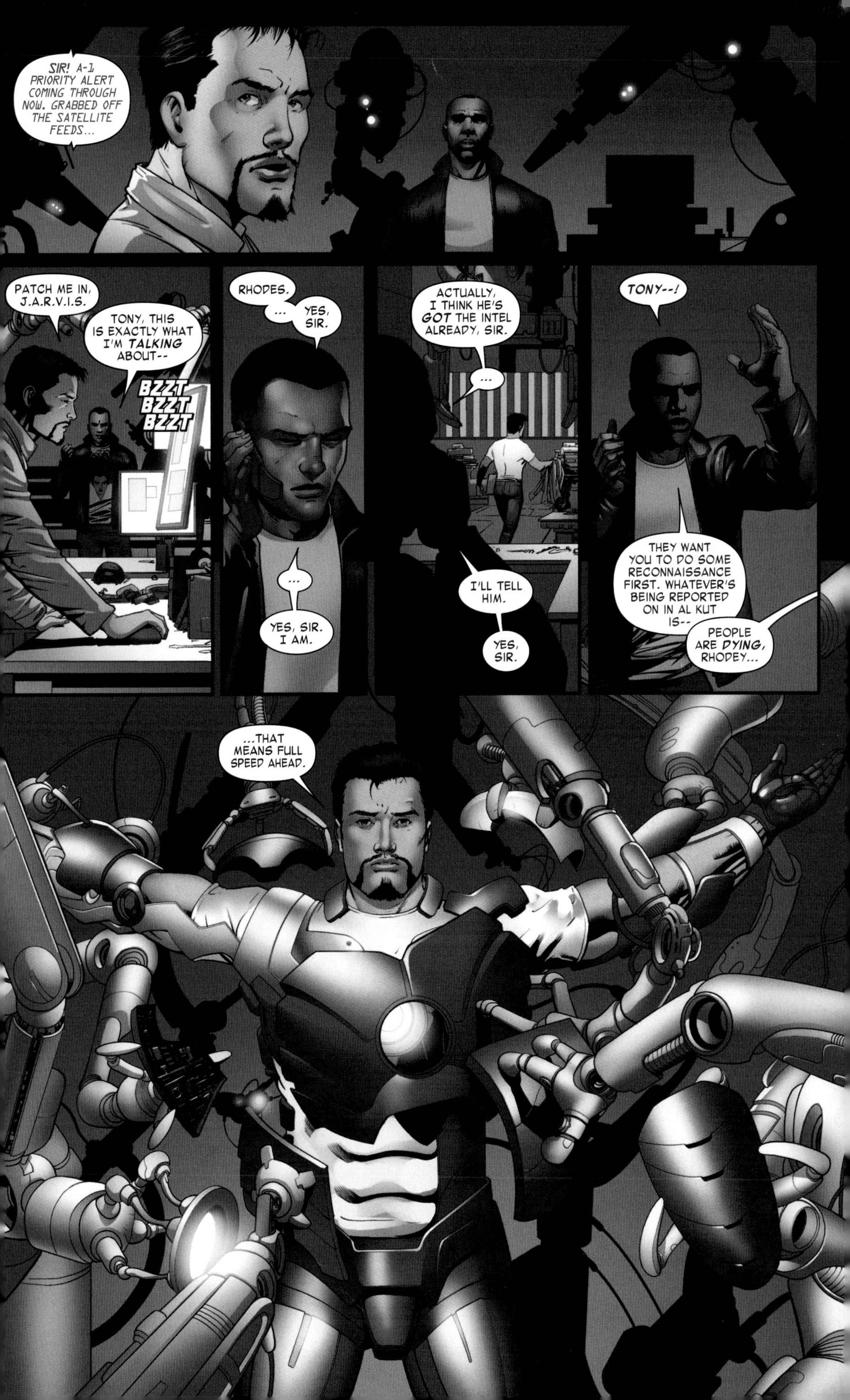
SIR! A-1 PRIORITY ALERT COMING THROUGH NOW. GRABBED OFF THE SATELLITE FEEDS...
PATCH ME IN, J.A.R.V.I.S.
TONY, THIS IS EXACTLY WHAT I'M TALKING ABOUT--
BZZT BZZT BZZT
RHODES.
...
YES, SIR.
...
YES, SIR. I AM.
ACTUALLY, I THINK HE'S GOT THE INTEL ALREADY, SIR.
...
I'LL TELL HIM.
YES, SIR.
TONY--!
THEY WANT YOU TO DO SOME RECONNAISSANCE FIRST. WHATEVER'S BEING REPORTED ON IN AL KUT IS--
PEOPLE ARE DYING, RHODEY...
...THAT MEANS FULL SPEED AHEAD.

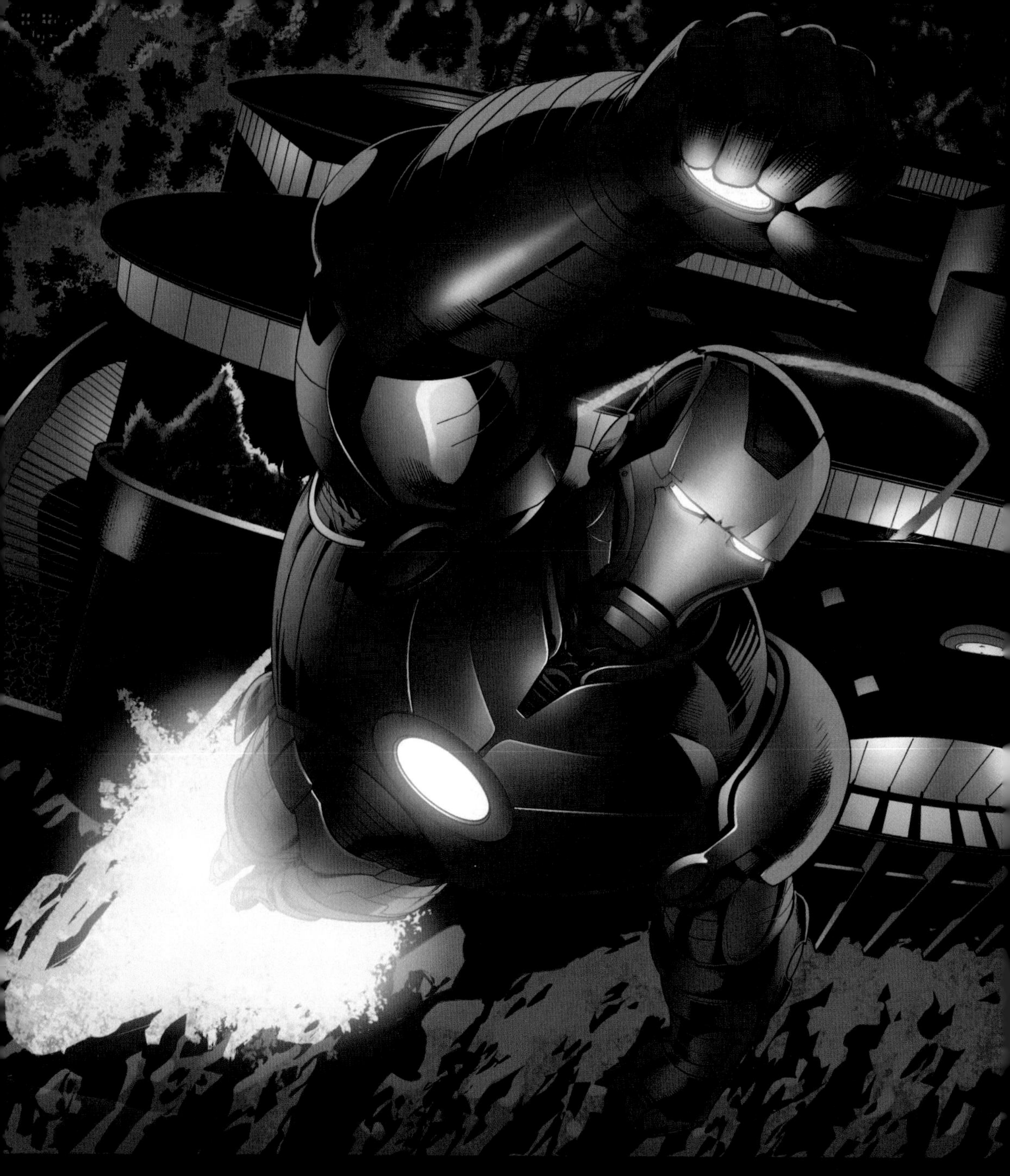

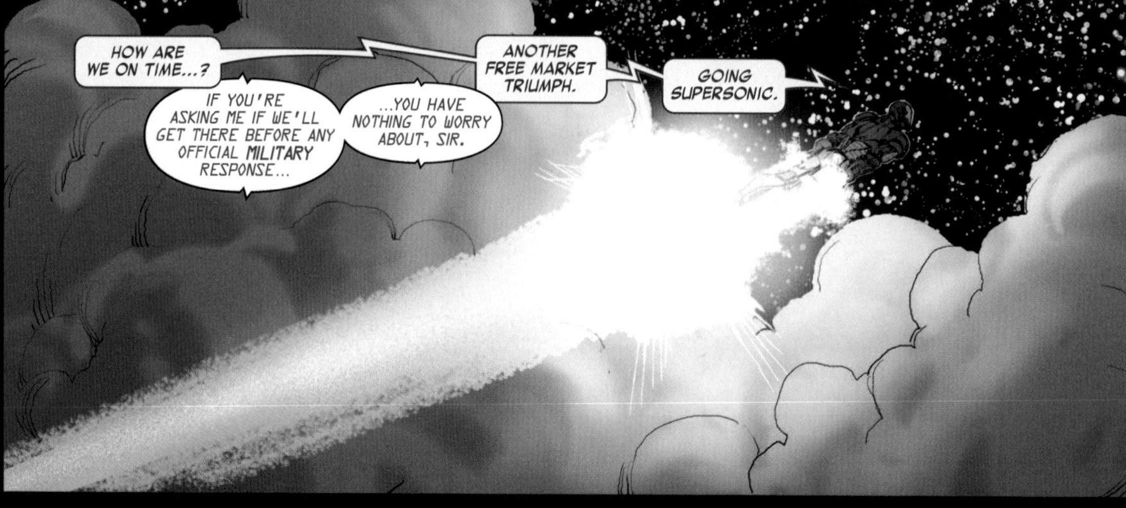
HOW ARE WE ON TIME...?
IF YOU'RE ASKING ME IF WE'LL GET THERE BEFORE ANY OFFICIAL MILITARY RESPONSE...
...YOU HAVE NOTHING TO WORRY ABOUT, SIR.
ANOTHER FREE MARKET TRIUMPH.
GOING SUPERSONIC.

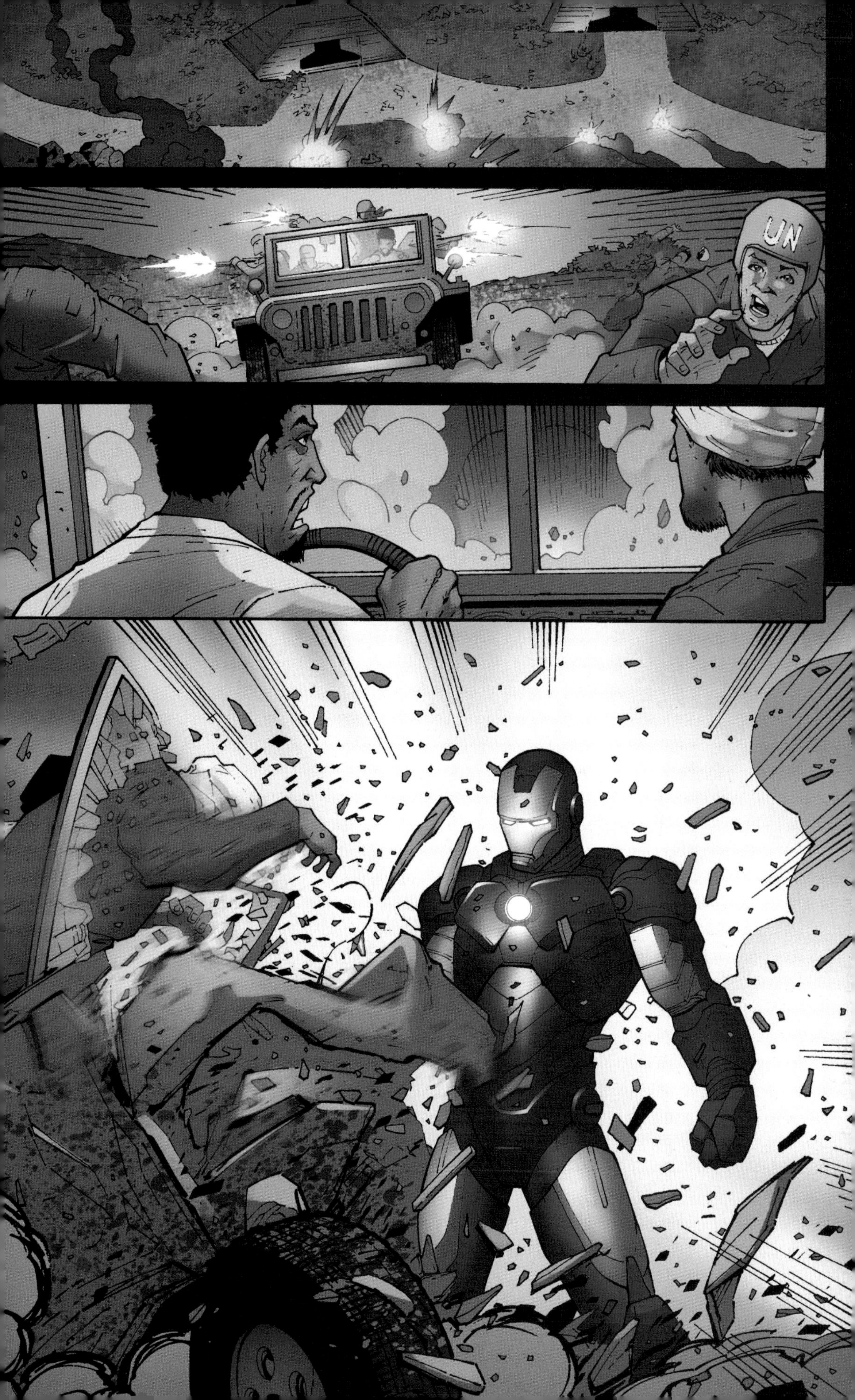
UN

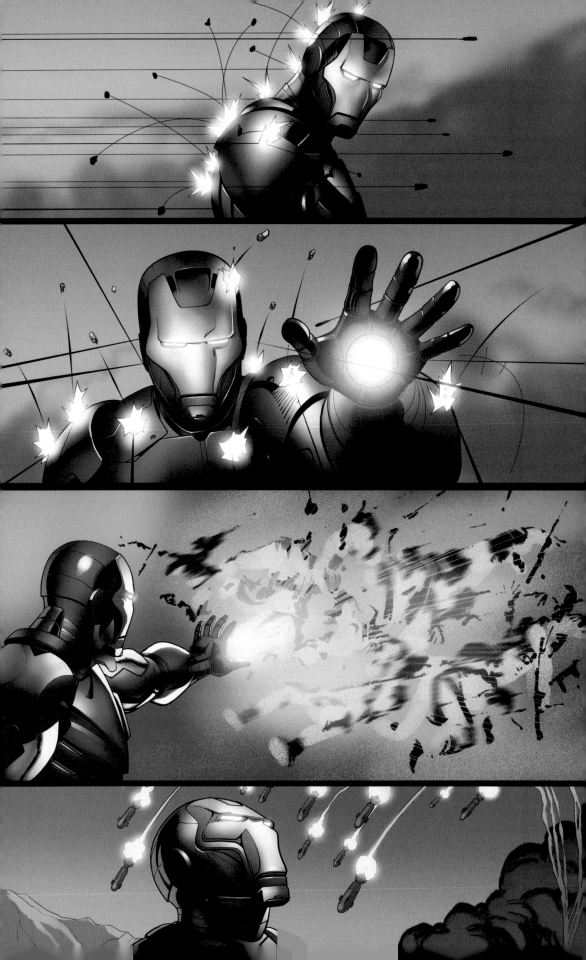

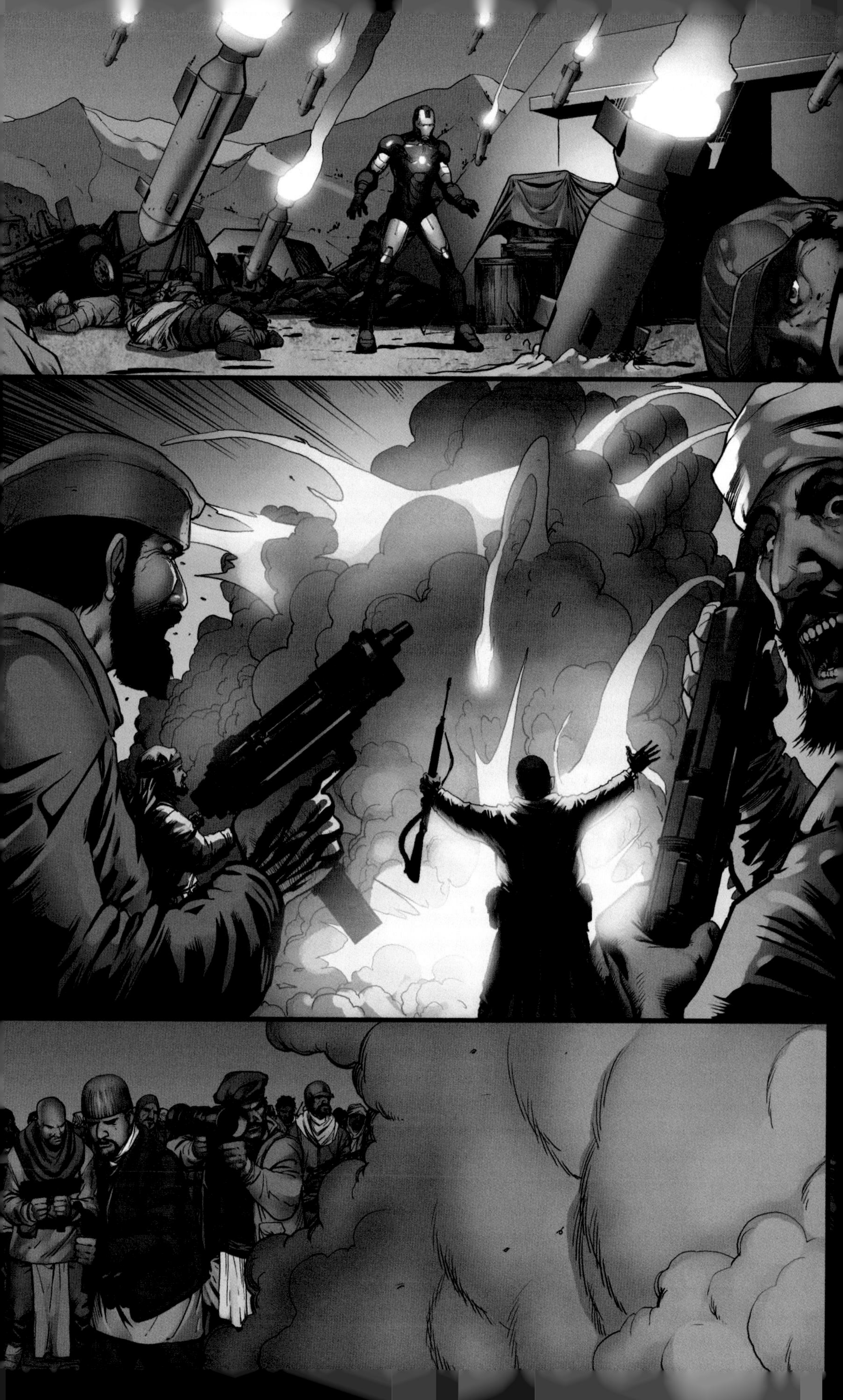

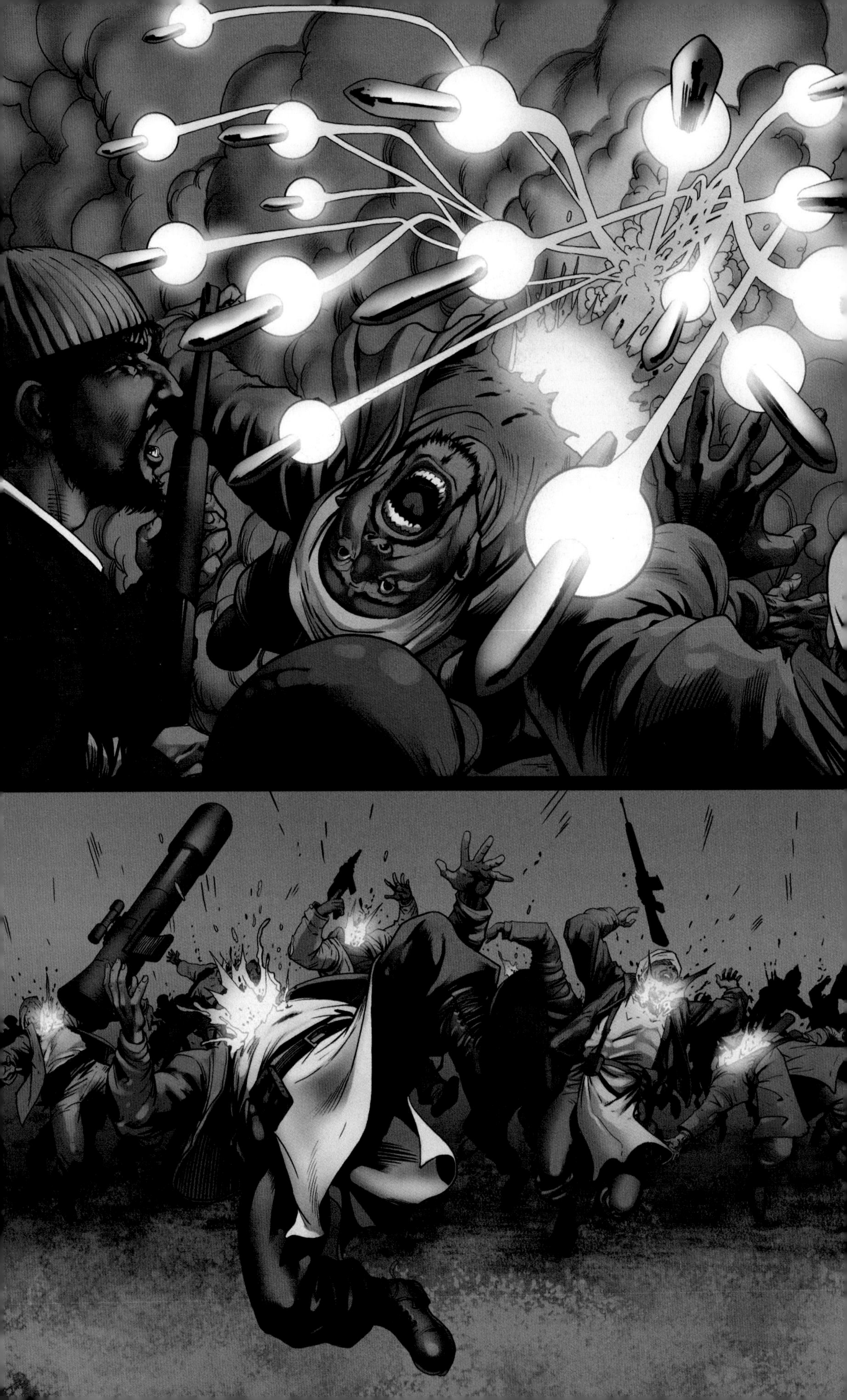

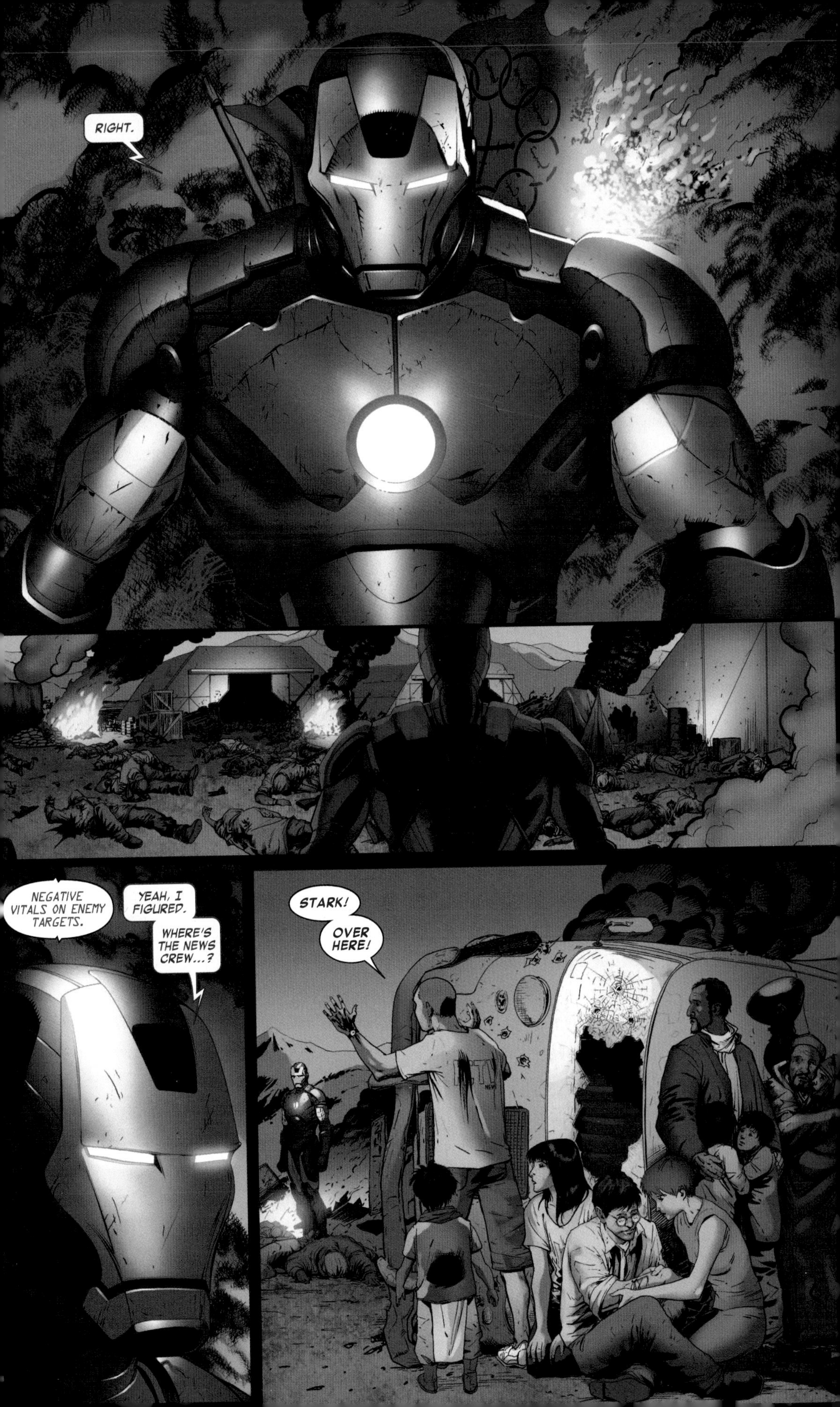
RIGHT.
NEGATIVE VITALS ON ENEMY TARGETS.
YEAH, I FIGURED.
WHERE'S THE NEWS CREW...?
STARK!
OVER HERE!

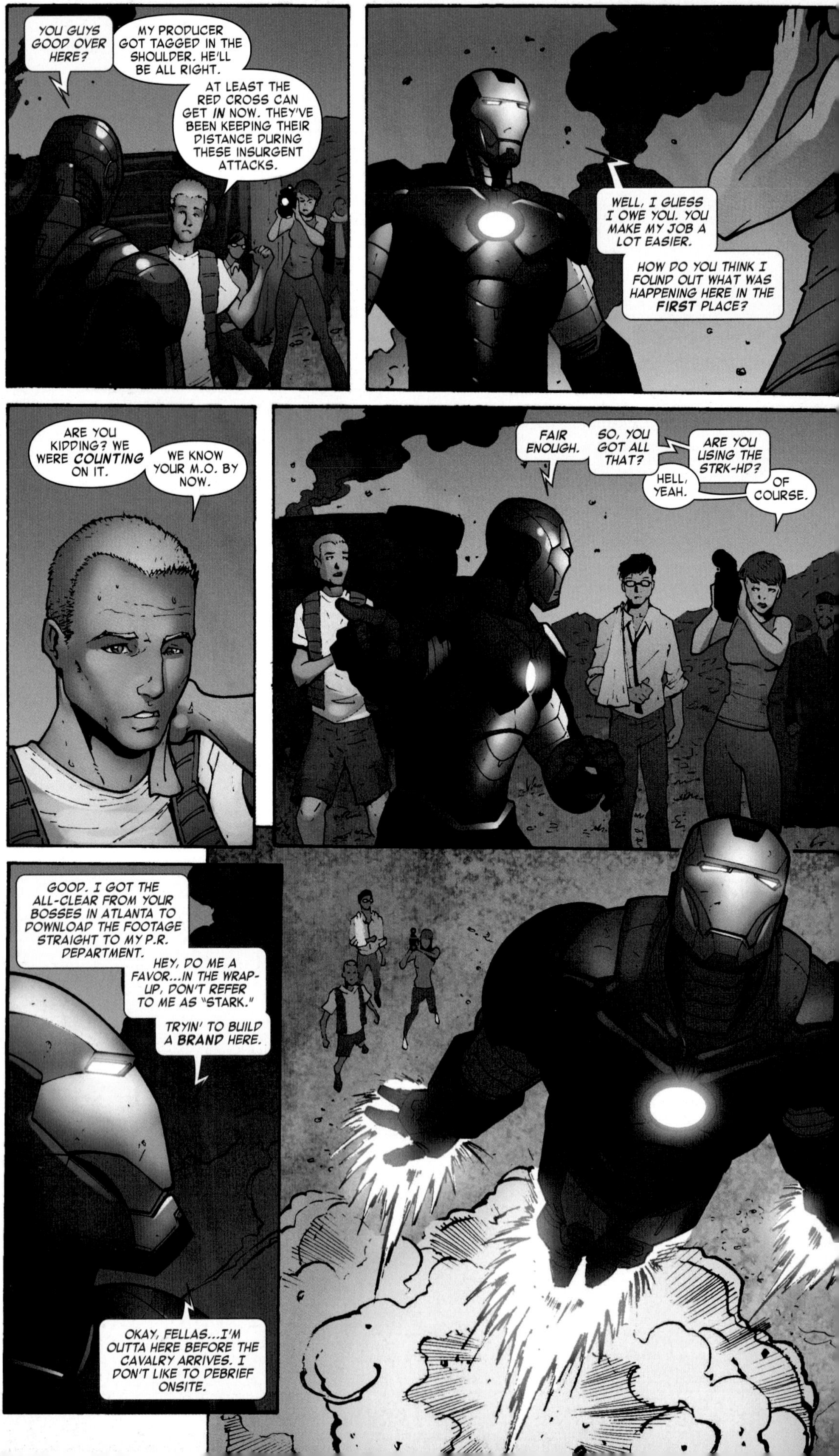

YOU GUYS GOOD OVER HERE?
MY PRODUCER GOT TAGGED IN THE SHOULDER. HE'LL BE ALL RIGHT.
AT LEAST THE RED CROSS CAN GET IN NOW. THEY'VE BEEN KEEPING THEIR DISTANCE DURING THESE INSURGENT ATTACKS.
WELL, I GUESS I OWE YOU. YOU MAKE MY JOB A LOT EASIER.
HOW DO YOU THINK I FOUND OUT WHAT WAS HAPPENING HERE IN THE FIRST PLACE?
ARE YOU KIDDING? WE WERE COUNTING ON IT.
WE KNOW YOUR M.O. BY NOW.
FAIR ENOUGH.
SO, YOU GOT ALL THAT?
ARE YOU USING THE STRK-HD?
HELL, YEAH.
OF COURSE.
GOOD. I GOT THE ALL-CLEAR FROM YOUR BOSSES IN ATLANTA TO DOWNLOAD THE FOOTAGE STRAIGHT TO MY P.R. DEPARTMENT.
HEY, DO ME A FAVOR...IN THE WRAP-UP, DON'T REFER TO ME AS "STARK."
TRYIN' TO BUILD A BRAND HERE.
OKAY, FELLAS...I'M OUTTA HERE BEFORE THE CAVALRY ARRIVES. I DON'T LIKE TO DEBRIEF ONSITE.

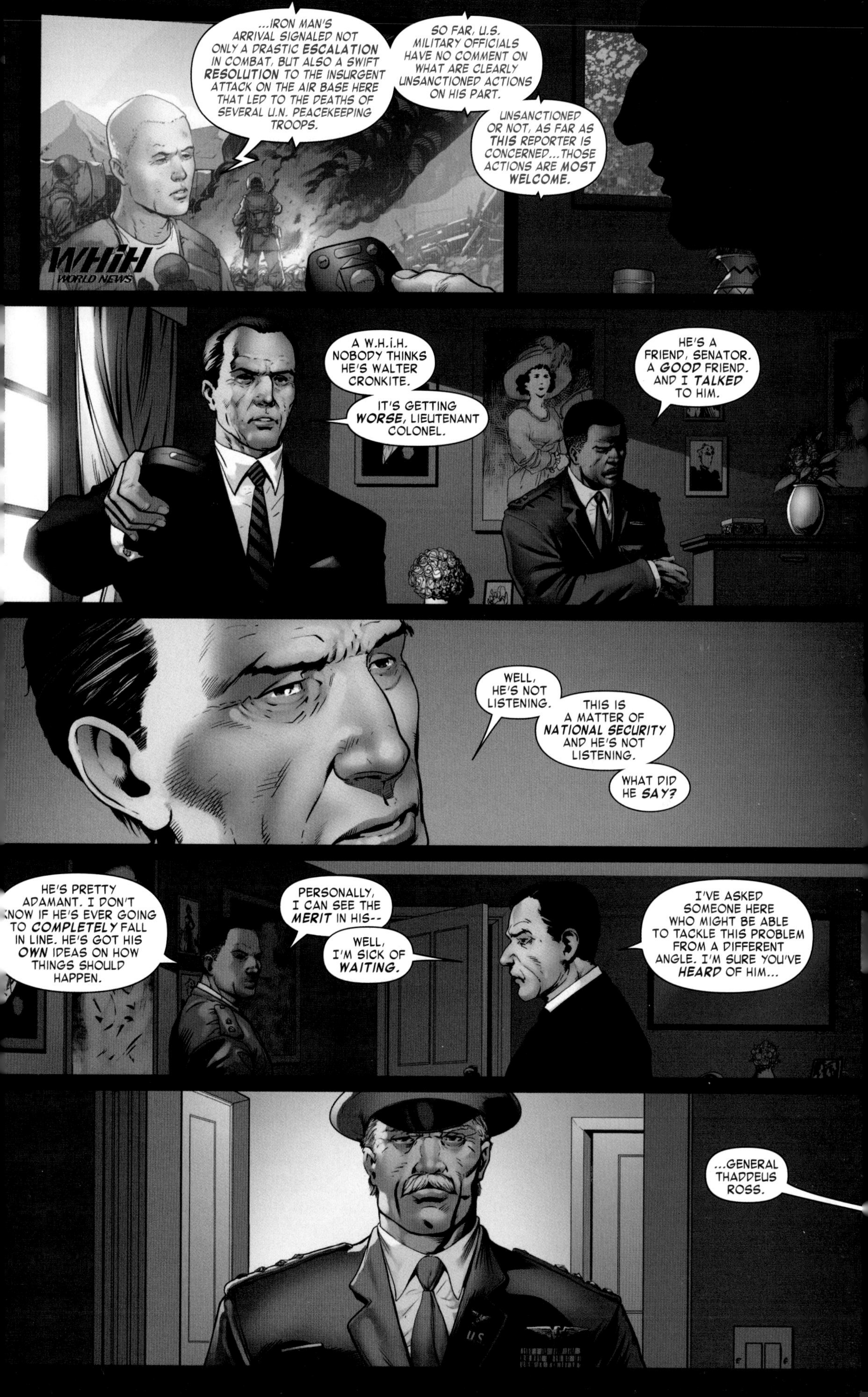
...IRON MAN'S ARRIVAL SIGNALED NOT ONLY A DRASTIC ESCALATION IN COMBAT, BUT ALSO A SWIFT RESOLUTION TO THE INSURGENT ATTACK ON THE AIR BASE HERE THAT LED TO THE DEATHS OF SEVERAL U.N. PEACEKEEPING TROOPS.
SO FAR, U.S. MILITARY OFFICIALS HAVE NO COMMENT ON WHAT ARE CLEARLY UNSANCTIONED ACTIONS ON HIS PART.
UNSANCTIONED OR NOT, AS FAR AS THIS REPORTER IS CONCERNED...THOSE ACTIONS ARE MOST WELCOME.
WHiH
WORLD NEWS
A W.H.i.H. NOBODY THINKS HE'S WALTER CRONKITE.
IT'S GETTING WORSE, LIEUTENANT COLONEL.
HE'S A FRIEND, SENATOR. A GOOD FRIEND. AND I TALKED TO HIM.
WELL, HE'S NOT LISTENING.
THIS IS A MATTER OF NATIONAL SECURITY AND HE'S NOT LISTENING.
WHAT DID HE SAY?
HE'S PRETTY ADAMANT. I DON'T NOW IF HE'S EVER GOING TO COMPLETELY FALL IN LINE. HE'S GOT HIS OWN IDEAS ON HOW THINGS SHOULD HAPPEN.
PERSONALLY, I CAN SEE THE MERIT IN HIS--
WELL, I'M SICK OF WAITING.
I'VE ASKED SOMEONE HERE WHO MIGHT BE ABLE TO TACKLE THIS PROBLEM FROM A DIFFERENT ANGLE. I'M SURE YOU'VE HEARD OF HIM...
...GENERAL THADDEUS ROSS.

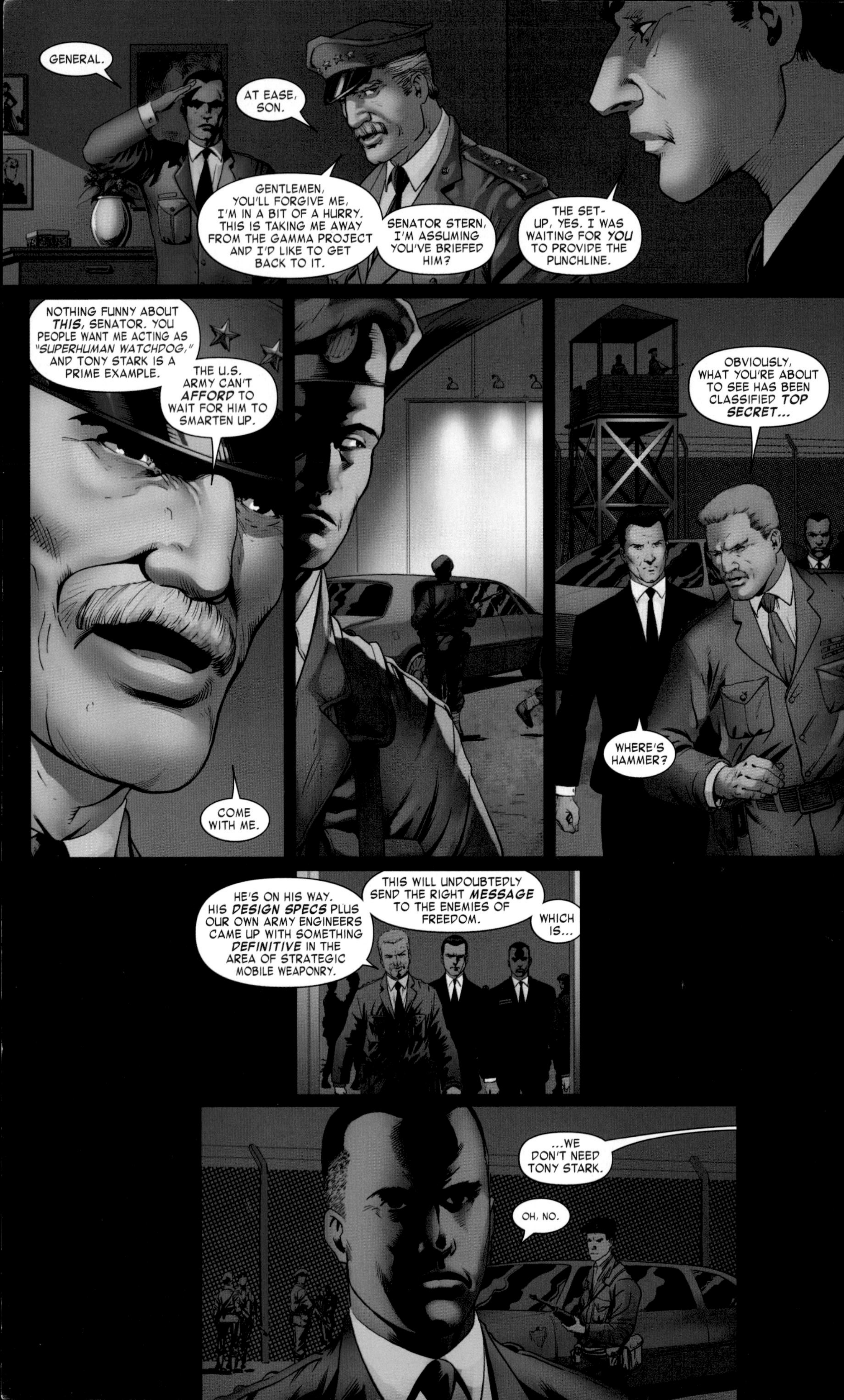
GENERAL.
AT EASE, SON.
GENTLEMEN, YOU'LL FORGIVE ME, I'M IN A BIT OF A HURRY. THIS IS TAKING ME AWAY FROM THE GAMMA PROJECT AND I'D LIKE TO GET BACK TO IT.
SENATOR STERN, I'M ASSUMING YOU'VE BRIEFED HIM?
THE SET-UP, YES. I WAS WAITING FOR YOU TO PROVIDE THE PUNCHLINE.
NOTHING FUNNY ABOUT THIS, SENATOR. YOU PEOPLE WANT ME ACTING AS "SUPERHUMAN WATCHDOG," AND TONY STARK IS A PRIME EXAMPLE.
THE U.S. ARMY CAN'T AFFORD TO WAIT FOR HIM TO SMARTEN UP.
COME WITH ME.
OBVIOUSLY, WHAT YOU'RE ABOUT TO SEE HAS BEEN CLASSIFIED TOP SECRET...
WHERE'S HAMMER?
HE'S ON HIS WAY. HIS DESIGN SPECS PLUS OUR OWN ARMY ENGINEERS CAME UP WITH SOMETHING DEFINITIVE IN THE AREA OF STRATEGIC MOBILE WEAPONRY.
THIS WILL UNDOUBTEDLY SEND THE RIGHT MESSAGE TO THE ENEMIES OF FREEDOM.
WHICH IS...
...WE DON'T NEED TONY STARK.
OH, NO.

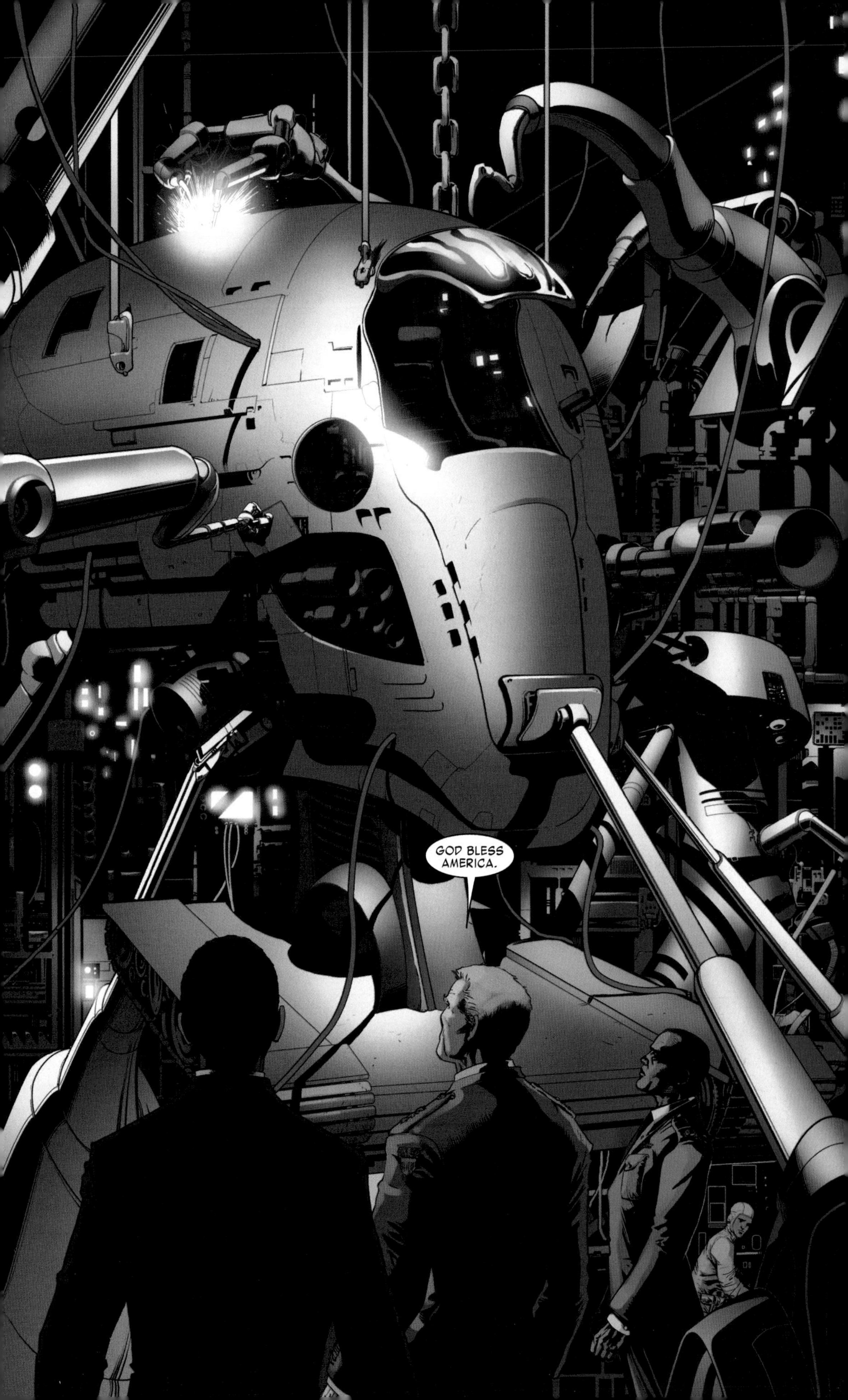
GOD BLESS AMERICA.

MARVEL STUDIOS

IRON MAN 2

PUBLIC IDENTITY

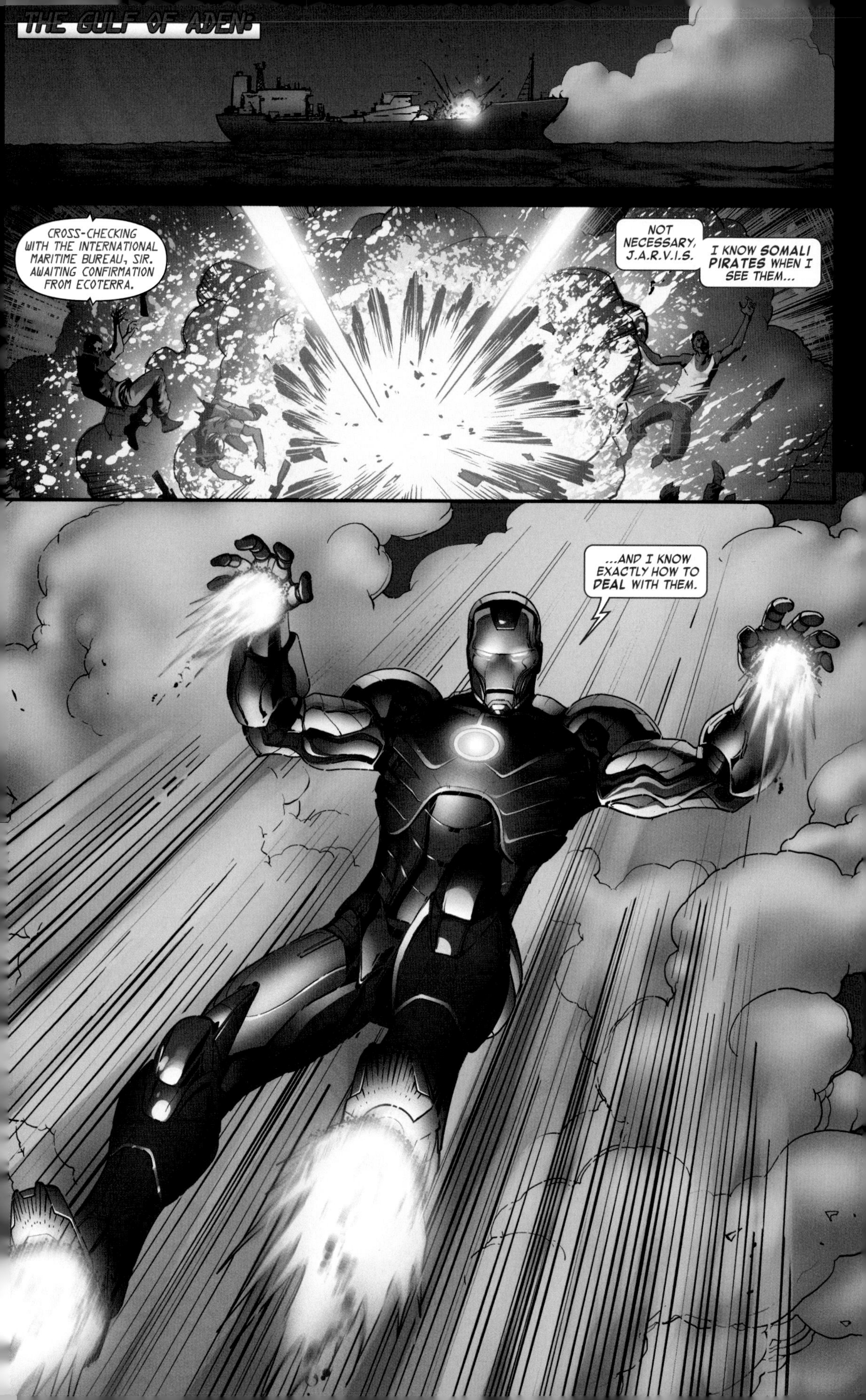
THE GULF OF ADEN:
CROSS-CHECKING WITH THE INTERNATIONAL MARITIME BUREAU, SIR. AWAITING CONFIRMATION FROM ECOTERRA.
NOT NECESSARY, J.A.R.V.I.S.
I KNOW SOMALI PIRATES WHEN I SEE THEM...
...AND I KNOW EXACTLY HOW TO DEAL WITH THEM.

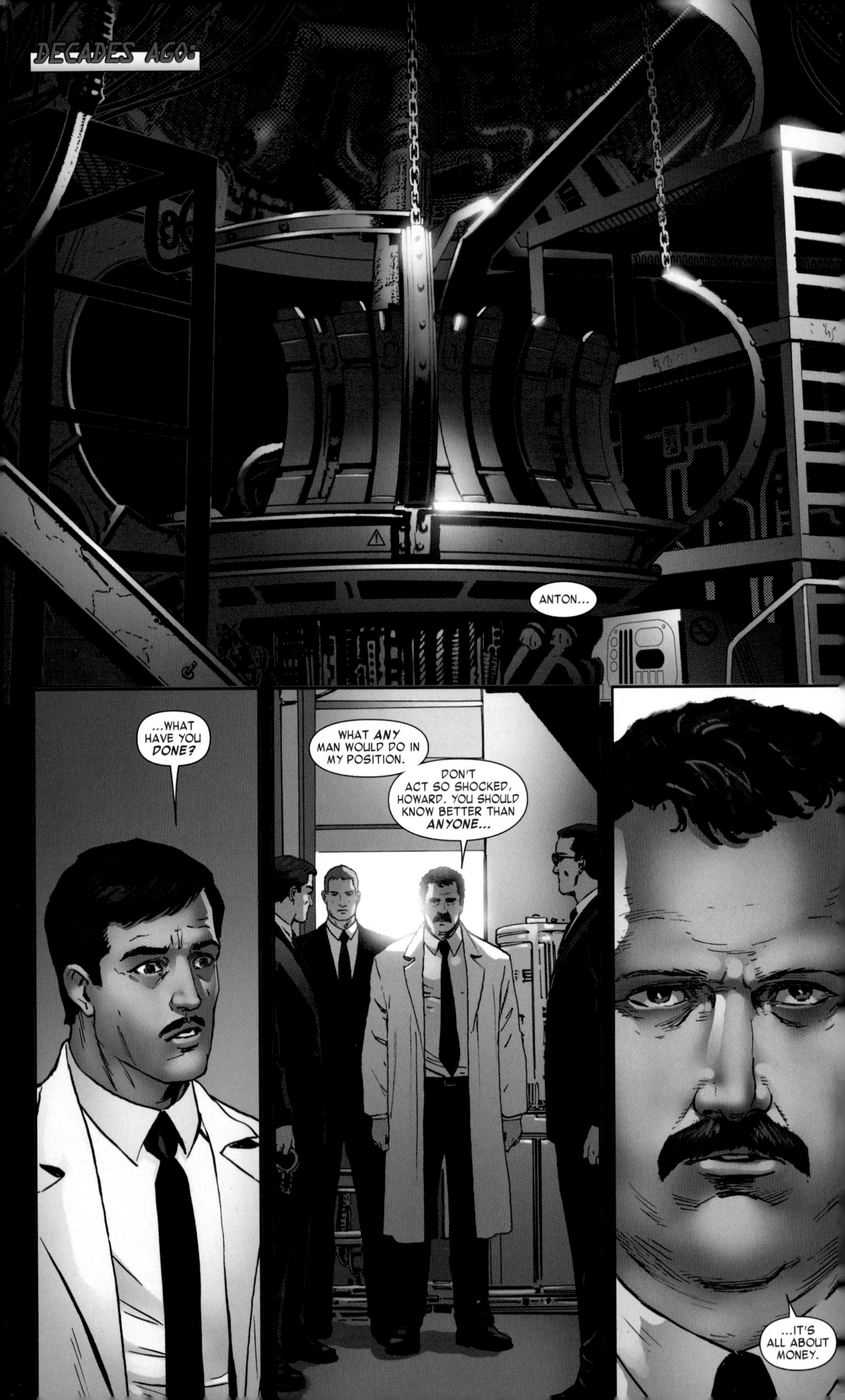
DECADES AGO:
ANTON...
...WHAT HAVE YOU DONE?
WHAT ANY MAN WOULD DO IN MY POSITION.
DON'T ACT SO SHOCKED, HOWARD. YOU SHOULD KNOW BETTER THAN ANYONE...
...IT'S ALL ABOUT MONEY.

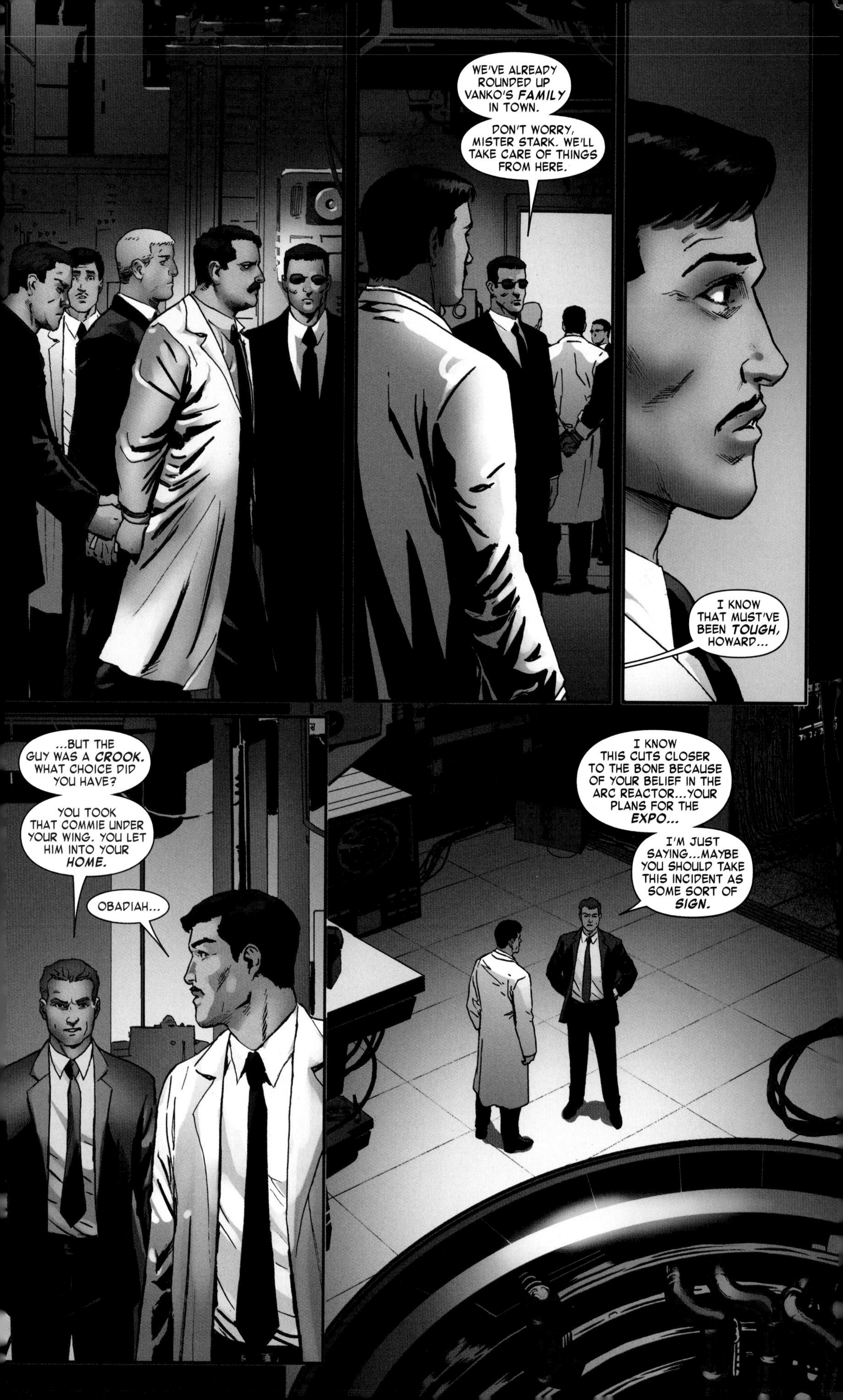
WE'VE ALREADY ROUNDED UP VANKO'S FAMILY IN TOWN.
DON'T WORRY, MISTER STARK. WE'LL TAKE CARE OF THINGS FROM HERE.
I KNOW THAT MUST'VE BEEN TOUGH, HOWARD...
...BUT THE GUY WAS A CROOK. WHAT CHOICE DID YOU HAVE?
YOU TOOK THAT COMMIE UNDER YOUR WING. YOU LET HIM INTO YOUR HOME.
OBADIAH...
I KNOW THIS CUTS CLOSER TO THE BONE BECAUSE OF YOUR BELIEF IN THE ARC REACTOR...YOUR PLANS FOR THE EXPO...
I'M JUST SAYING...MAYBE YOU SHOULD TAKE THIS INCIDENT AS SOME SORT OF SIGN.

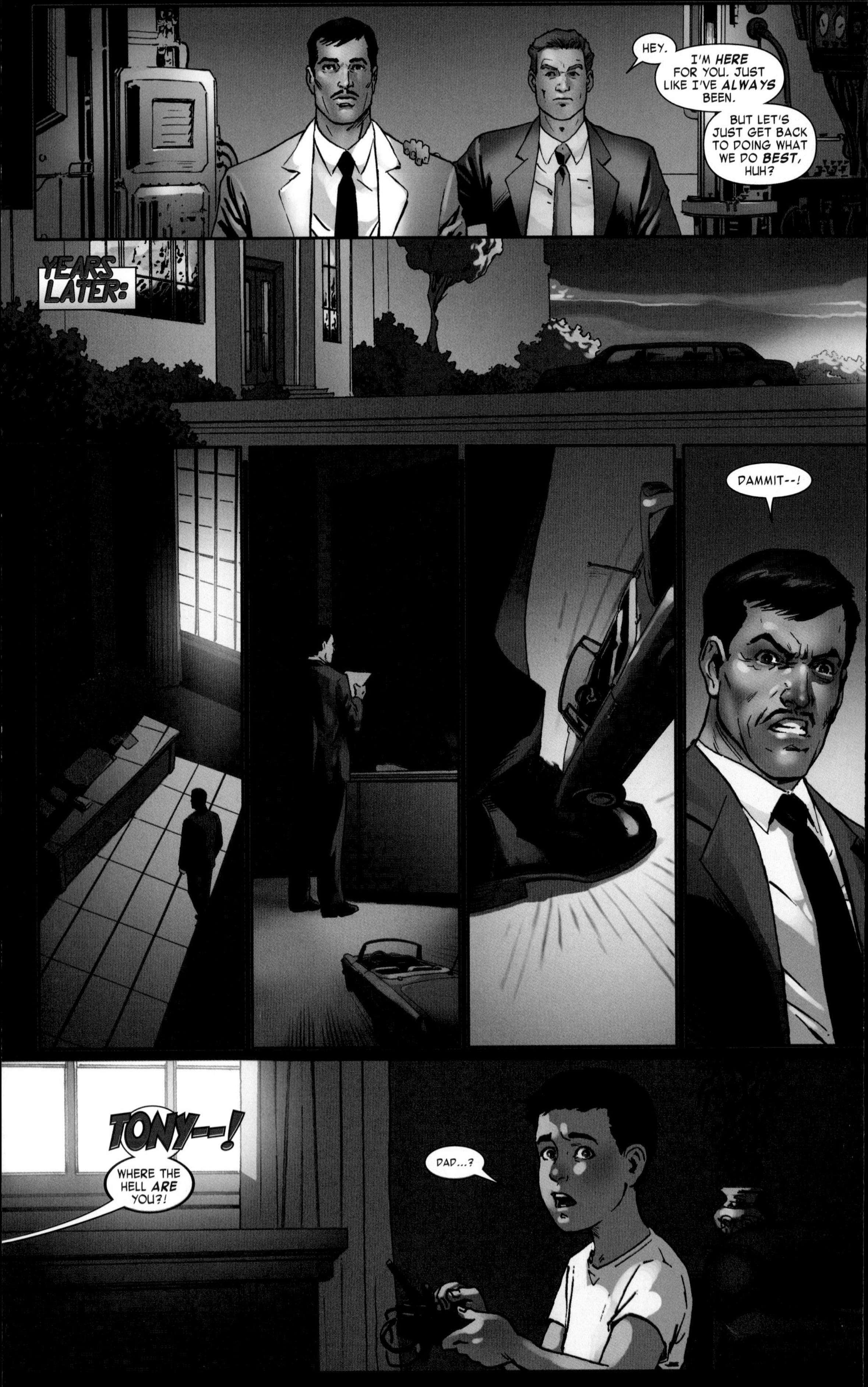

HEY.
I'M HERE FOR YOU. JUST LIKE I'VE ALWAYS BEEN.
BUT LET'S JUST GET BACK TO DOING WHAT WE DO BEST, HUH?
YEARS LATER:
DAMMIT--!
TONY--!
WHERE THE HELL ARE YOU?!
DAD...?

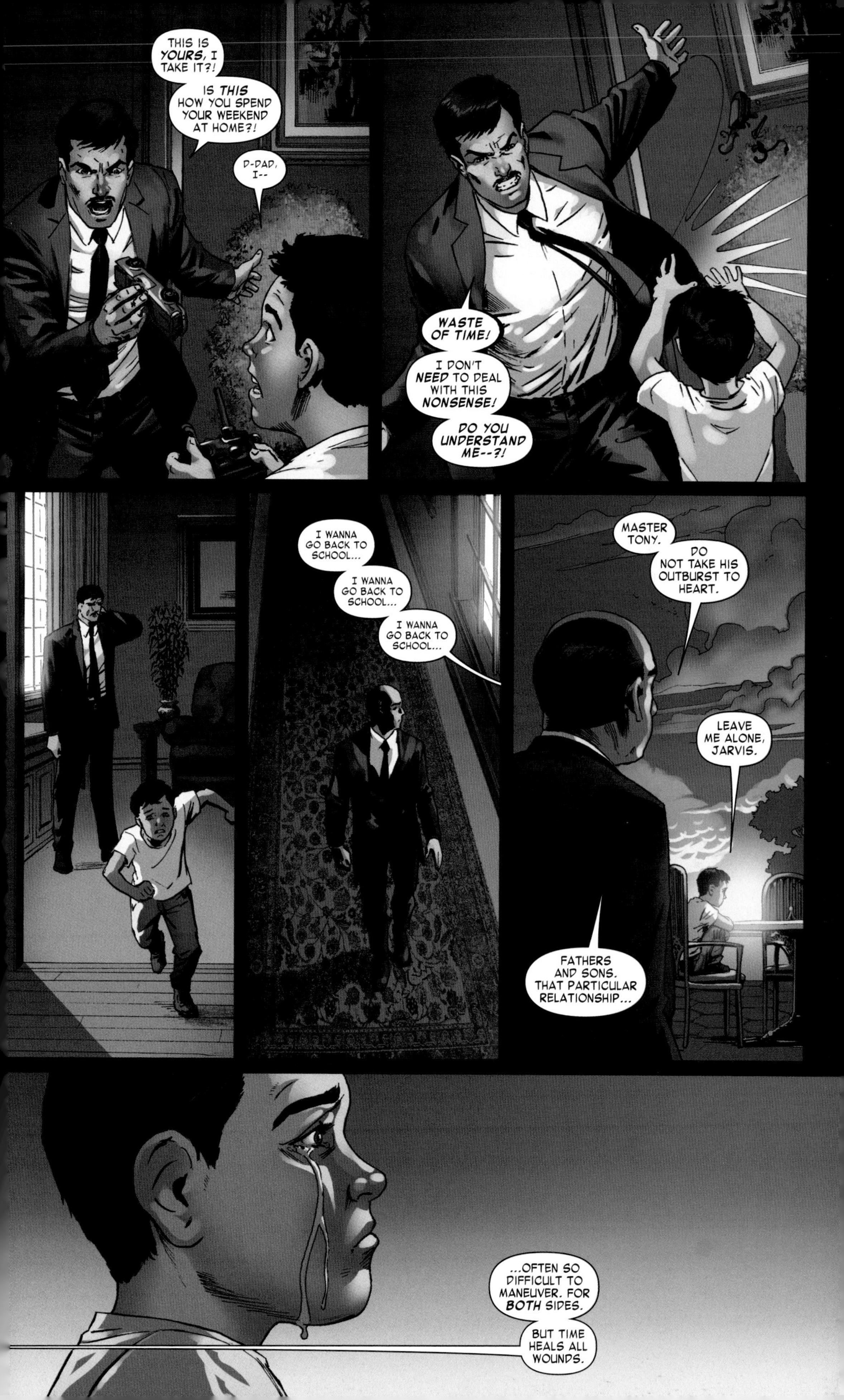

THIS IS YOURS, I TAKE IT?!
IS THIS HOW YOU SPEND YOUR WEEKEND AT HOME?!
D-DAD, I--
WASTE OF TIME!
I DON'T NEED TO DEAL WITH THIS NONSENSE!
DO YOU UNDERSTAND ME--?!
I WANNA GO BACK TO SCHOOL...
I WANNA GO BACK TO SCHOOL...
I WANNA GO BACK TO SCHOOL...
MASTER TONY.
DO NOT TAKE HIS OUTBURST TO HEART.
LEAVE ME ALONE, JARVIS.
FATHERS AND SONS. THAT PARTICULAR RELATIONSHIP...
...OFTEN SO DIFFICULT TO MANEUVER. FOR BOTH SIDES.
BUT TIME HEALS ALL WOUNDS.

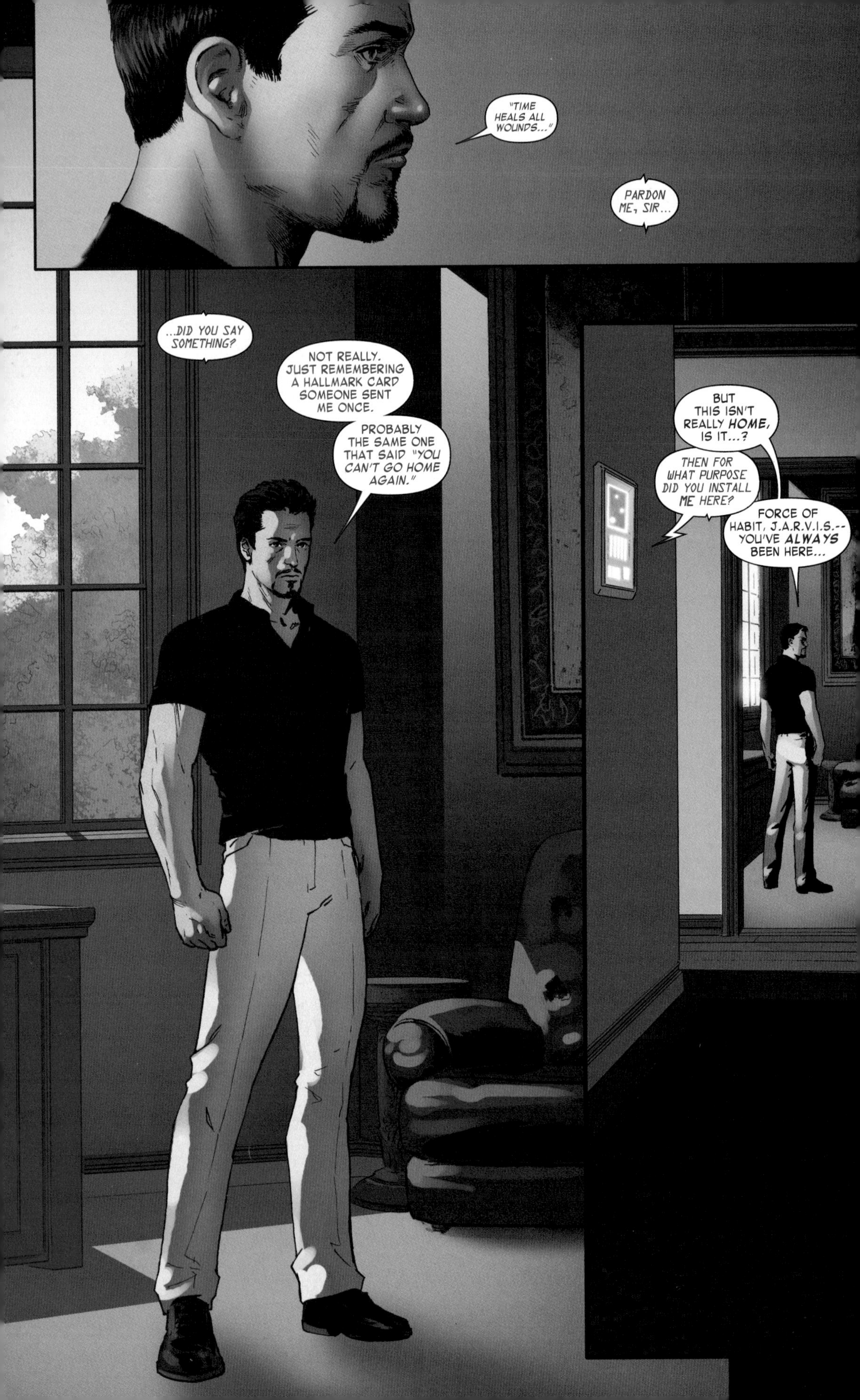
"TIME HEALS ALL WOUNDS..."
PARDON ME, SIR...
...DID YOU SAY SOMETHING?
NOT REALLY. JUST REMEMBERING A HALLMARK CARD SOMEONE SENT ME ONCE.
PROBABLY THE SAME ONE THAT SAID "YOU CAN'T GO HOME AGAIN."
BUT THIS ISN'T REALLY HOME, IS IT...?
THEN FOR WHAT PURPOSE DID YOU INSTALL ME HERE?
FORCE OF HABIT, J.A.R.V.I.S.-- YOU'VE ALWAYS BEEN HERE...

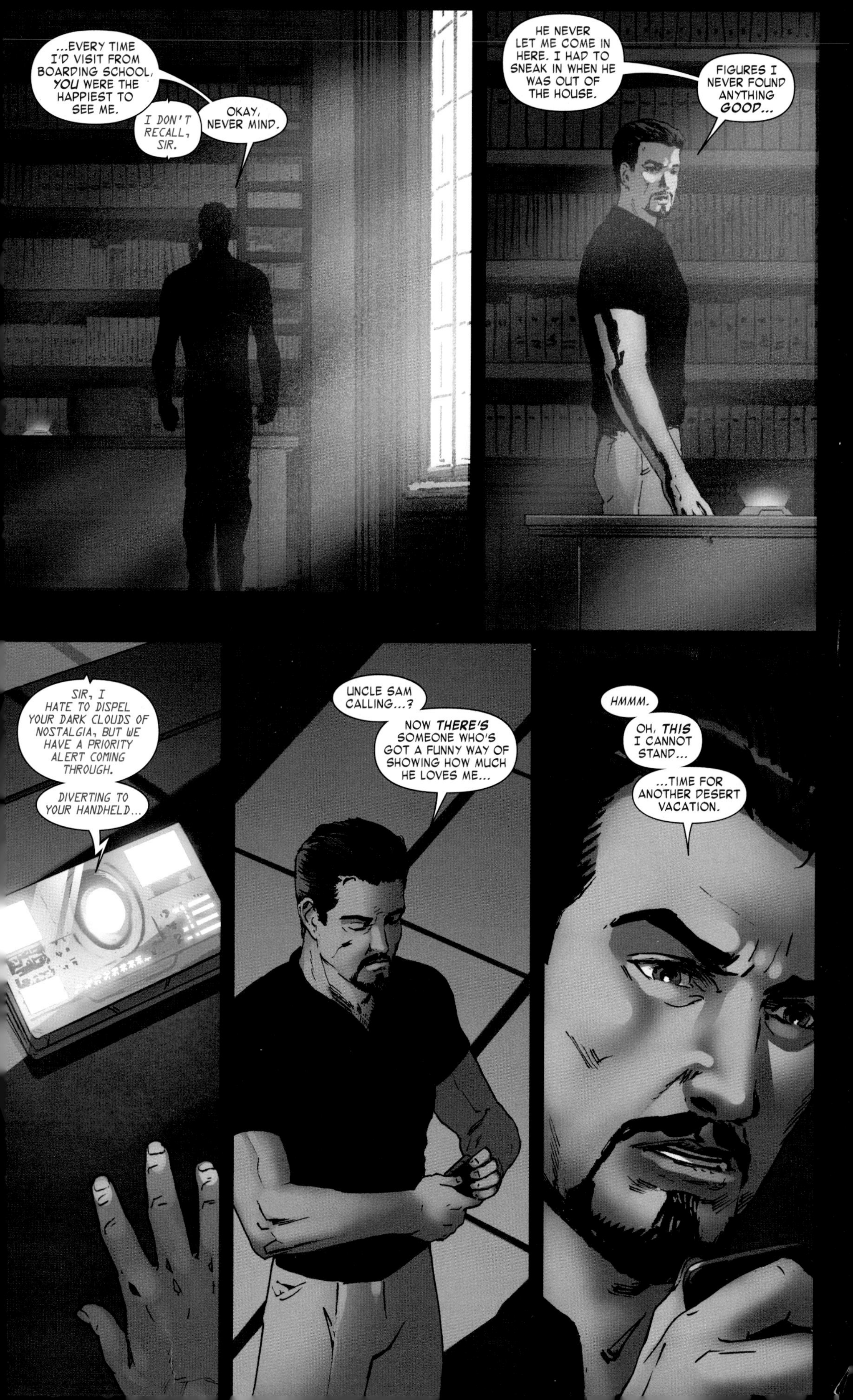
...EVERY TIME I'D VISIT FROM BOARDING SCHOOL, YOU WERE THE HAPPIEST TO SEE ME.
I DON'T RECALL, SIR.
OKAY, NEVER MIND.
HE NEVER LET ME COME IN HERE. I HAD TO SNEAK IN WHEN HE WAS OUT OF THE HOUSE.
FIGURES I NEVER FOUND ANYTHING GOOD...
SIR, I HATE TO DISPEL YOUR DARK CLOUDS OF NOSTALGIA, BUT WE HAVE A PRIORITY ALERT COMING THROUGH.
DIVERTING TO YOUR HANDHELD...
UNCLE SAM CALLING...?
NOW THERE'S SOMEONE WHO'S GOT A FUNNY WAY OF SHOWING HOW MUCH HE LOVES ME...
HMMM.
OH, THIS I CANNOT STAND...
...TIME FOR ANOTHER DESERT VACATION.

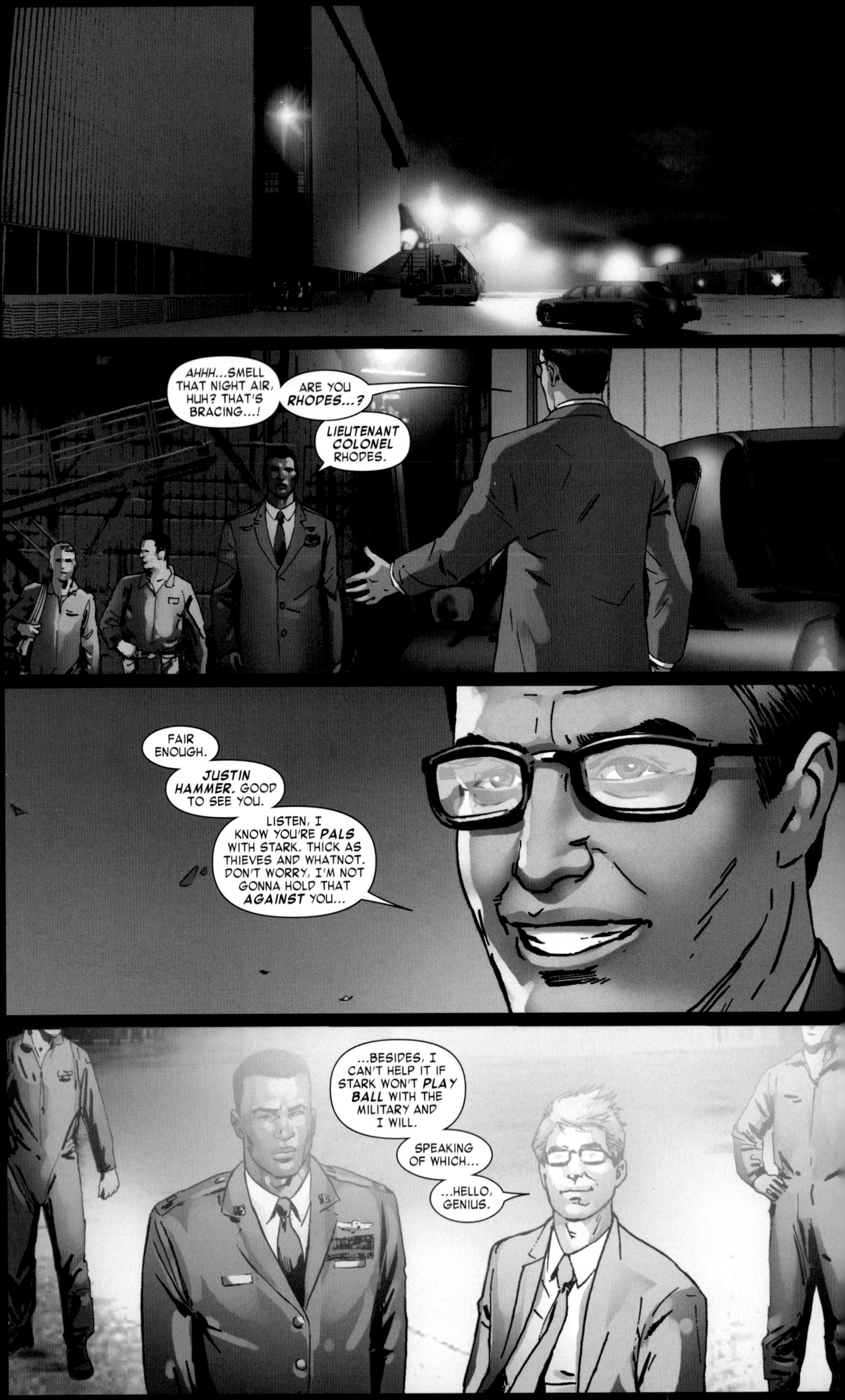
AHHH...SMELL THAT NIGHT AIR, HUH? THAT'S BRACING...!
ARE YOU RHODES...?
LIEUTENANT COLONEL RHODES.
FAIR ENOUGH.
JUSTIN HAMMER. GOOD TO SEE YOU.
LISTEN, I KNOW YOU'RE PALS WITH STARK. THICK AS THIEVES AND WHATNOT. DON'T WORRY, I'M NOT GONNA HOLD THAT AGAINST YOU...
...BESIDES, I CAN'T HELP IT IF STARK WON'T PLAY BALL WITH THE MILITARY AND I WILL.
SPEAKING OF WHICH...
...HELLO, GENIUS.

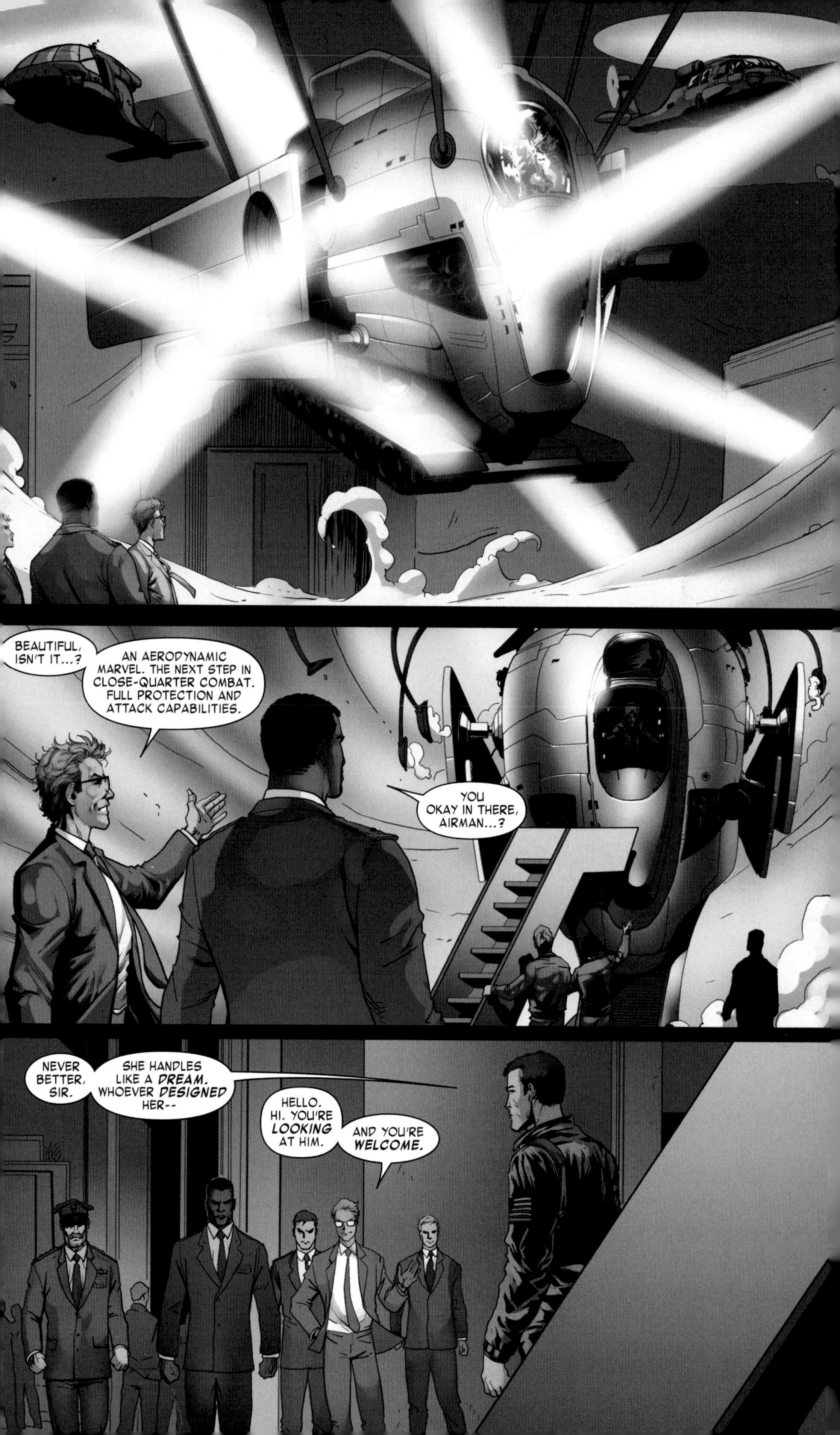
BEAUTIFUL, ISN'T IT...?
AN AERODYNAMIC MARVEL. THE NEXT STEP IN CLOSE-QUARTER COMBAT. FULL PROTECTION AND ATTACK CAPABILITIES.
YOU OKAY IN THERE, AIRMAN...?
NEVER BETTER, SIR.
SHE HANDLES LIKE A DREAM. WHOEVER DESIGNED HER--
HELLO. HI. YOU'RE LOOKING AT HIM.
AND YOU'RE WELCOME.

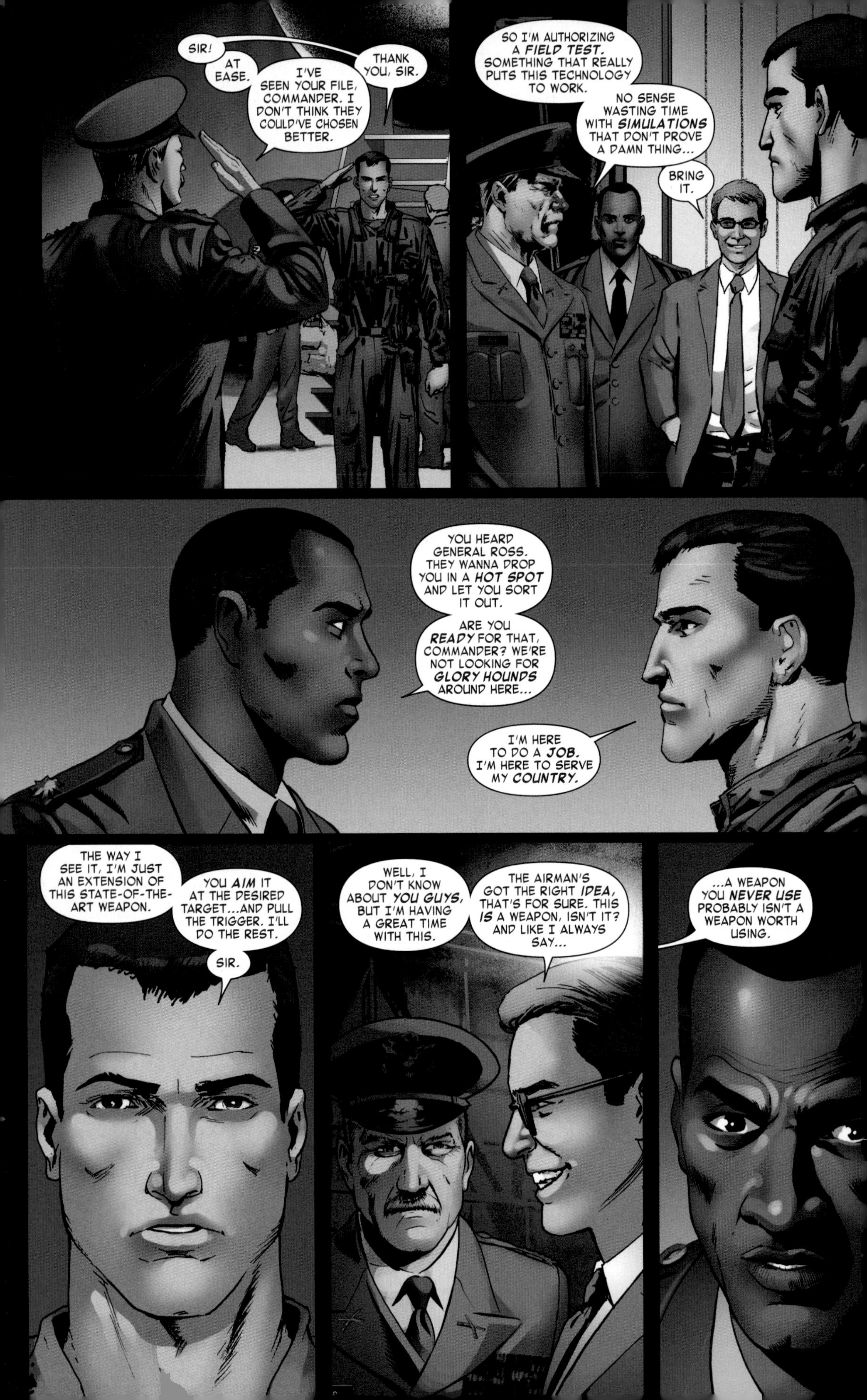
SIR!
AT EASE.
THANK YOU, SIR.
I'VE SEEN YOUR FILE, COMMANDER. I DON'T THINK THEY COULD'VE CHOSEN BETTER.
SO I'M AUTHORIZING A FIELD TEST. SOMETHING THAT REALLY PUTS THIS TECHNOLOGY TO WORK.
NO SENSE WASTING TIME WITH SIMULATIONS THAT DON'T PROVE A DAMN THING...
BRING IT.
YOU HEARD GENERAL ROSS. THEY WANNA DROP YOU IN A HOT SPOT AND LET YOU SORT IT OUT.
ARE YOU READY FOR THAT, COMMANDER? WE'RE NOT LOOKING FOR GLORY HOUNDS AROUND HERE...
I'M HERE TO DO A JOB. I'M HERE TO SERVE MY COUNTRY.
THE WAY I SEE IT, I'M JUST AN EXTENSION OF THIS STATE-OF-THE-ART WEAPON.
YOU AIM IT AT THE DESIRED TARGET...AND PULL THE TRIGGER. I'LL DO THE REST.
SIR.
WELL, I DON'T KNOW ABOUT YOU GUYS, BUT I'M HAVING A GREAT TIME WITH THIS.
THE AIRMAN'S GOT THE RIGHT IDEA, THAT'S FOR SURE. THIS IS A WEAPON, ISN'T IT? AND LIKE I ALWAYS SAY...
...A WEAPON YOU NEVER USE PROBABLY ISN'T A WEAPON WORTH USING.

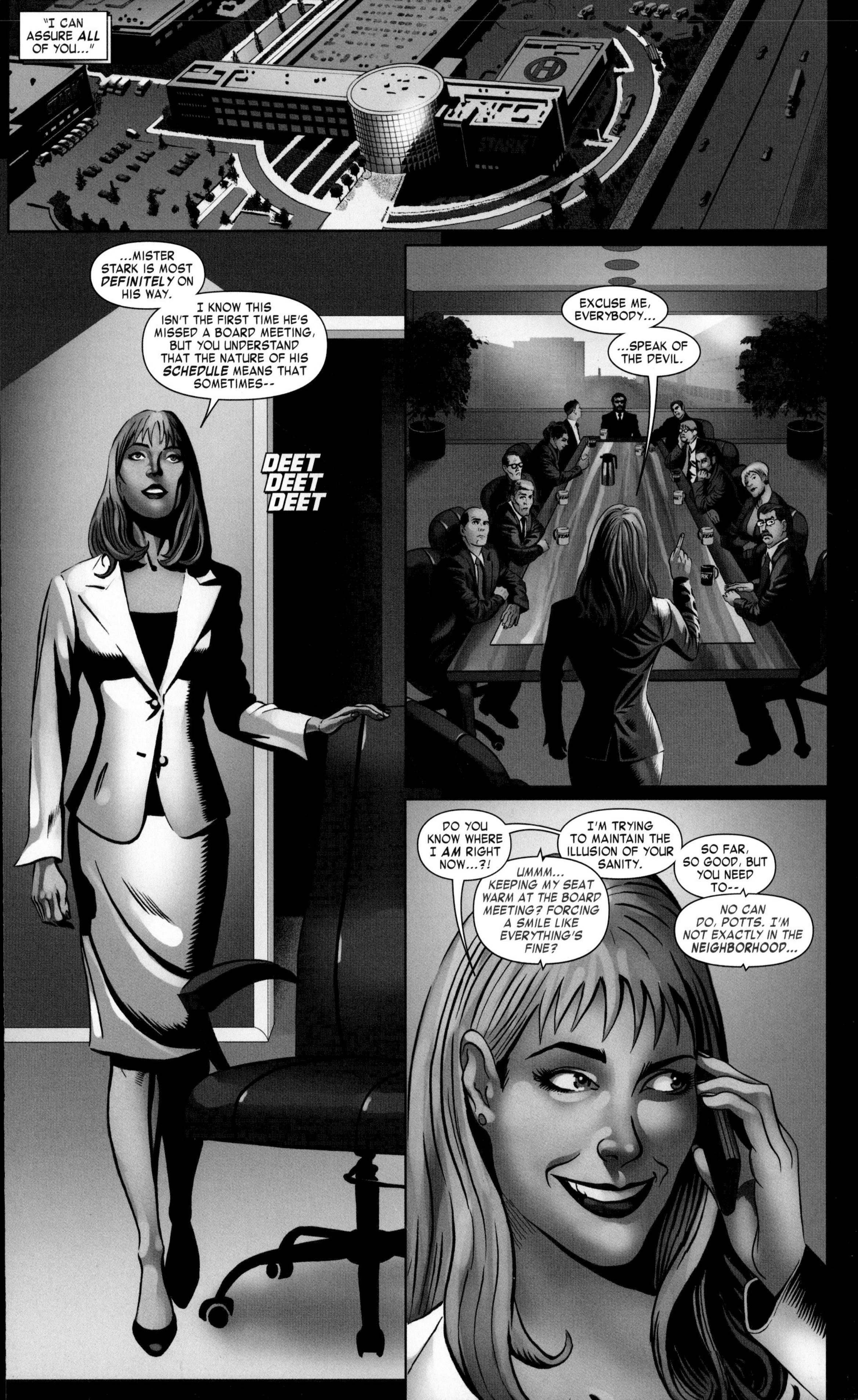
"I CAN ASSURE ALL OF YOU..."
...MISTER STARK IS MOST DEFINITELY ON HIS WAY.
I KNOW THIS ISN'T THE FIRST TIME HE'S MISSED A BOARD MEETING, BUT YOU UNDERSTAND THAT THE NATURE OF HIS SCHEDULE MEANS THAT SOMETIMES--
DEET DEET DEET
EXCUSE ME, EVERYBODY...
...SPEAK OF THE DEVIL.
DO YOU KNOW WHERE I AM RIGHT NOW...?!
UMMM... KEEPING MY SEAT WARM AT THE BOARD MEETING? FORCING A SMILE LIKE EVERYTHING'S FINE?
I'M TRYING TO MAINTAIN THE ILLUSION OF YOUR SANITY.
SO FAR, SO GOOD, BUT YOU NEED TO--
NO CAN DO, POTTS. I'M NOT EXACTLY IN THE NEIGHBORHOOD...

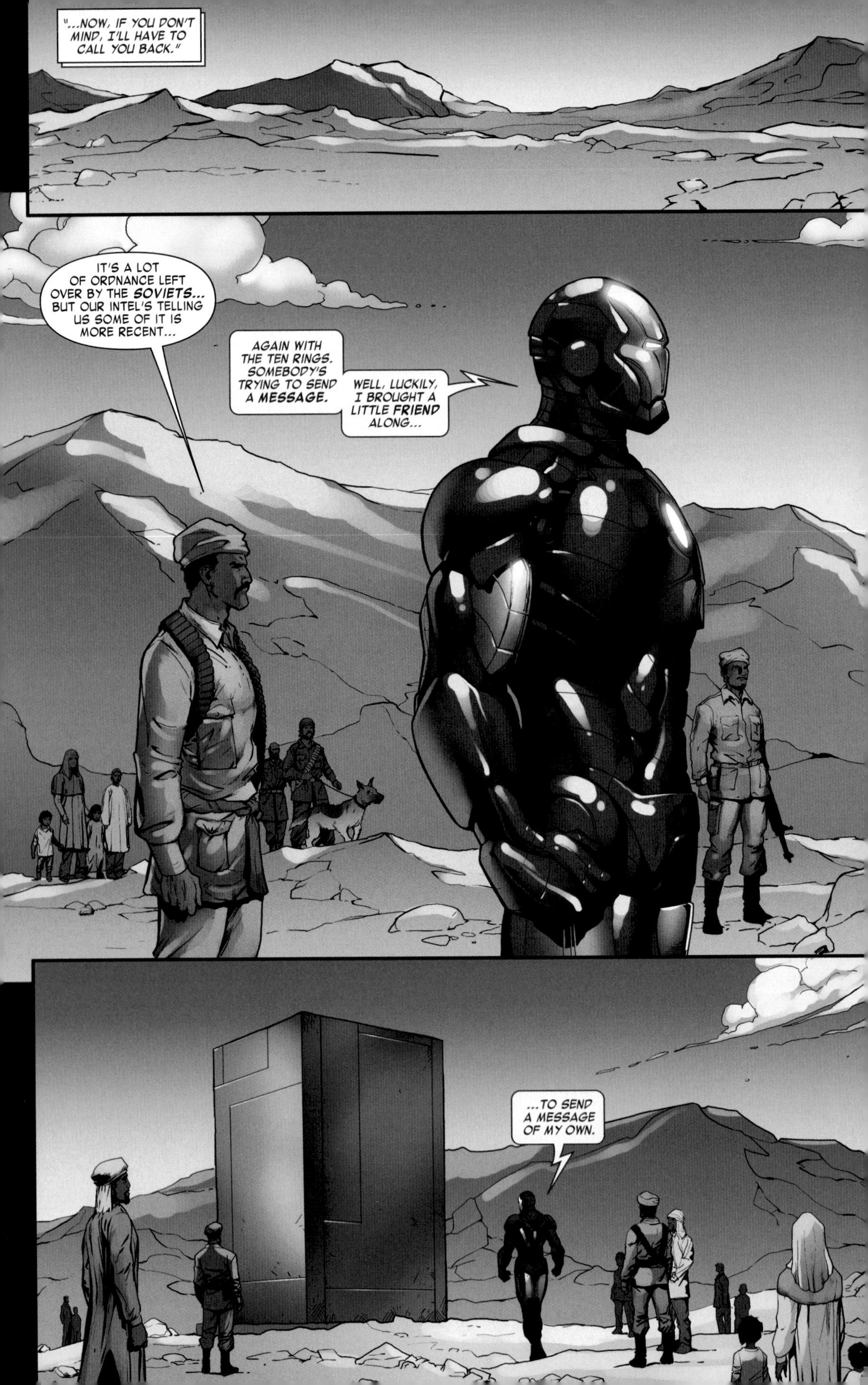
"...NOW, IF YOU DON'T MIND, I'LL HAVE TO CALL YOU BACK."
IT'S A LOT OF ORDNANCE LEFT OVER BY THE SOVIETS... BUT OUR INTEL'S TELLING US SOME OF IT IS MORE RECENT...
AGAIN WITH THE TEN RINGS. SOMEBODY'S TRYING TO SEND A MESSAGE.
WELL, LUCKILY, I BROUGHT A LITTLE FRIEND ALONG...
...TO SEND A MESSAGE OF MY OWN.

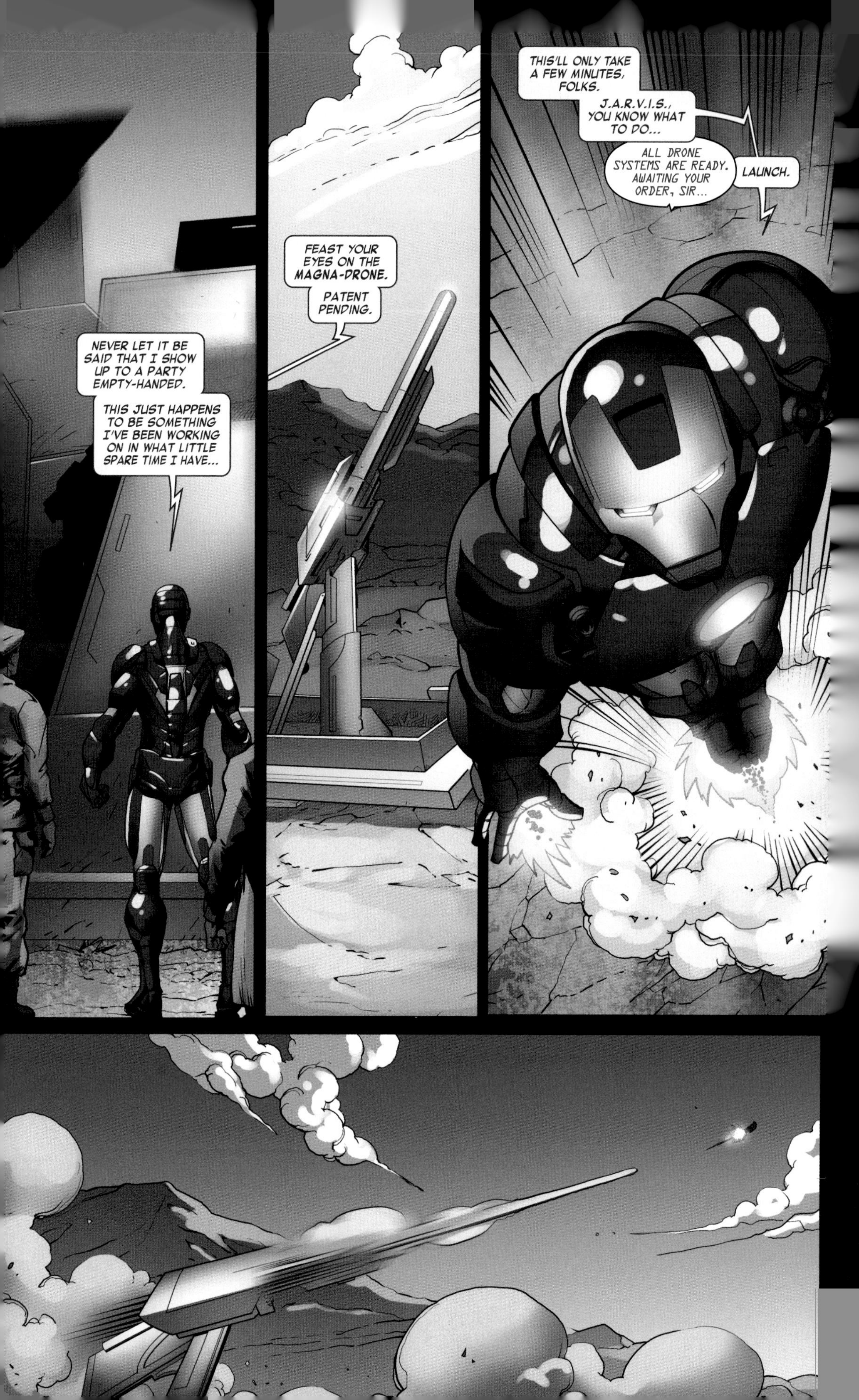
NEVER LET IT BE SAID THAT I SHOW UP TO A PARTY EMPTY-HANDED.
THIS JUST HAPPENS TO BE SOMETHING I'VE BEEN WORKING ON IN WHAT LITTLE SPARE TIME I HAVE...
FEAST YOUR EYES ON THE MAGNA-DRONE.
PATENT PENDING.
THIS'LL ONLY TAKE A FEW MINUTES, FOLKS.
J.A.R.V.I.S., YOU KNOW WHAT TO DO...
ALL DRONE SYSTEMS ARE READY. AWAITING YOUR ORDER, SIR...
LAUNCH.

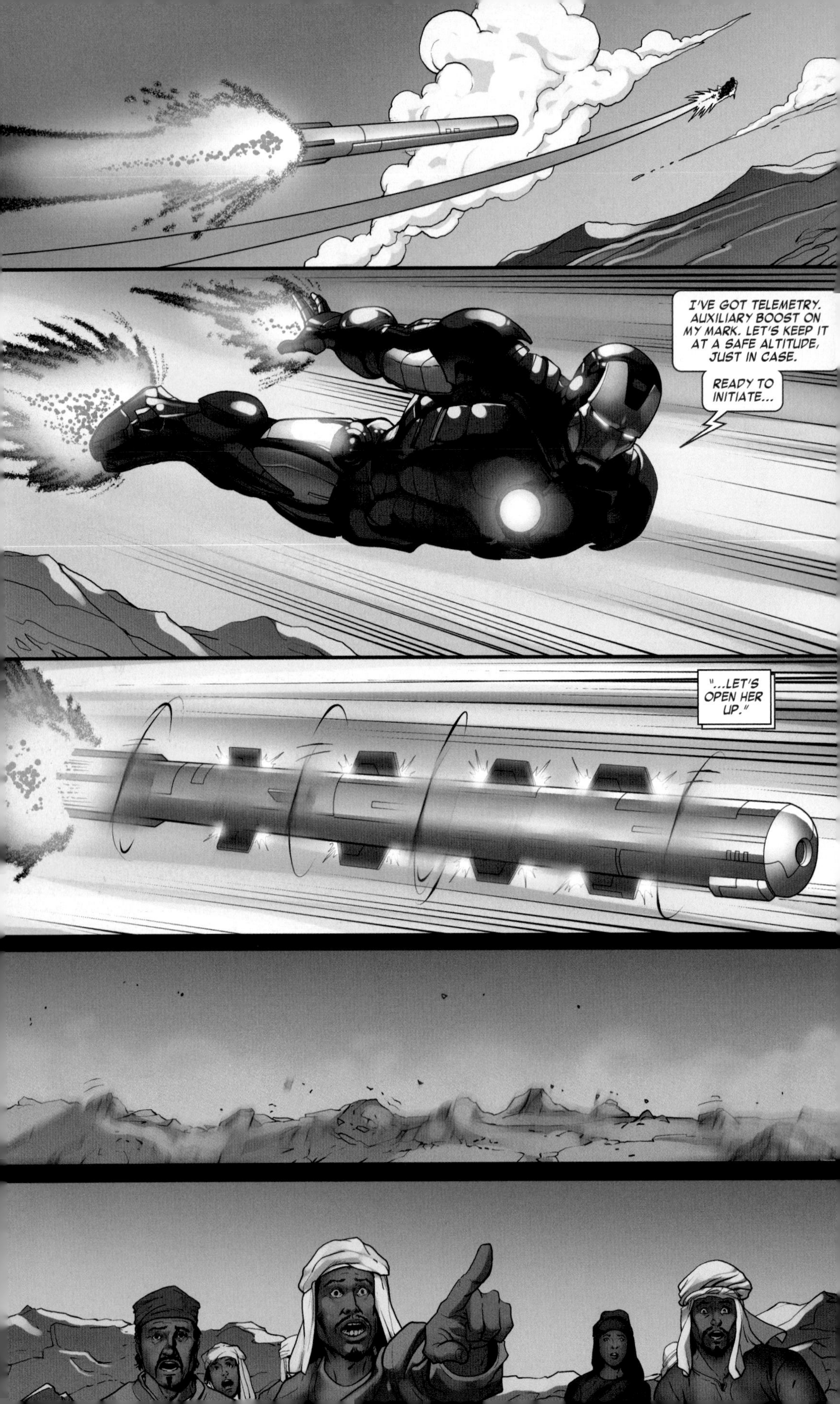
I'VE GOT TELEMETRY. AUXILIARY BOOST ON MY MARK. LET'S KEEP IT AT A SAFE ALTITUDE, JUST IN CASE.
READY TO INITIATE...
"...LET'S OPEN HER UP."

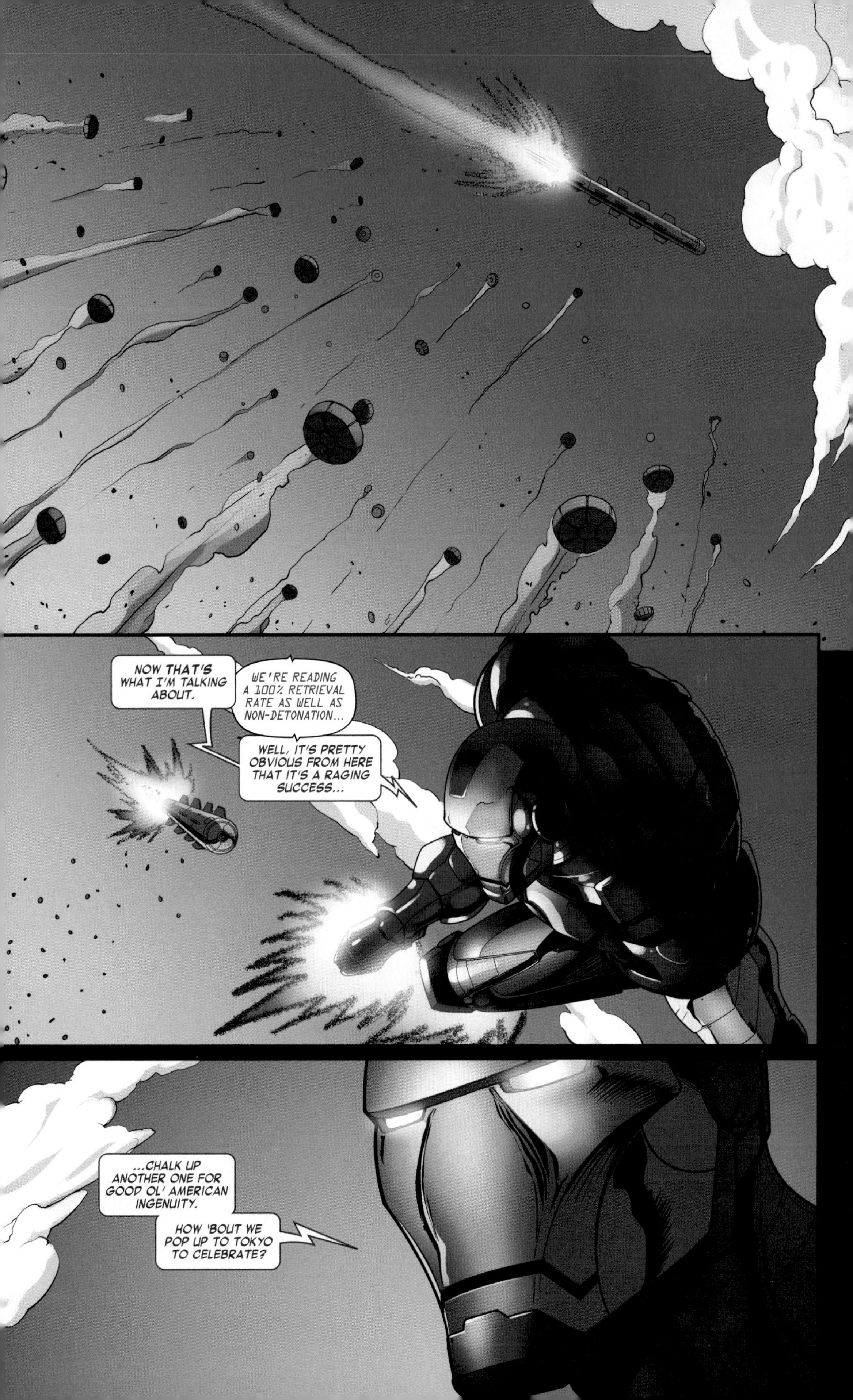
NOW THAT'S WHAT I'M TALKING ABOUT.
WE'RE READING A 100% RETRIEVAL RATE AS WELL AS NON-DETONATION...
WELL, IT'S PRETTY OBVIOUS FROM HERE THAT IT'S A RAGING SUCCESS...
...CHALK UP ANOTHER ONE FOR GOOD OL' AMERICAN INGENUITY.
HOW 'BOUT WE POP UP TO TOKYO TO CELEBRATE?

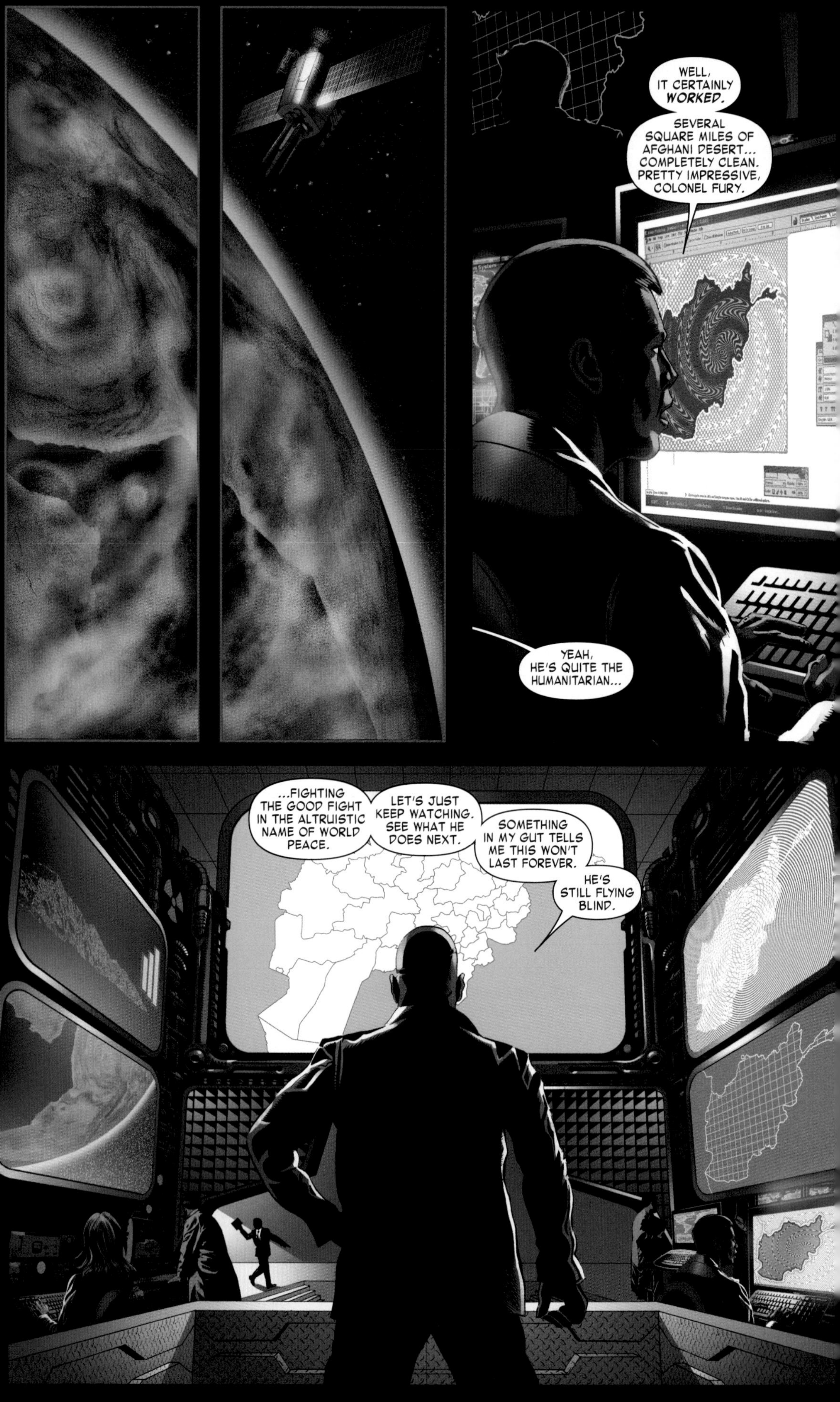
WELL, IT CERTAINLY *WORKED.*
SEVERAL SQUARE MILES OF AFGHANI DESERT... COMPLETELY CLEAN. PRETTY IMPRESSIVE, COLONEL FURY.
YEAH, HE'S QUITE THE HUMANITARIAN...
...FIGHTING THE GOOD FIGHT IN THE ALTRUISTIC NAME OF WORLD PEACE.
LET'S JUST KEEP WATCHING. SEE WHAT HE DOES NEXT.
SOMETHING IN MY GUT TELLS ME THIS WON'T LAST FOREVER.
HE'S STILL FLYING BLIND.

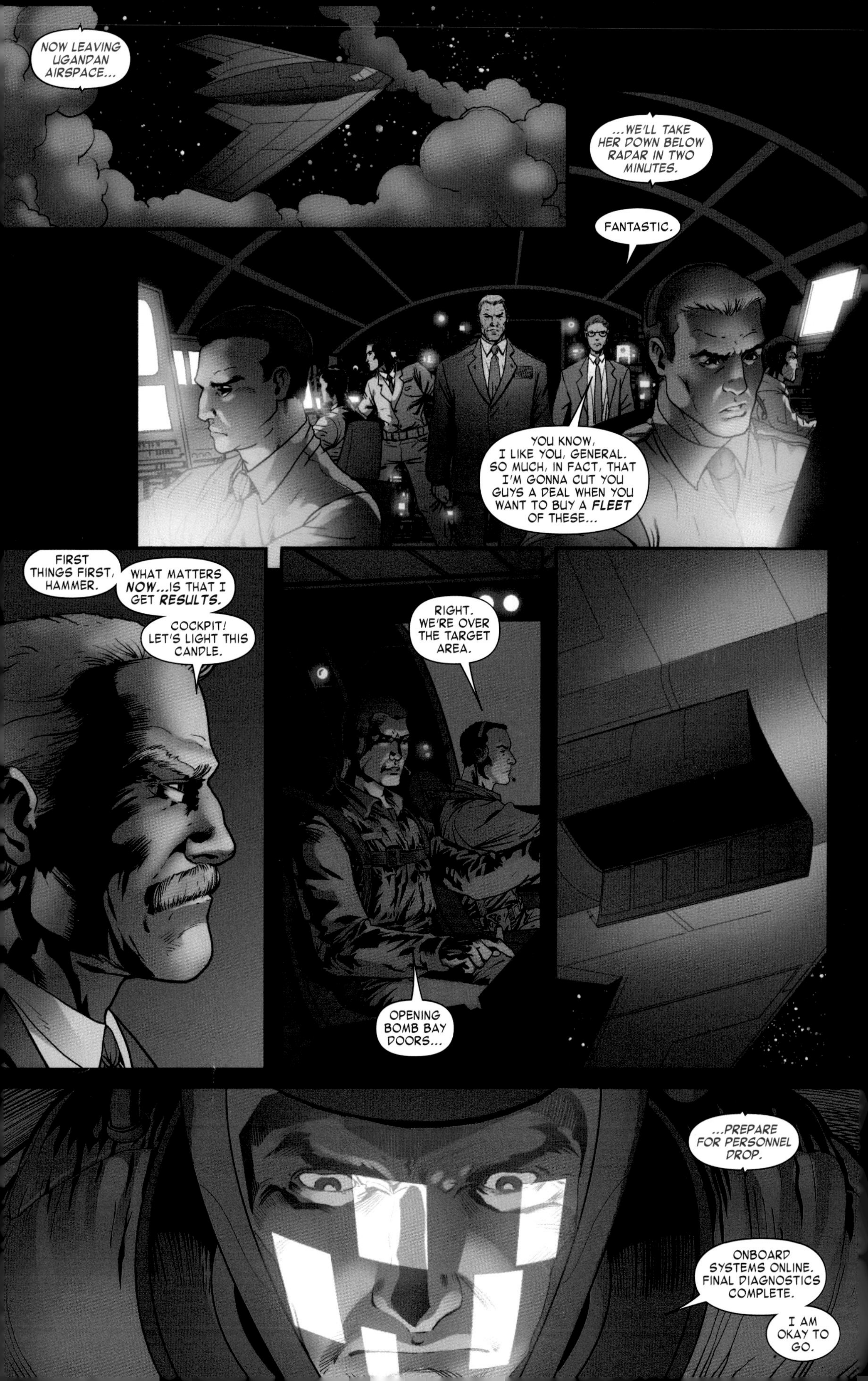
NOW LEAVING UGANDAN AIRSPACE...
...WE'LL TAKE HER DOWN BELOW RADAR IN TWO MINUTES.
FANTASTIC.
YOU KNOW, I LIKE YOU, GENERAL. SO MUCH, IN FACT, THAT I'M GONNA CUT YOU GUYS A DEAL WHEN YOU WANT TO BUY A FLEET OF THESE...
FIRST THINGS FIRST, HAMMER.
WHAT MATTERS NOW...IS THAT I GET RESULTS.
COCKPIT! LET'S LIGHT THIS CANDLE.
RIGHT. WE'RE OVER THE TARGET AREA.
OPENING BOMB BAY DOORS...
...PREPARE FOR PERSONNEL DROP.
ONBOARD SYSTEMS ONLINE. FINAL DIAGNOSTICS COMPLETE.
I AM OKAY TO GO.

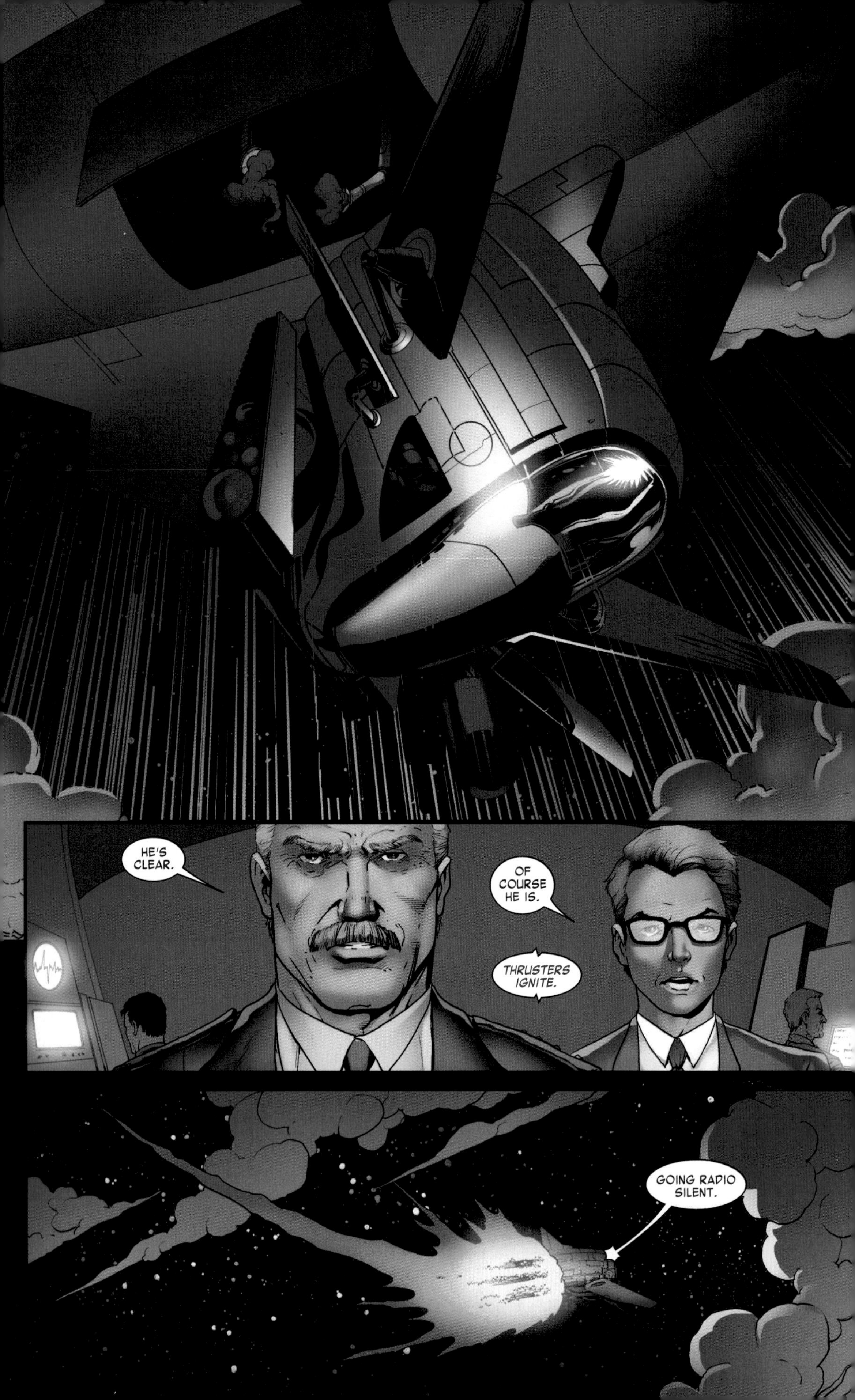
HE'S CLEAR.
OF COURSE HE IS.
THRUSTERS IGNITE.
GOING RADIO SILENT.

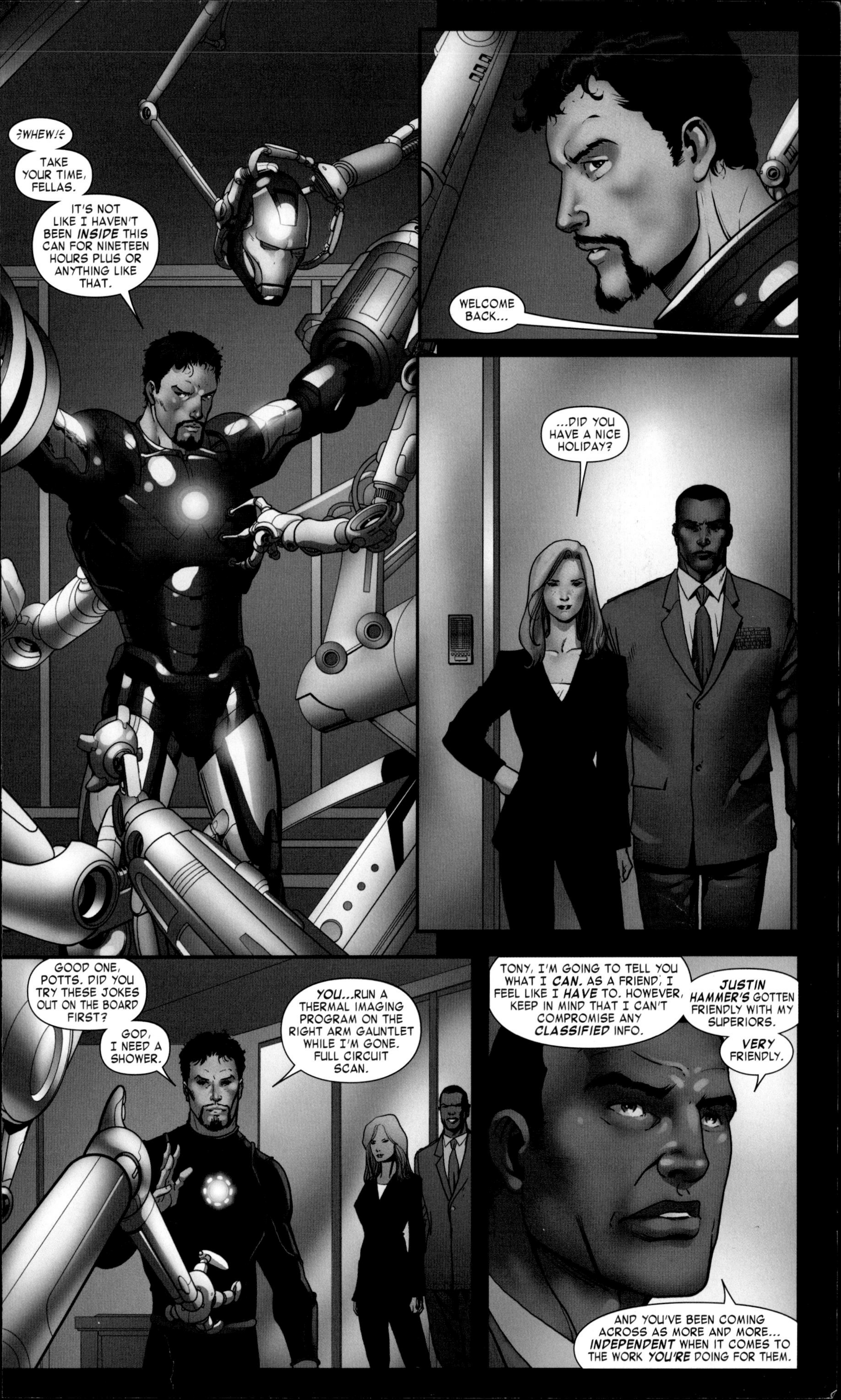

WHEW!
TAKE YOUR TIME, FELLAS.
IT'S NOT LIKE I HAVEN'T BEEN INSIDE THIS CAN FOR NINETEEN HOURS PLUS OR ANYTHING LIKE THAT.
WELCOME BACK...
...DID YOU HAVE A NICE HOLIDAY?
GOOD ONE, POTTS. DID YOU TRY THESE JOKES OUT ON THE BOARD FIRST?
GOD, I NEED A SHOWER.
YOU...RUN A THERMAL IMAGING PROGRAM ON THE RIGHT ARM GAUNTLET WHILE I'M GONE. FULL CIRCUIT SCAN.
TONY, I'M GOING TO TELL YOU WHAT I CAN. AS A FRIEND, I FEEL LIKE I HAVE TO. HOWEVER, KEEP IN MIND THAT I CAN'T COMPROMISE ANY CLASSIFIED INFO.
JUSTIN HAMMER'S GOTTEN FRIENDLY WITH MY SUPERIORS.
VERY FRIENDLY.
AND YOU'VE BEEN COMING ACROSS AS MORE AND MORE... INDEPENDENT WHEN IT COMES TO THE WORK YOU'RE DOING FOR THEM.

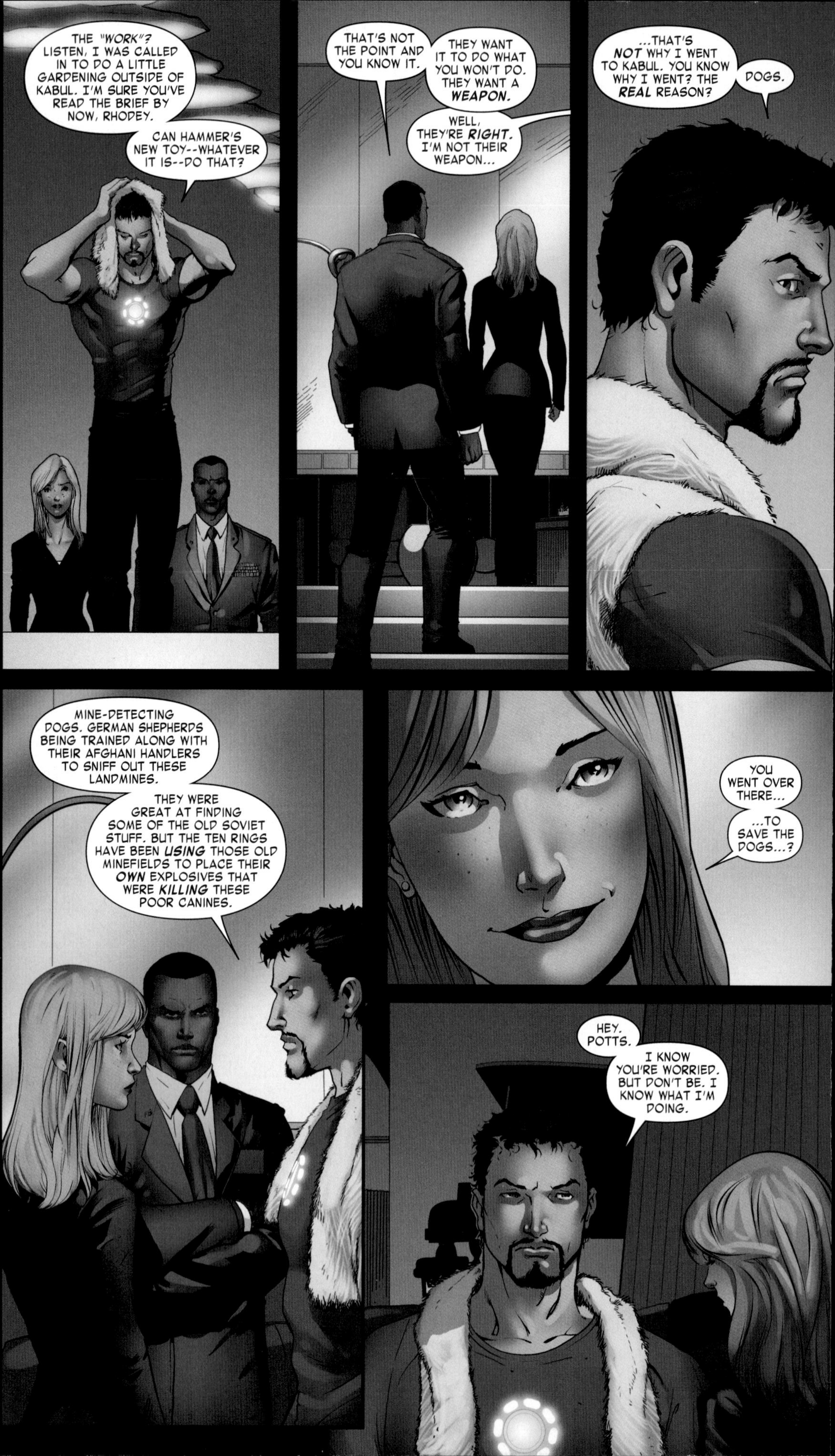
THE "WORK"? LISTEN, I WAS CALLED IN TO DO A LITTLE GARDENING OUTSIDE OF KABUL. I'M SURE YOU'VE READ THE BRIEF BY NOW, RHODEY.
CAN HAMMER'S NEW TOY--WHATEVER IT IS--DO THAT?
THAT'S NOT THE POINT AND YOU KNOW IT.
THEY WANT IT TO DO WHAT YOU WON'T DO. THEY WANT A WEAPON.
WELL, THEY'RE RIGHT. I'M NOT THEIR WEAPON...
...THAT'S NOT WHY I WENT TO KABUL. YOU KNOW WHY I WENT? THE REAL REASON?
DOGS.
MINE-DETECTING DOGS. GERMAN SHEPHERDS BEING TRAINED ALONG WITH THEIR AFGHANI HANDLERS TO SNIFF OUT THESE LANDMINES.
THEY WERE GREAT AT FINDING SOME OF THE OLD SOVIET STUFF. BUT THE TEN RINGS HAVE BEEN USING THOSE OLD MINEFIELDS TO PLACE THEIR OWN EXPLOSIVES THAT WERE KILLING THESE POOR CANINES.
YOU WENT OVER THERE...
...TO SAVE THE DOGS...?
HEY. POTTS.
I KNOW YOU'RE WORRIED. BUT DON'T BE. I KNOW WHAT I'M DOING.

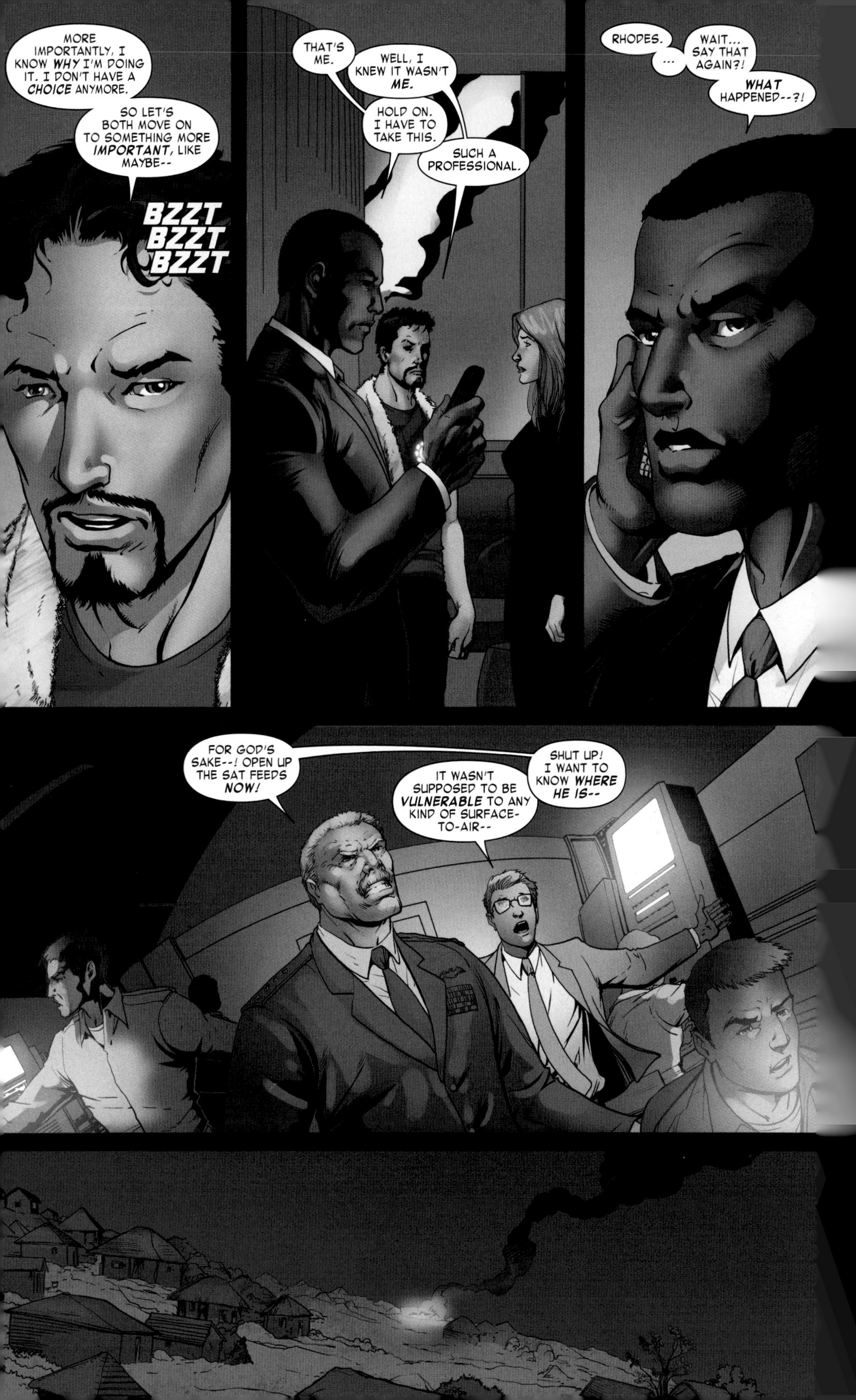

MORE IMPORTANTLY, I KNOW WHY I'M DOING IT. I DON'T HAVE A CHOICE ANYMORE.
SO LET'S BOTH MOVE ON TO SOMETHING MORE IMPORTANT, LIKE MAYBE--
BZZT BZZT BZZT
THAT'S ME.
WELL, I KNEW IT WASN'T ME.
HOLD ON. I HAVE TO TAKE THIS.
SUCH A PROFESSIONAL.
RHODES.
...
WAIT... SAY THAT AGAIN?!
WHAT HAPPENED--?!
FOR GOD'S SAKE--! OPEN UP THE SAT FEEDS NOW!
IT WASN'T SUPPOSED TO BE VULNERABLE TO ANY KIND OF SURFACE-TO-AIR--
SHUT UP! I WANT TO KNOW WHERE HE IS--

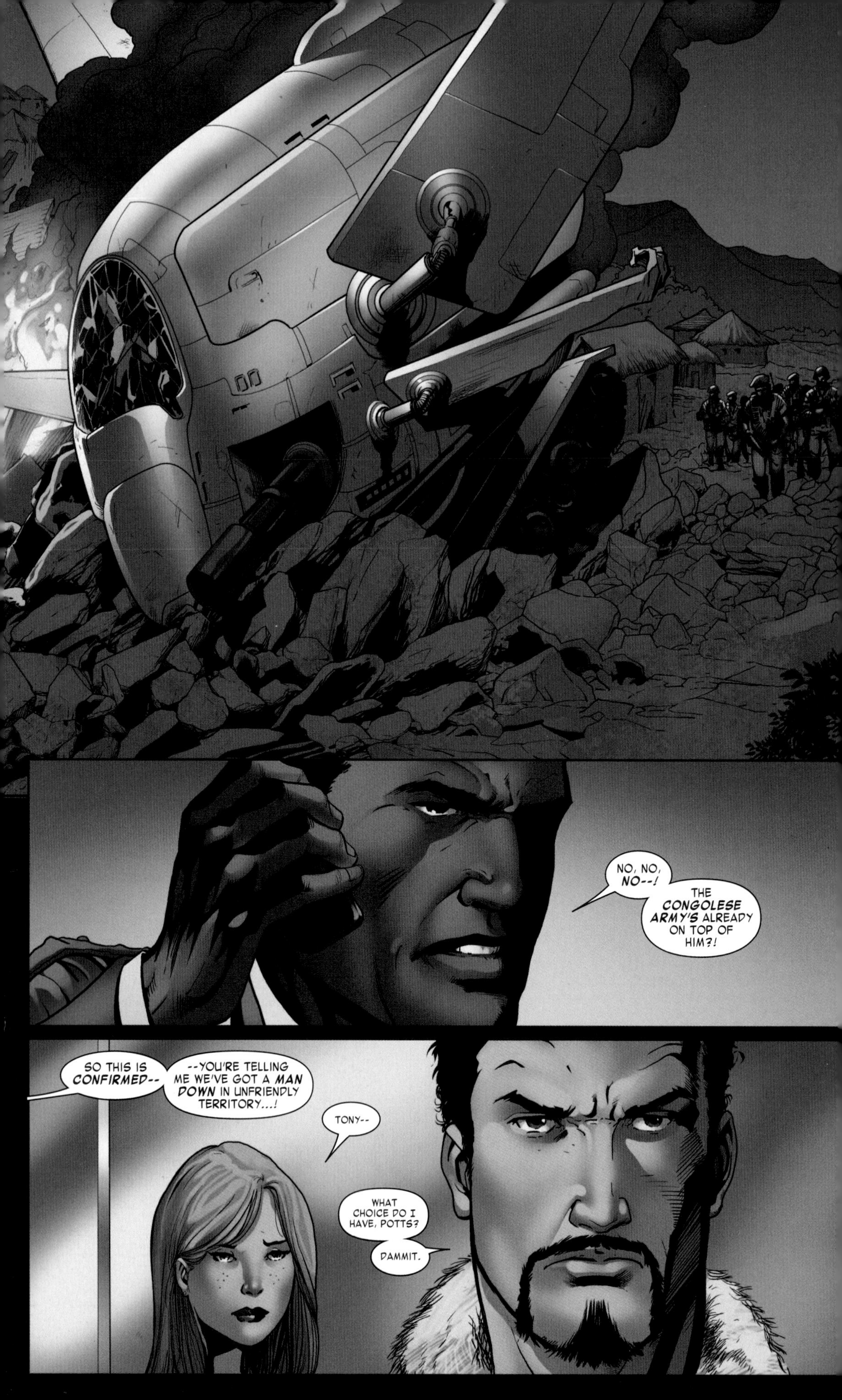
NO, NO, NO--!
THE CONGOLESE ARMY'S ALREADY ON TOP OF HIM?!
SO THIS IS CONFIRMED--
--YOU'RE TELLING ME WE'VE GOT A MAN DOWN IN UNFRIENDLY TERRITORY...!
TONY--
WHAT CHOICE DO I HAVE, POTTS?
DAMMIT.

MARVEL STUDIOS

IRON MAN 2

PUBLIC IDENTITY

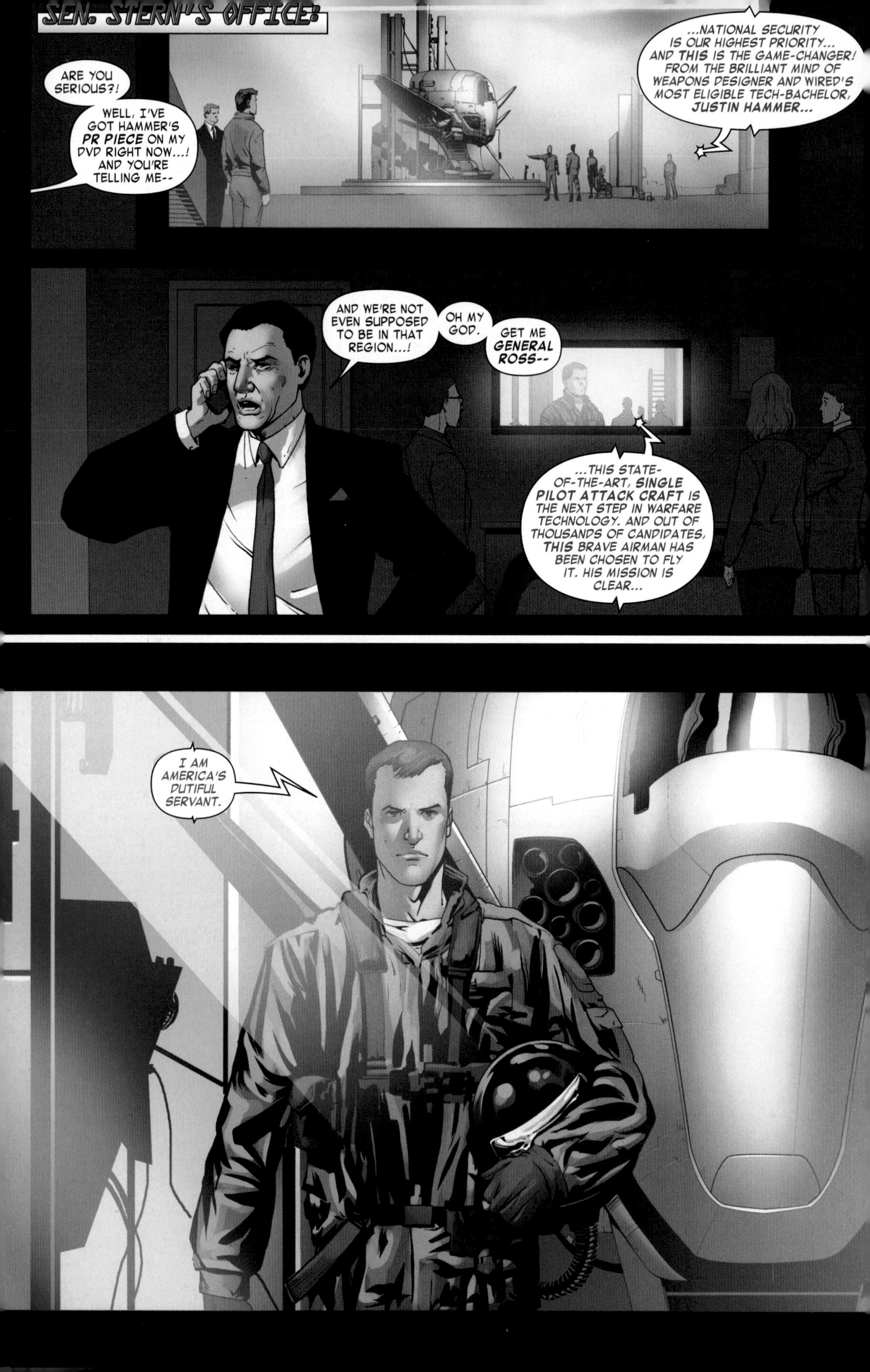
SEN. STERN'S OFFICE:
ARE YOU SERIOUS?!
WELL, I'VE GOT HAMMER'S PR PIECE ON MY DVD RIGHT NOW...! AND YOU'RE TELLING ME--
...NATIONAL SECURITY IS OUR HIGHEST PRIORITY... AND THIS IS THE GAME-CHANGER! FROM THE BRILLIANT MIND OF WEAPONS DESIGNER AND WIRED'S MOST ELIGIBLE TECH-BACHELOR, JUSTIN HAMMER...
AND WE'RE NOT EVEN SUPPOSED TO BE IN THAT REGION...!
OH MY GOD.
GET ME GENERAL ROSS--
...THIS STATE-OF-THE-ART, SINGLE PILOT ATTACK CRAFT IS THE NEXT STEP IN WARFARE TECHNOLOGY. AND OUT OF THOUSANDS OF CANDIDATES, THIS BRAVE AIRMAN HAS BEEN CHOSEN TO FLY IT. HIS MISSION IS CLEAR...
I AM AMERICA'S DUTIFUL SERVANT.

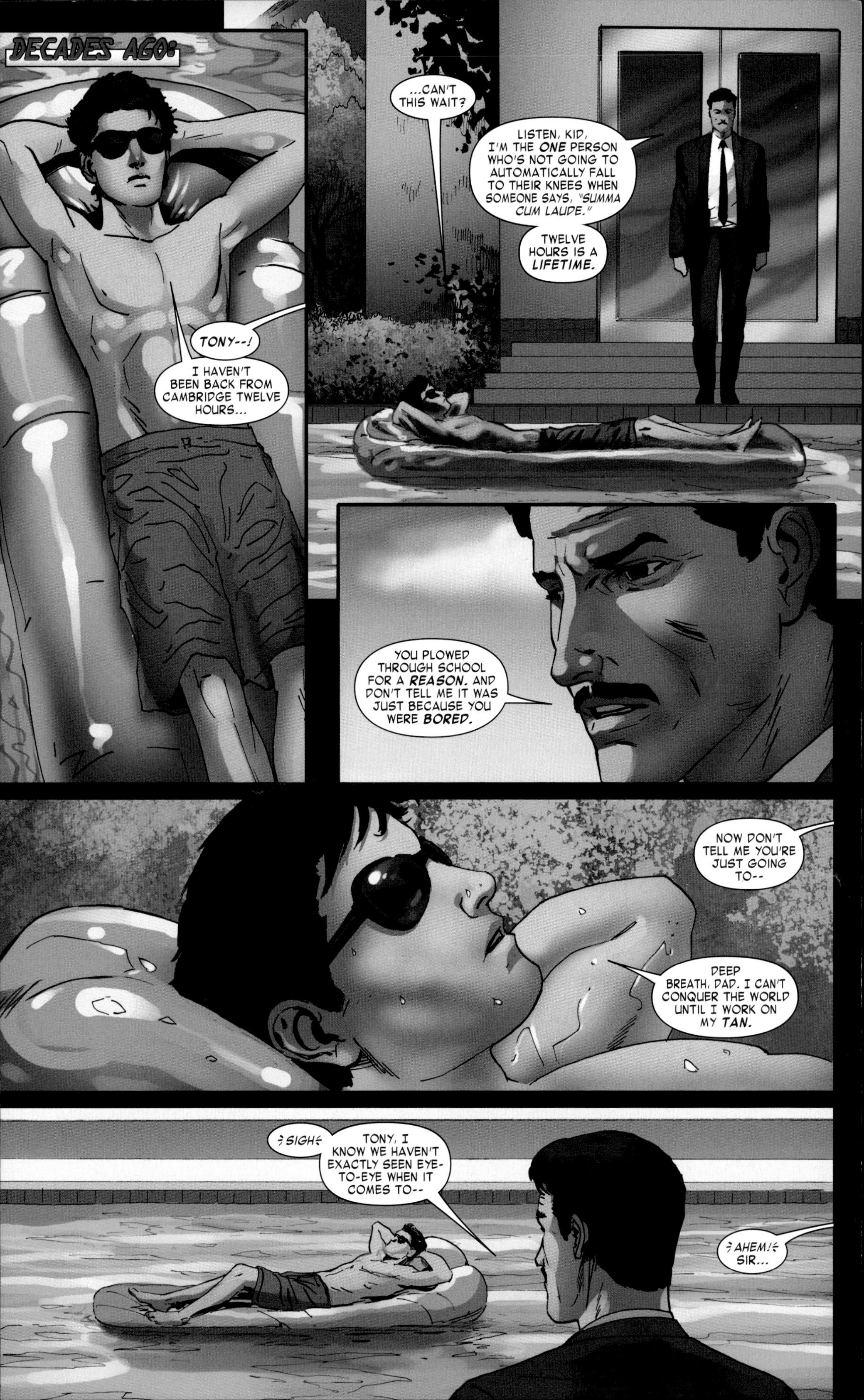
DECADES AGO:
TONY--!
I HAVEN'T BEEN BACK FROM CAMBRIDGE TWELVE HOURS...
...CAN'T THIS WAIT?
LISTEN, KID, I'M THE ONE PERSON WHO'S NOT GOING TO AUTOMATICALLY FALL TO THEIR KNEES WHEN SOMEONE SAYS, "SUMMA CUM LAUDE."
TWELVE HOURS IS A LIFETIME.
YOU PLOWED THROUGH SCHOOL FOR A REASON. AND DON'T TELL ME IT WAS JUST BECAUSE YOU WERE BORED.
NOW DON'T TELL ME YOU'RE JUST GOING TO--
DEEP BREATH, DAD. I CAN'T CONQUER THE WORLD UNTIL I WORK ON MY TAN.
SIGH
TONY, I KNOW WE HAVEN'T EXACTLY SEEN EYE-TO-EYE WHEN IT COMES TO--
AHEM! SIR...

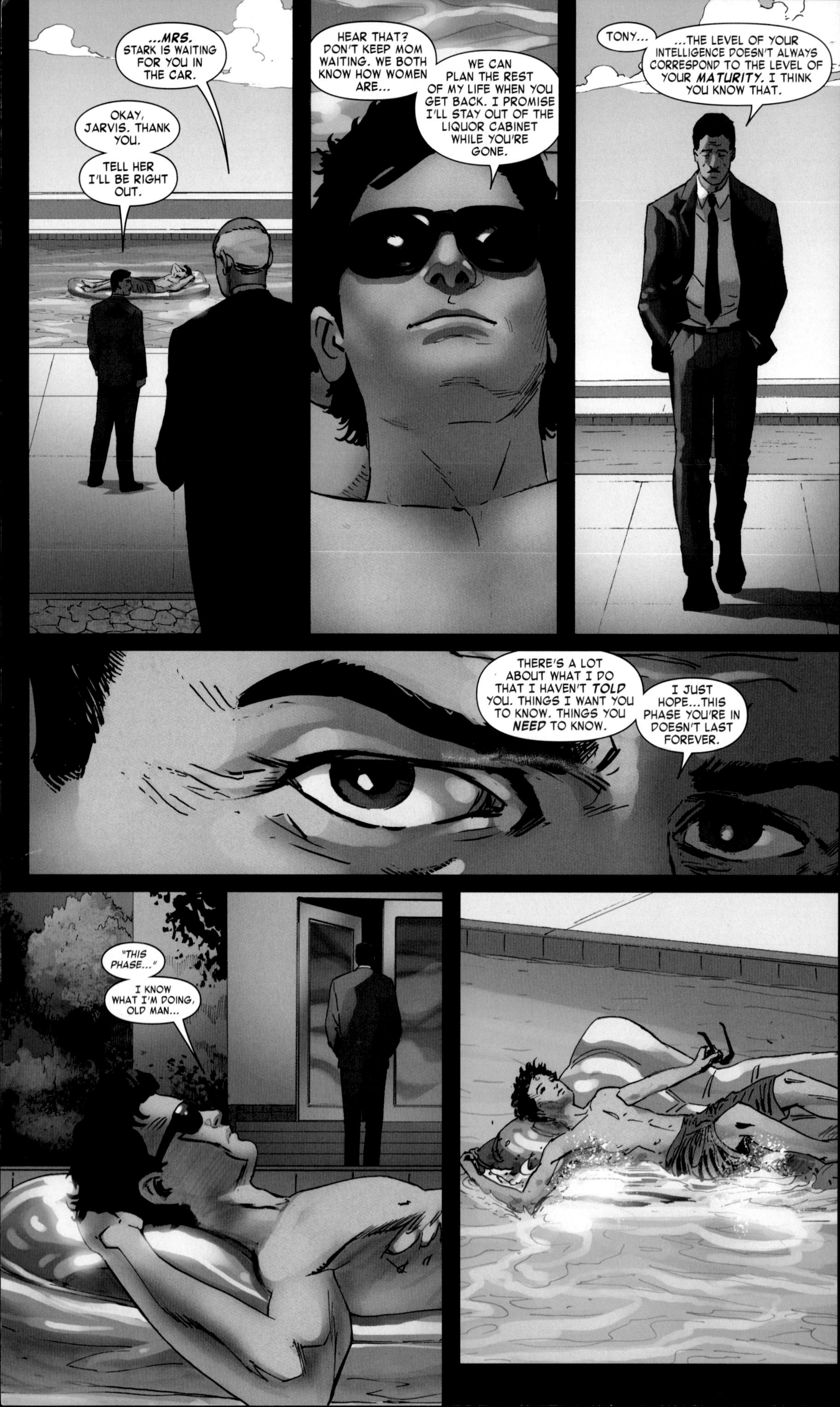
...MRS. STARK IS WAITING FOR YOU IN THE CAR.
OKAY, JARVIS. THANK YOU.
TELL HER I'LL BE RIGHT OUT.
HEAR THAT? DON'T KEEP MOM WAITING. WE BOTH KNOW HOW WOMEN ARE...
WE CAN PLAN THE REST OF MY LIFE WHEN YOU GET BACK. I PROMISE I'LL STAY OUT OF THE LIQUOR CABINET WHILE YOU'RE GONE.
TONY...
...THE LEVEL OF YOUR INTELLIGENCE DOESN'T ALWAYS CORRESPOND TO THE LEVEL OF YOUR MATURITY. I THINK YOU KNOW THAT.
THERE'S A LOT ABOUT WHAT I DO THAT I HAVEN'T TOLD YOU. THINGS I WANT YOU TO KNOW. THINGS YOU NEED TO KNOW.
I JUST HOPE...THIS PHASE YOU'RE IN DOESN'T LAST FOREVER.
"THIS PHASE..."
I KNOW WHAT I'M DOING, OLD MAN...

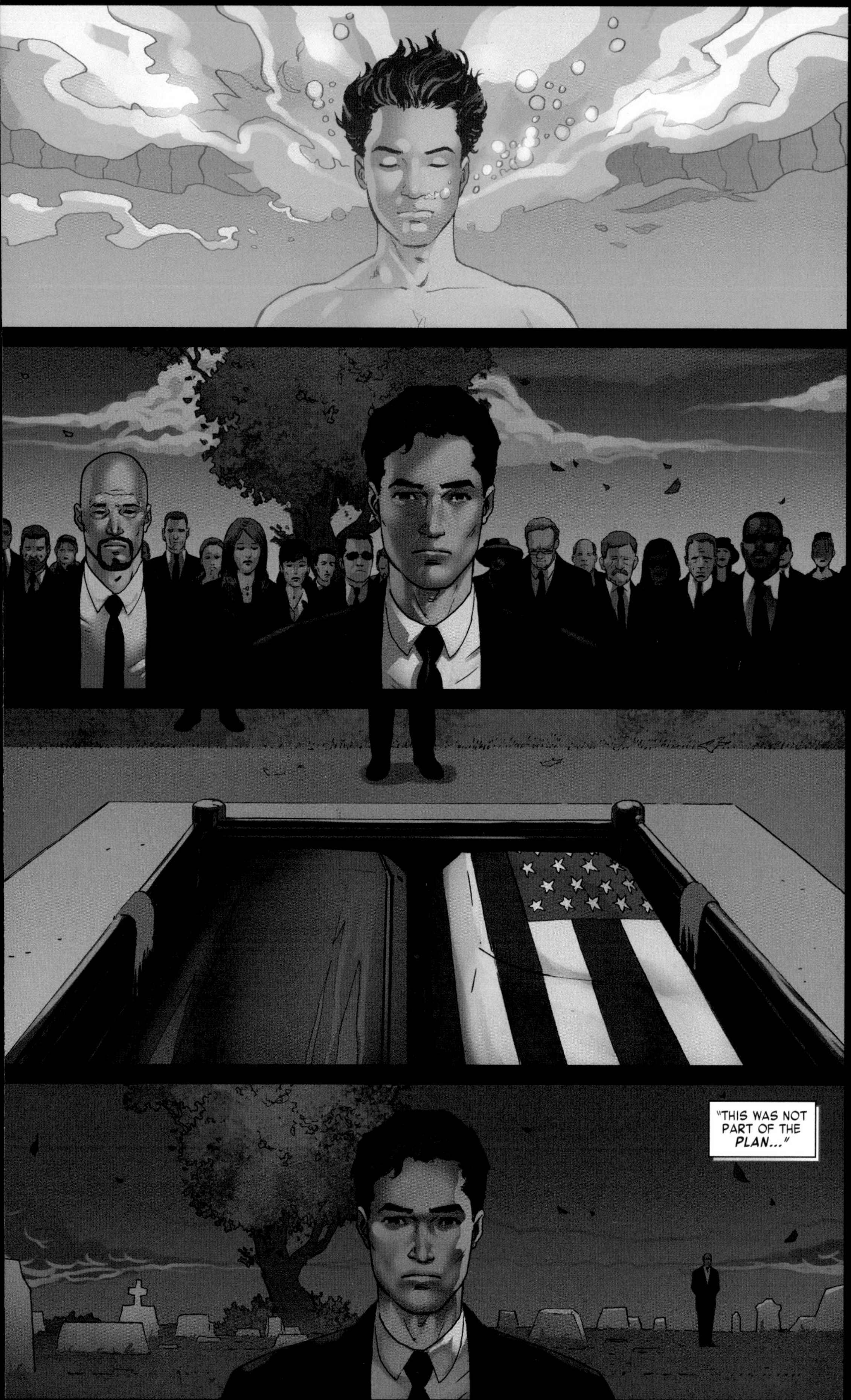
"THIS WAS NOT PART OF THE PLAN..."

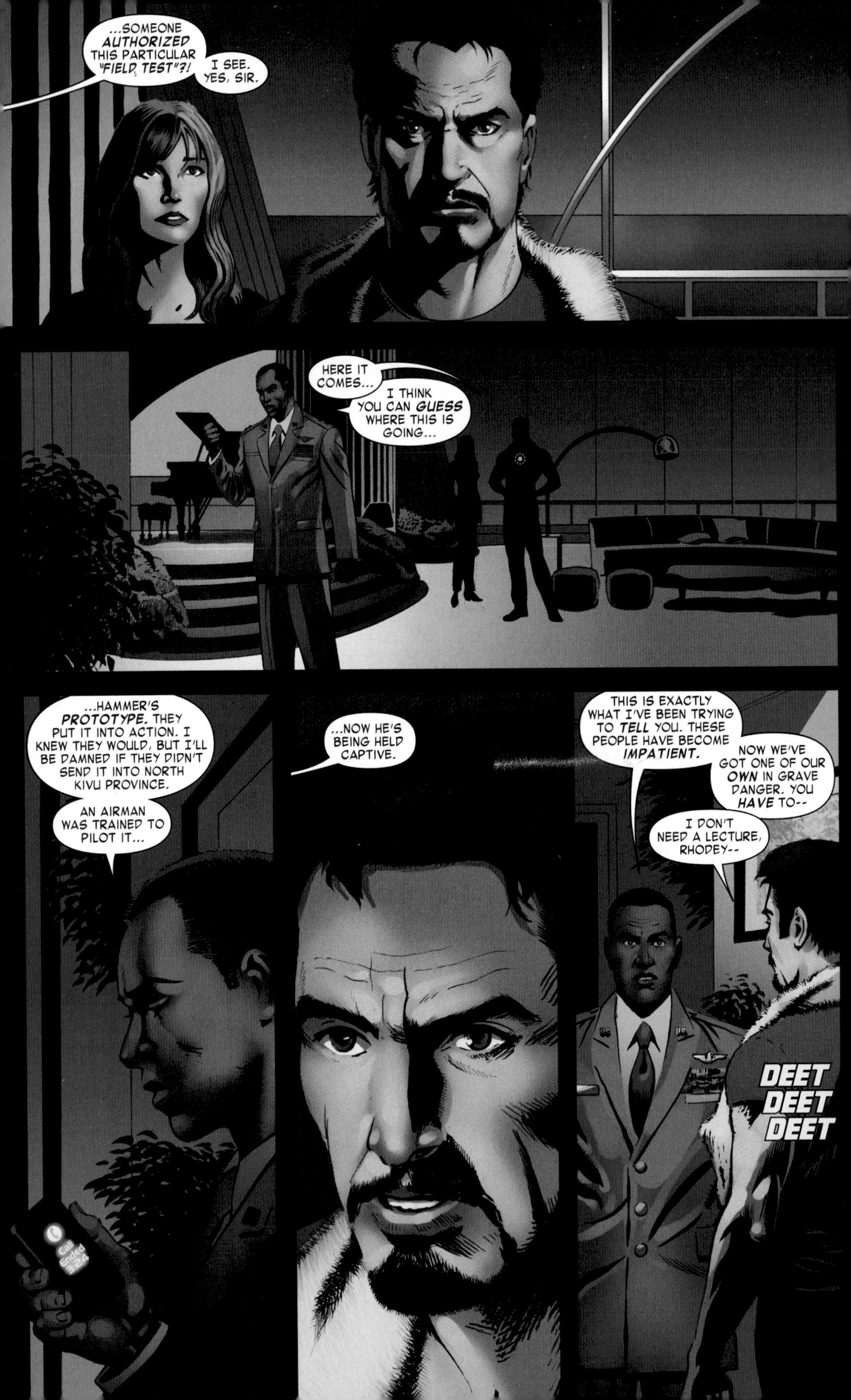
...SOMEONE AUTHORIZED THIS PARTICULAR "FIELD TEST"?!
I SEE. YES, SIR.
HERE IT COMES...
I THINK YOU CAN GUESS WHERE THIS IS GOING...
...HAMMER'S PROTOTYPE. THEY PUT IT INTO ACTION. I KNEW THEY WOULD, BUT I'LL BE DAMNED IF THEY DIDN'T SEND IT INTO NORTH KIVU PROVINCE.
AN AIRMAN WAS TRAINED TO PILOT IT...
Call Ended 3:24
...NOW HE'S BEING HELD CAPTIVE.
THIS IS EXACTLY WHAT I'VE BEEN TRYING TO TELL YOU. THESE PEOPLE HAVE BECOME IMPATIENT.
NOW WE'VE GOT ONE OF OUR OWN IN GRAVE DANGER. YOU HAVE TO--
I DON'T NEED A LECTURE, RHODEY--
DEET DEET DEET

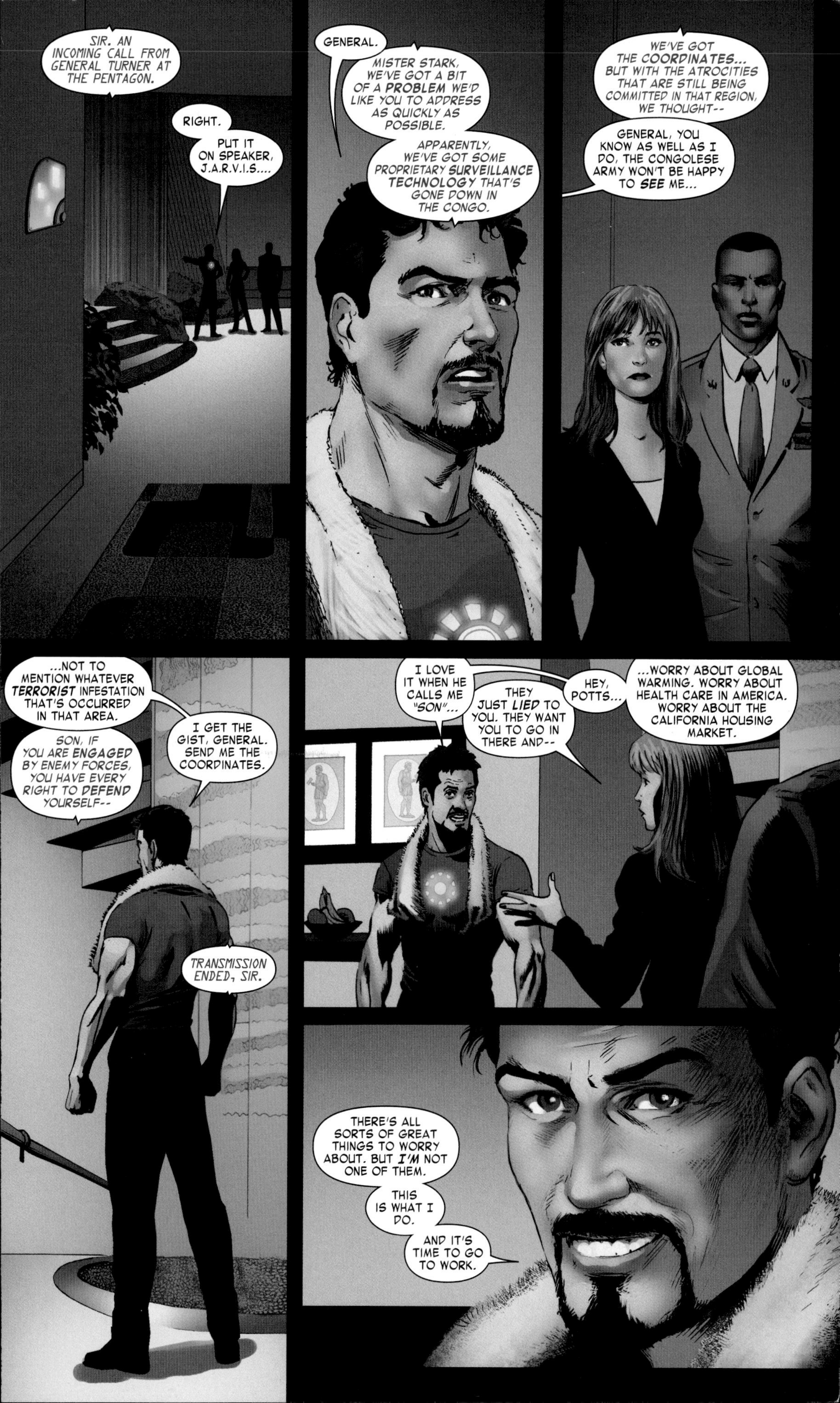
SIR. AN INCOMING CALL FROM GENERAL TURNER AT THE PENTAGON.
RIGHT.
PUT IT ON SPEAKER, J.A.R.V.I.S....
GENERAL.
MISTER STARK, WE'VE GOT A BIT OF A PROBLEM WE'D LIKE YOU TO ADDRESS AS QUICKLY AS POSSIBLE.
APPARENTLY, WE'VE GOT SOME PROPRIETARY SURVEILLANCE TECHNOLOGY THAT'S GONE DOWN IN THE CONGO.
WE'VE GOT THE COORDINATES... BUT WITH THE ATROCITIES THAT ARE STILL BEING COMMITTED IN THAT REGION, WE THOUGHT--
GENERAL, YOU KNOW AS WELL AS I DO, THE CONGOLESE ARMY WON'T BE HAPPY TO SEE ME...
...NOT TO MENTION WHATEVER TERRORIST INFESTATION THAT'S OCCURRED IN THAT AREA.
SON, IF YOU ARE ENGAGED BY ENEMY FORCES, YOU HAVE EVERY RIGHT TO DEFEND YOURSELF--
I GET THE GIST, GENERAL. SEND ME THE COORDINATES.
TRANSMISSION ENDED, SIR.
I LOVE IT WHEN HE CALLS ME "SON"...
HEY, POTTS...
THEY JUST LIED TO YOU. THEY WANT YOU TO GO IN THERE AND--
...WORRY ABOUT GLOBAL WARMING. WORRY ABOUT HEALTH CARE IN AMERICA. WORRY ABOUT THE CALIFORNIA HOUSING MARKET.
THERE'S ALL SORTS OF GREAT THINGS TO WORRY ABOUT. BUT I'M NOT ONE OF THEM.
THIS IS WHAT I DO.
AND IT'S TIME TO GO TO WORK.

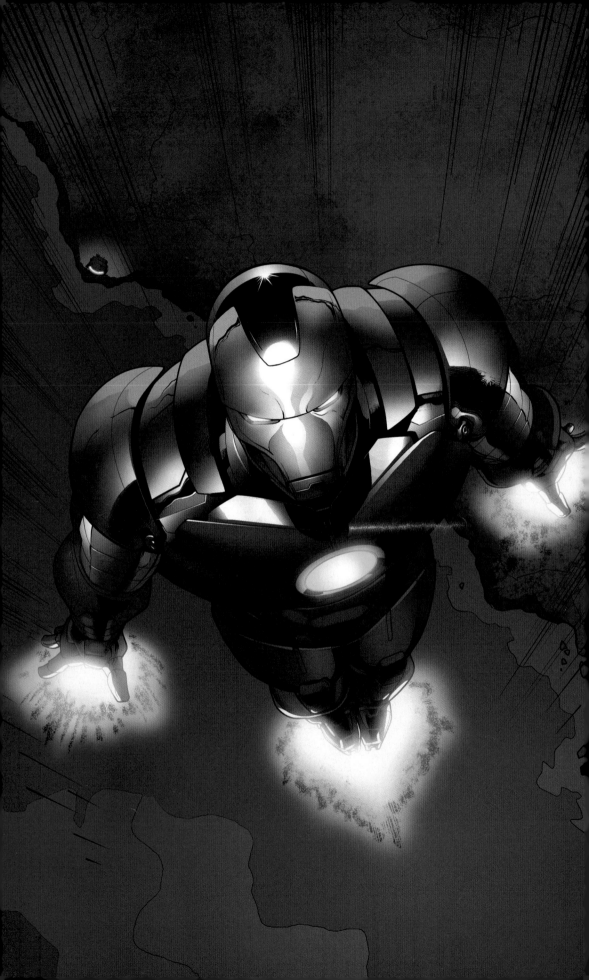

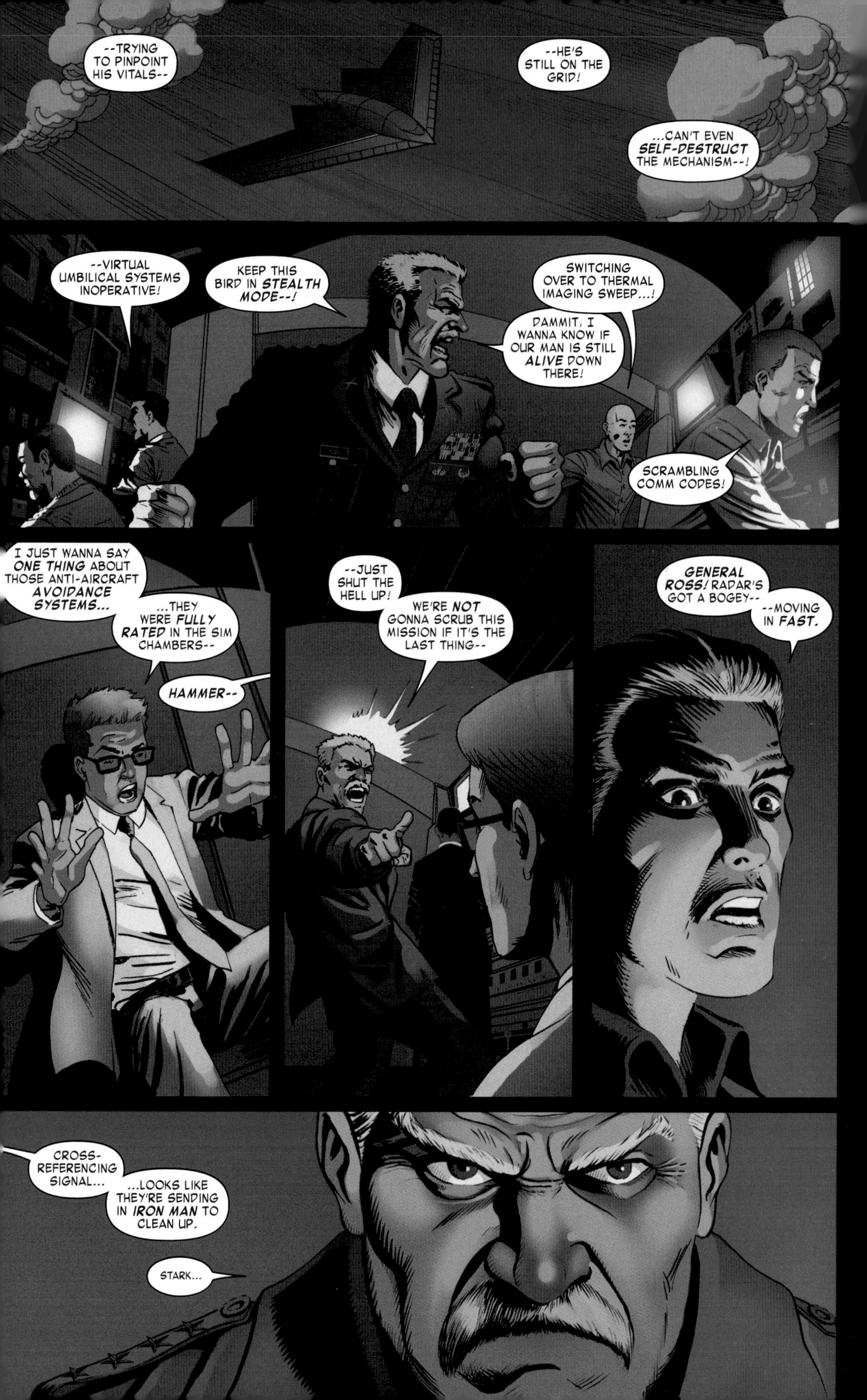
--TRYING TO PINPOINT HIS VITALS--
--HE'S STILL ON THE GRID!
...CAN'T EVEN SELF-DESTRUCT THE MECHANISM--!
--VIRTUAL UMBILICAL SYSTEMS INOPERATIVE!
KEEP THIS BIRD IN STEALTH MODE--!
SWITCHING OVER TO THERMAL IMAGING SWEEP...!
DAMMIT, I WANNA KNOW IF OUR MAN IS STILL ALIVE DOWN THERE!
SCRAMBLING COMM CODES!
I JUST WANNA SAY ONE THING ABOUT THOSE ANTI-AIRCRAFT AVOIDANCE SYSTEMS...
...THEY WERE FULLY RATED IN THE SIM CHAMBERS--
HAMMER--
--JUST SHUT THE HELL UP!
WE'RE NOT GONNA SCRUB THIS MISSION IF IT'S THE LAST THING--
GENERAL ROSS! RADAR'S GOT A BOGEY--
--MOVING IN FAST.
CROSS-REFERENCING SIGNAL...
...LOOKS LIKE THEY'RE SENDING IN IRON MAN TO CLEAN UP.
STARK...

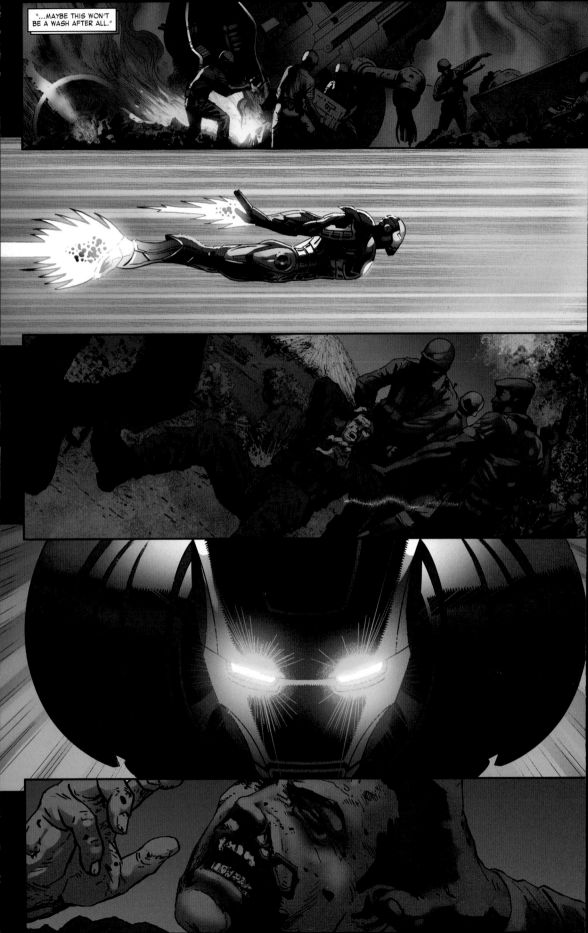

"...MAYBE THIS WON'T BE A WASH AFTER ALL."

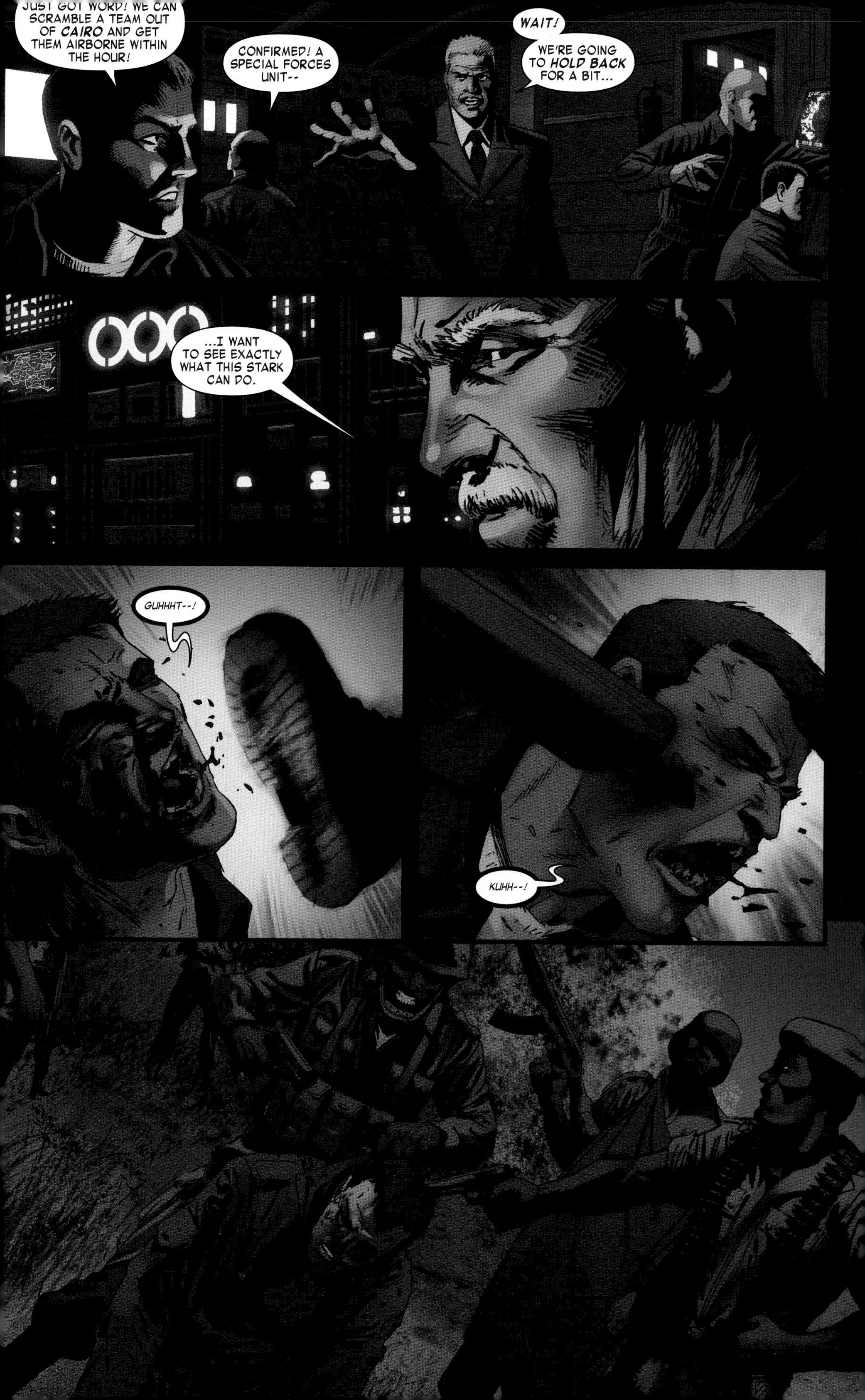
JUST GOT WORD! WE CAN SCRAMBLE A TEAM OUT OF CAIRO AND GET THEM AIRBORNE WITHIN THE HOUR!
CONFIRMED! A SPECIAL FORCES UNIT--
WAIT!
WE'RE GOING TO HOLD BACK FOR A BIT...
...I WANT TO SEE EXACTLY WHAT THIS STARK CAN DO.
GUHHHT--!
KUHH--!

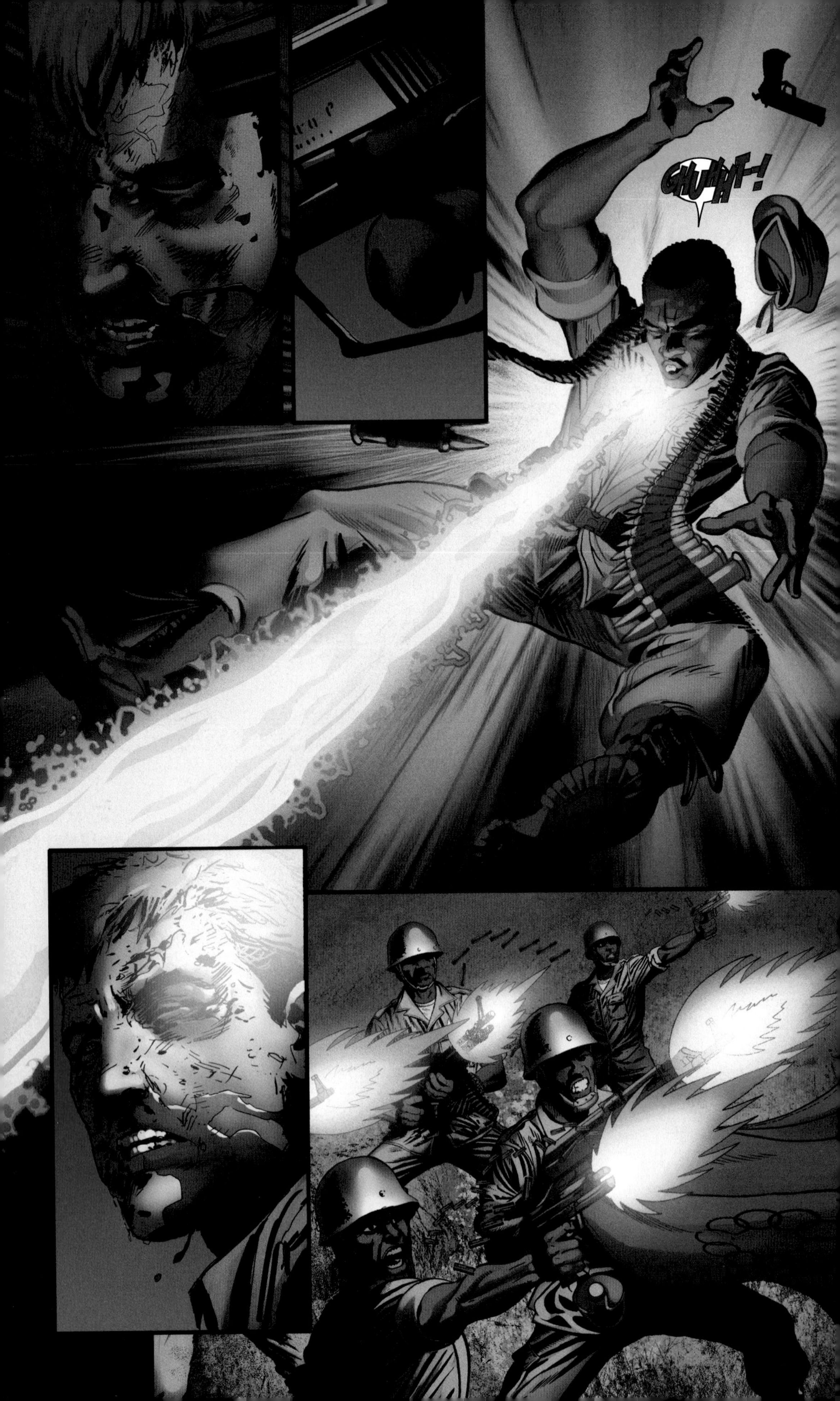
GHUHHT-!

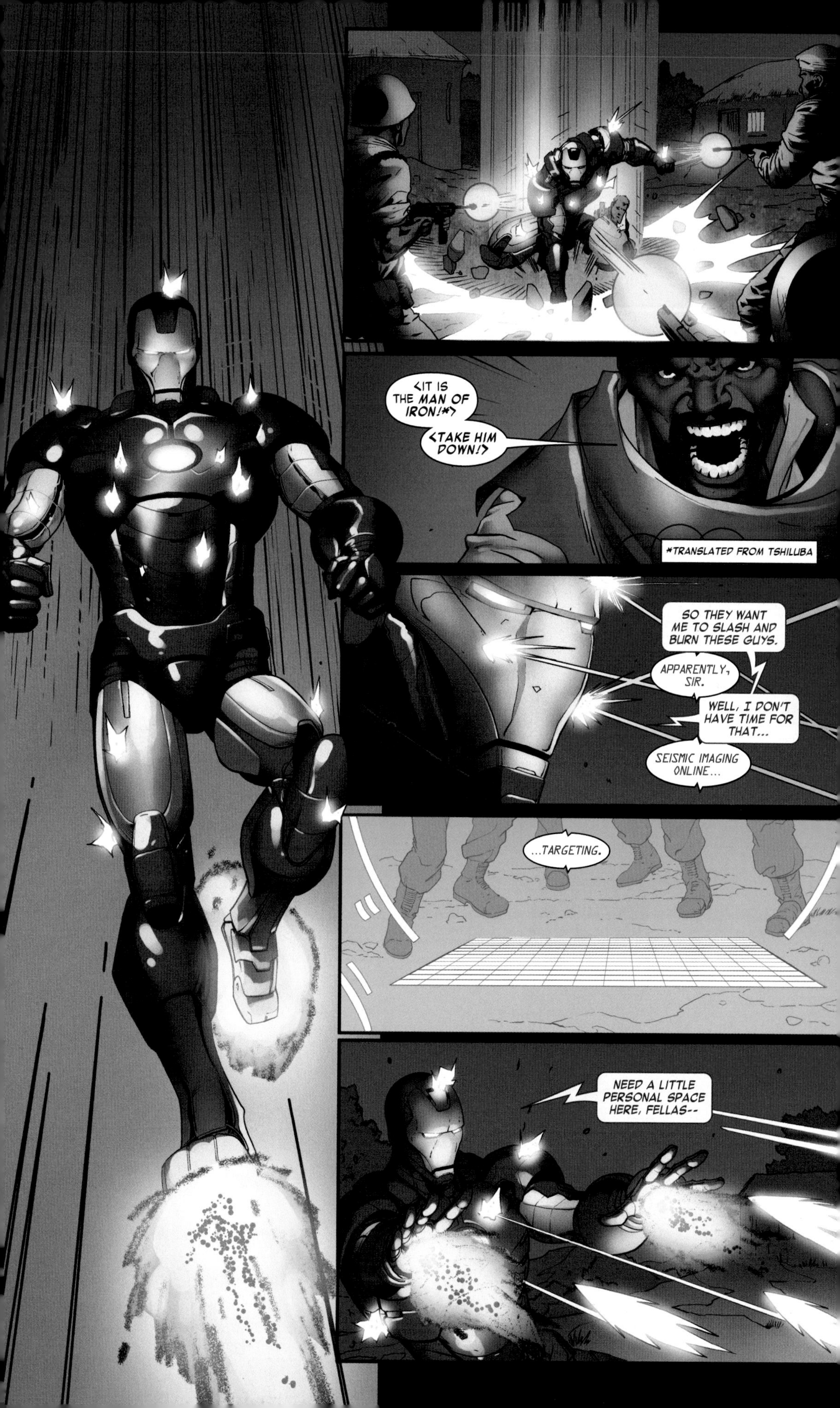

<IT IS THE MAN OF IRON!*>
<TAKE HIM DOWN!>
*TRANSLATED FROM TSHILUBA
SO THEY WANT ME TO SLASH AND BURN THESE GUYS.
APPARENTLY, SIR.
WELL, I DON'T HAVE TIME FOR THAT...
SEISMIC IMAGING ONLINE...
...TARGETING.
NEED A LITTLE PERSONAL SPACE HERE, FELLAS--

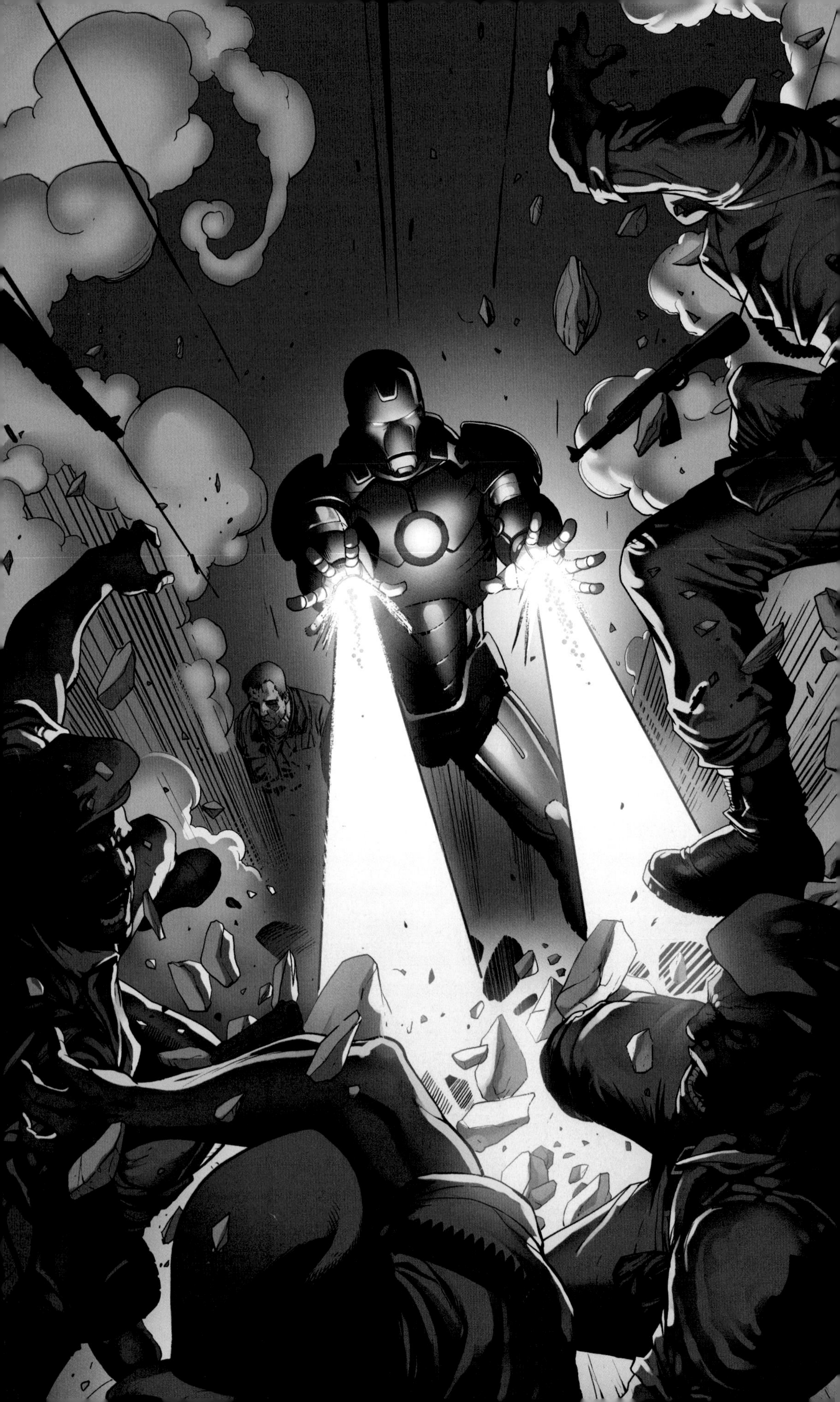

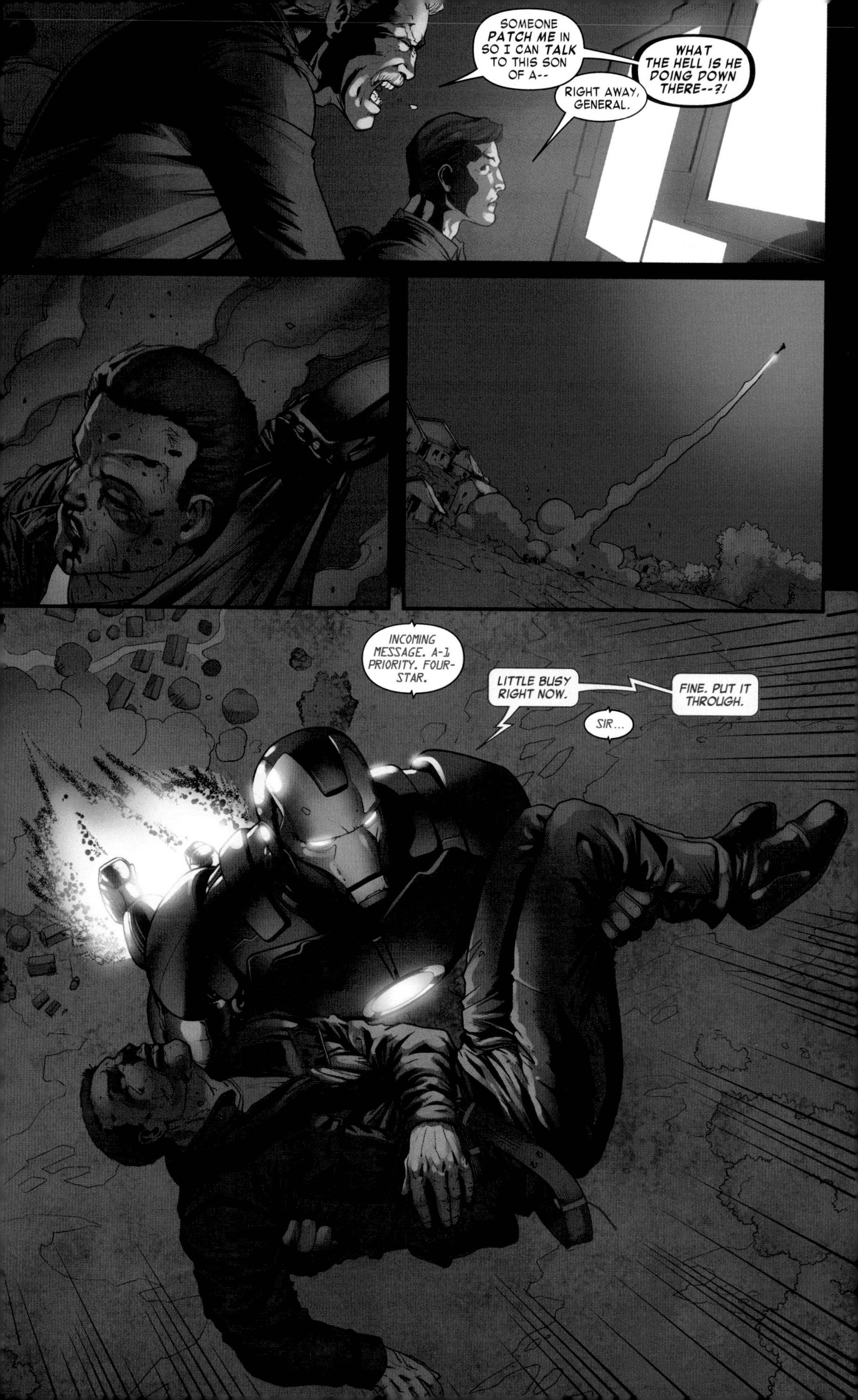
SOMEONE PATCH ME IN SO I CAN TALK TO THIS SON OF A--
WHAT THE HELL IS HE DOING DOWN THERE--?!
RIGHT AWAY, GENERAL.
INCOMING MESSAGE. A-1 PRIORITY. FOUR-STAR.
LITTLE BUSY RIGHT NOW.
FINE. PUT IT THROUGH.
SIR...

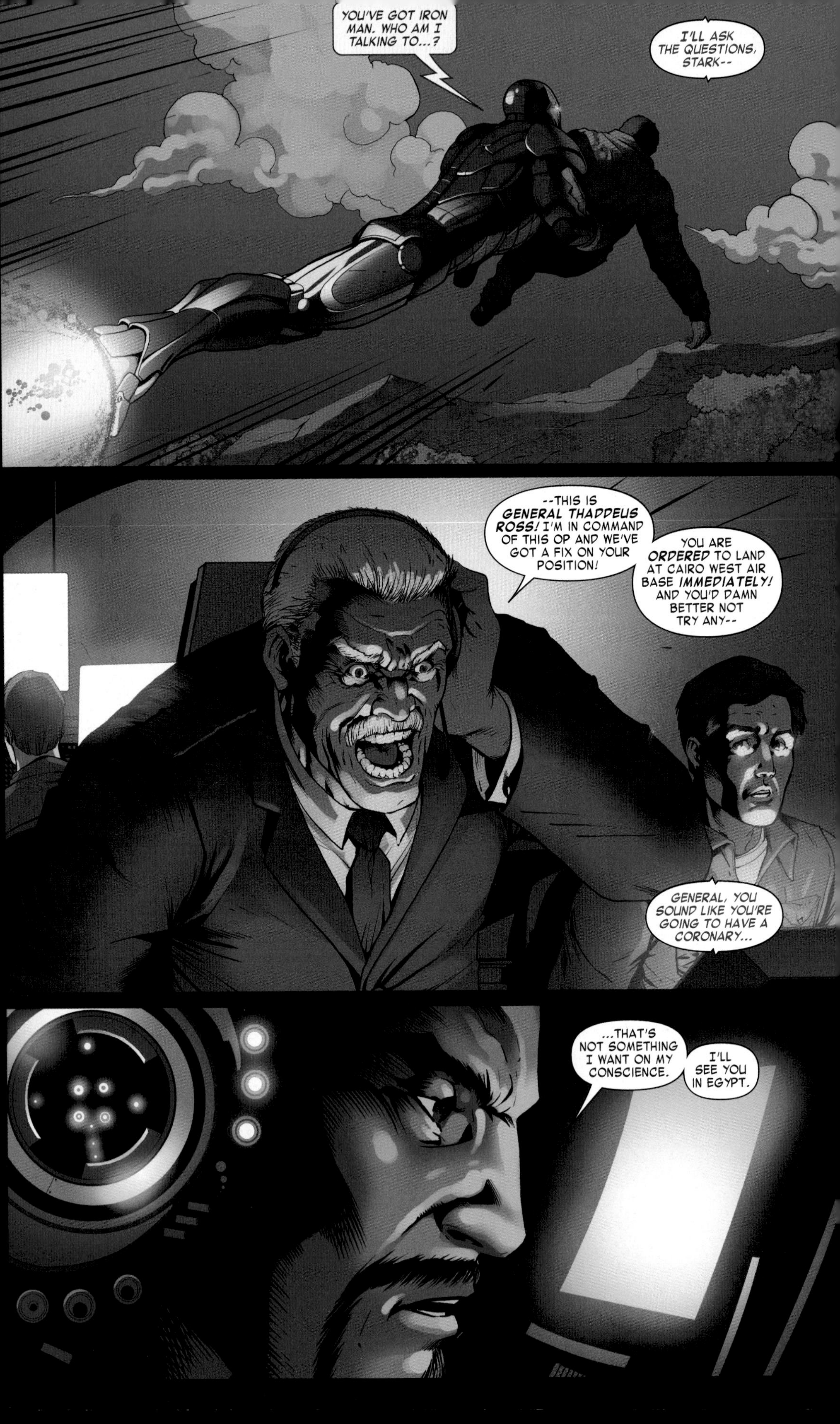
YOU'VE GOT IRON MAN. WHO AM I TALKING TO...?
I'LL ASK THE QUESTIONS, STARK--
--THIS IS GENERAL THADDEUS ROSS! I'M IN COMMAND OF THIS OP AND WE'VE GOT A FIX ON YOUR POSITION!
YOU ARE ORDERED TO LAND AT CAIRO WEST AIR BASE IMMEDIATELY! AND YOU'D DAMN BETTER NOT TRY ANY--
GENERAL, YOU SOUND LIKE YOU'RE GOING TO HAVE A CORONARY...
...THAT'S NOT SOMETHING I WANT ON MY CONSCIENCE.
I'LL SEE YOU IN EGYPT.

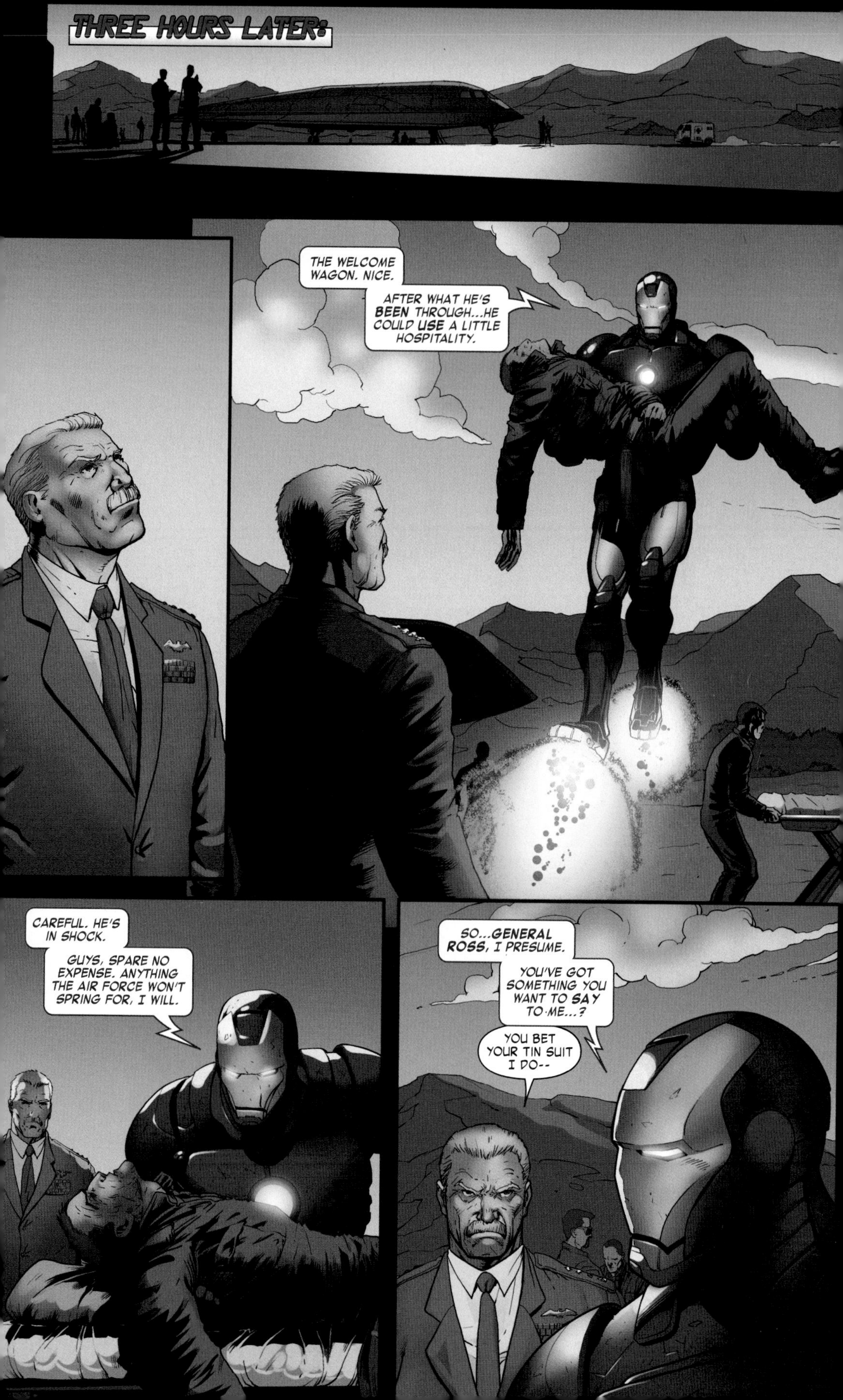
THREE HOURS LATER:
THE WELCOME WAGON. NICE.
AFTER WHAT HE'S BEEN THROUGH...HE COULD USE A LITTLE HOSPITALITY.
CAREFUL. HE'S IN SHOCK.
GUYS, SPARE NO EXPENSE. ANYTHING THE AIR FORCE WON'T SPRING FOR, I WILL.
SO...GENERAL ROSS, I PRESUME.
YOU'VE GOT SOMETHING YOU WANT TO SAY TO ME...?
YOU BET YOUR TIN SUIT I DO--

--SATS PICKED UP A *SHOOTOUT* WITH THE CONGOLESE ARMY AND YOU DON'T *RETURN FIRE*?!

SOMEONE FIRES ON AN *AMERICAN*-- THAT AMERICAN *FIRES BACK*!

YEAH...I FIGURED THAT'S WHAT YOU GUYS WANTED ME TO DO.

THAT IS, IF HAMMER'S FOLLY COULDN'T DO THE JOB FOR YOU FIRST.

DON'T CONFUSE THE ISSUE, STARK! I KNOW YOU'VE BEEN *DISTANCING* YOURSELF FROM YOUR FATHER'S LEGACY--

--YOU CLAIM YOU'RE NO LONGER A WEAPONS MAKER-- BUT NOW YOU *ARE* THE WEAPON!

INTERESTING ANALYSIS OF MY LIFE'S WORK.

Y'KNOW, ON MY WAY *HERE*, I DECIDED TO RESEARCH *YOU*.

DID A LITTLE *DIGGING*. PULLED UP YOUR *FILE*...

THADDEUS ROSS
a.k.a. THUNDERBOLT

Lorem ipsum dolor sit amet, consectetur adipiscing elit. Integer et orci massa, eu aliquet lacus. Etiam placerat, leo quis varius volutpat, elit dolor iaculis sem, eget pretium mi leo vitae lectus. In hac habitasse platea dictumst. Mauris vel sapien nec urna vulputate eleifend nec quis nulla. Vestibulum quis sem dolor, vitae sagittis justo. Pellentesque convallis velit cursus purus sollicitudin egestas nec hendrerit augue. Sed nisi purus, porttitor vel molestie eu, lacinia eu nulla. Donec purus dui, placerat id vehicula eu, pulvinar eu tortor. Aenean eleifend turpis porttitor lectus ultrices accumsan. Nunc rutrum gravida eros, non viverra justo lacinia sit. Sed commodo, nisi ut sagittis lacinia, dolor risus mollis tortor, eu volutpat nibh tortor nec sem. In hac habitasse platea dictumst. Lorem ipsum dolor sit amet, consectetur adipiscing elit. Morbi aliquet lectus ligula, ut mattis ante. Sed vehicula neque ac mauris commodo sagittis. Pellentesque habitant morbi tristique senectus et netus et malesuada fames ac turpis egestas. Cras magna risus, aliquet non pretium eu, rhoncus id amet metus.

Suspendisse potenti. Quisque vulputate venenatis ligula, ut accumsan sapien ornare a. Mauris eget nibh leo, vitae sagittis felis. Sed laoreet urna eget diam ultrices sed bibendum est imperdiet. Aenean eleifend consequat augue ac aliquet. Aliquam eros lectus non velit ullamcorper porta. Praesent ut massa et erat tincidunt luctus eu quis ipsum. Vestibulum ut nunc dolor. Sed at massa nisl, ut iaculis dolor. Nam mattis erat, sagittis viverra vulputate vitae, viverra quis nisl. Mauris fringilla enim ne elit pharetra ultrices. Donec dolor dolor, blandit in mattis ac, tempor sed tortor. Duis erat dolor, cursus quis gravida id, molestie eget lorem. Mauris rhoncus lectus vel leo vehicula dignissim. In pellentesque tincidunt ante, et tempor ante vestibulum et.

...QUITE A *RESUME*. YOU'VE HAD YOUR FINGERS IN A LOT OF PIES.

GENETIC ENHANCEMENTS FOR MILITARY EXPLOITATION. PRETTY ADVANCED FOR A SACRED COW LIKE YOU. NOT TO MENTION *DICEY*.

AND *"THUNDERBOLT"*...KIND OF AN ODD NICKNAME. WHO *GAVE* THAT TO YOU? THAT'S A REAL SHAME.

ANYWAY...

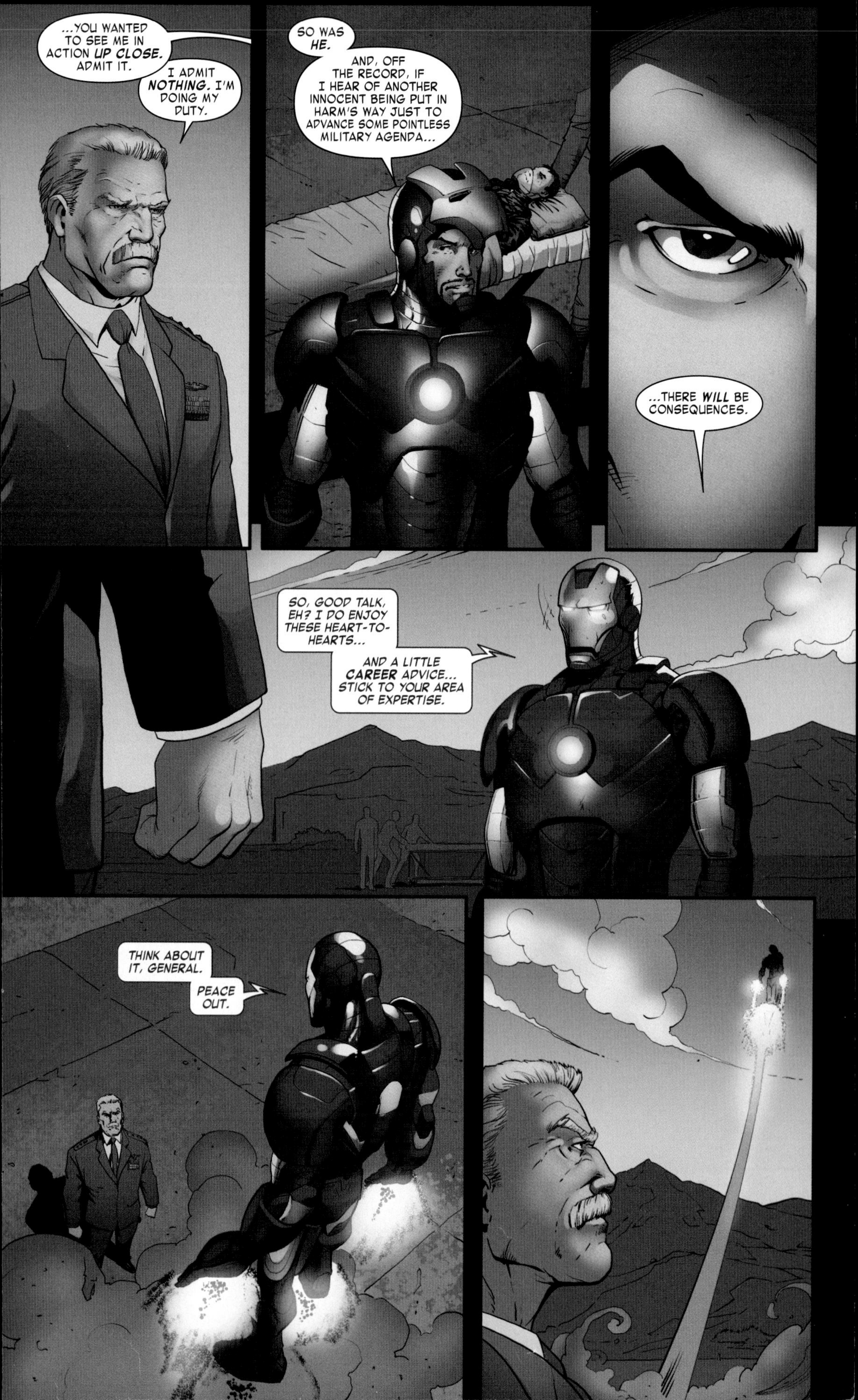
...YOU WANTED TO SEE ME IN ACTION UP CLOSE. ADMIT IT.
I ADMIT NOTHING. I'M DOING MY DUTY.
SO WAS HE.
AND, OFF THE RECORD, IF I HEAR OF ANOTHER INNOCENT BEING PUT IN HARM'S WAY JUST TO ADVANCE SOME POINTLESS MILITARY AGENDA...
...THERE WILL BE CONSEQUENCES.
SO, GOOD TALK, EH? I DO ENJOY THESE HEART-TO-HEARTS...
AND A LITTLE CAREER ADVICE... STICK TO YOUR AREA OF EXPERTISE.
THINK ABOUT IT, GENERAL.
PEACE OUT.

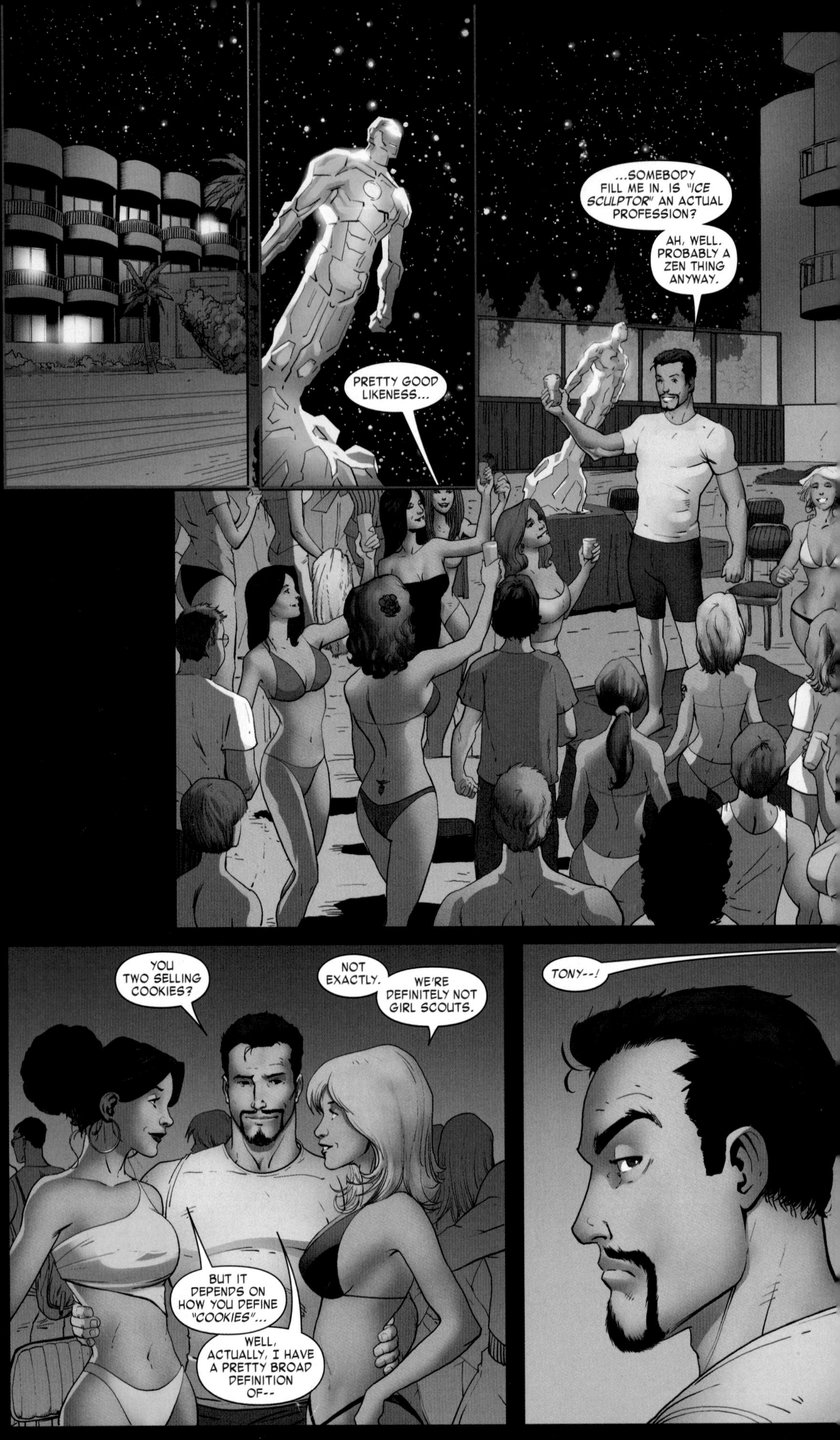
PRETTY GOOD LIKENESS...
...SOMEBODY FILL ME IN. IS "ICE SCULPTOR" AN ACTUAL PROFESSION?
AH, WELL. PROBABLY A ZEN THING ANYWAY.
YOU TWO SELLING COOKIES?
NOT EXACTLY.
WE'RE DEFINITELY NOT GIRL SCOUTS.
BUT IT DEPENDS ON HOW YOU DEFINE "COOKIES"...
WELL, ACTUALLY, I HAVE A PRETTY BROAD DEFINITION OF--
TONY--!

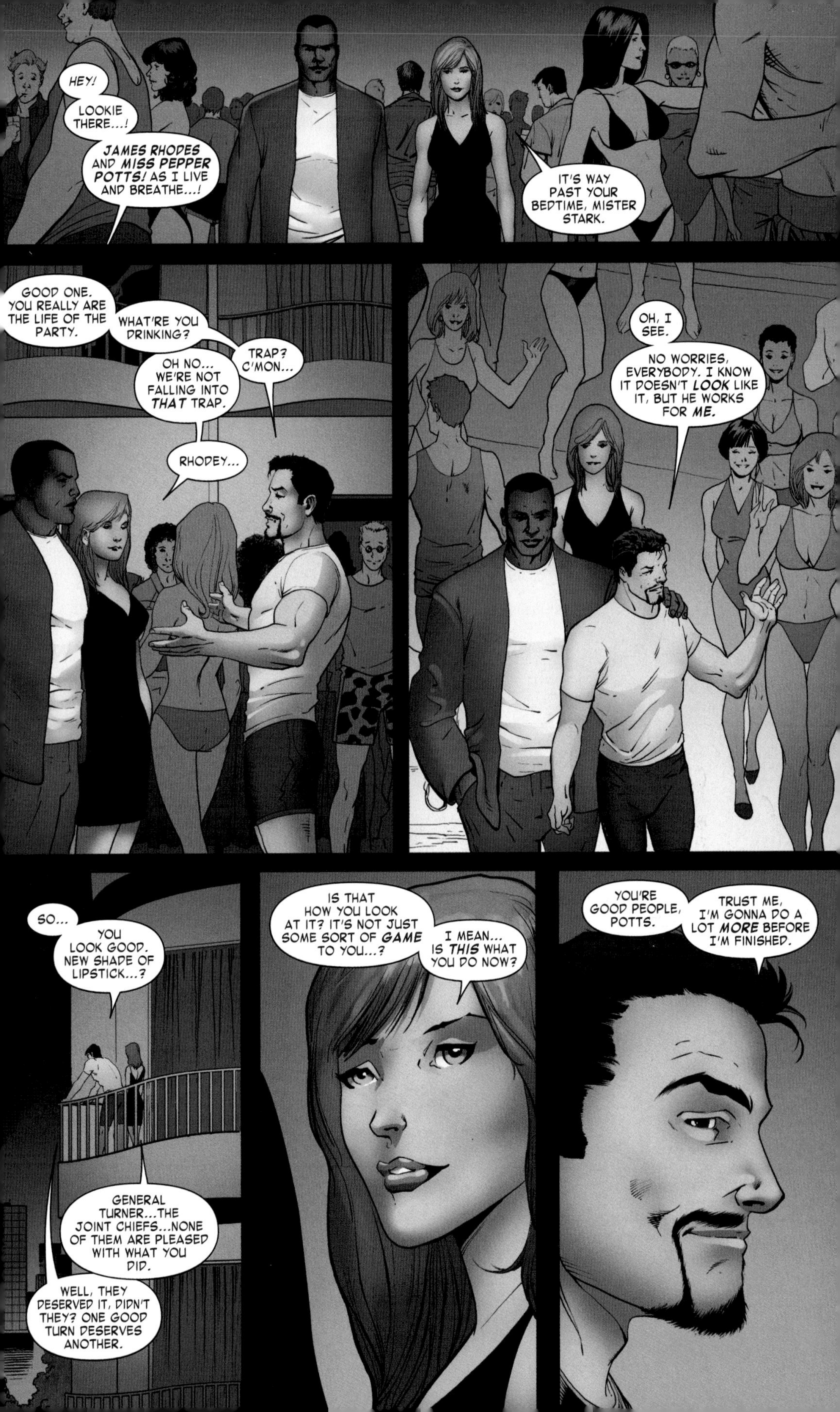
HEY!
LOOKIE THERE...!
JAMES RHODES AND MISS PEPPER POTTS! AS I LIVE AND BREATHE...!
IT'S WAY PAST YOUR BEDTIME, MISTER STARK.
GOOD ONE. YOU REALLY ARE THE LIFE OF THE PARTY.
WHAT'RE YOU DRINKING?
OH NO... WE'RE NOT FALLING INTO THAT TRAP.
TRAP? C'MON...
RHODEY...
OH, I SEE.
NO WORRIES, EVERYBODY. I KNOW IT DOESN'T LOOK LIKE IT, BUT HE WORKS FOR ME.
SO...
YOU LOOK GOOD. NEW SHADE OF LIPSTICK...?
GENERAL TURNER...THE JOINT CHIEFS...NONE OF THEM ARE PLEASED WITH WHAT YOU DID.
WELL, THEY DESERVED IT, DIDN'T THEY? ONE GOOD TURN DESERVES ANOTHER.
IS THAT HOW YOU LOOK AT IT? IT'S NOT JUST SOME SORT OF GAME TO YOU...?
I MEAN... IS THIS WHAT YOU DO NOW?
YOU'RE GOOD PEOPLE, POTTS.
TRUST ME, I'M GONNA DO A LOT MORE BEFORE I'M FINISHED.

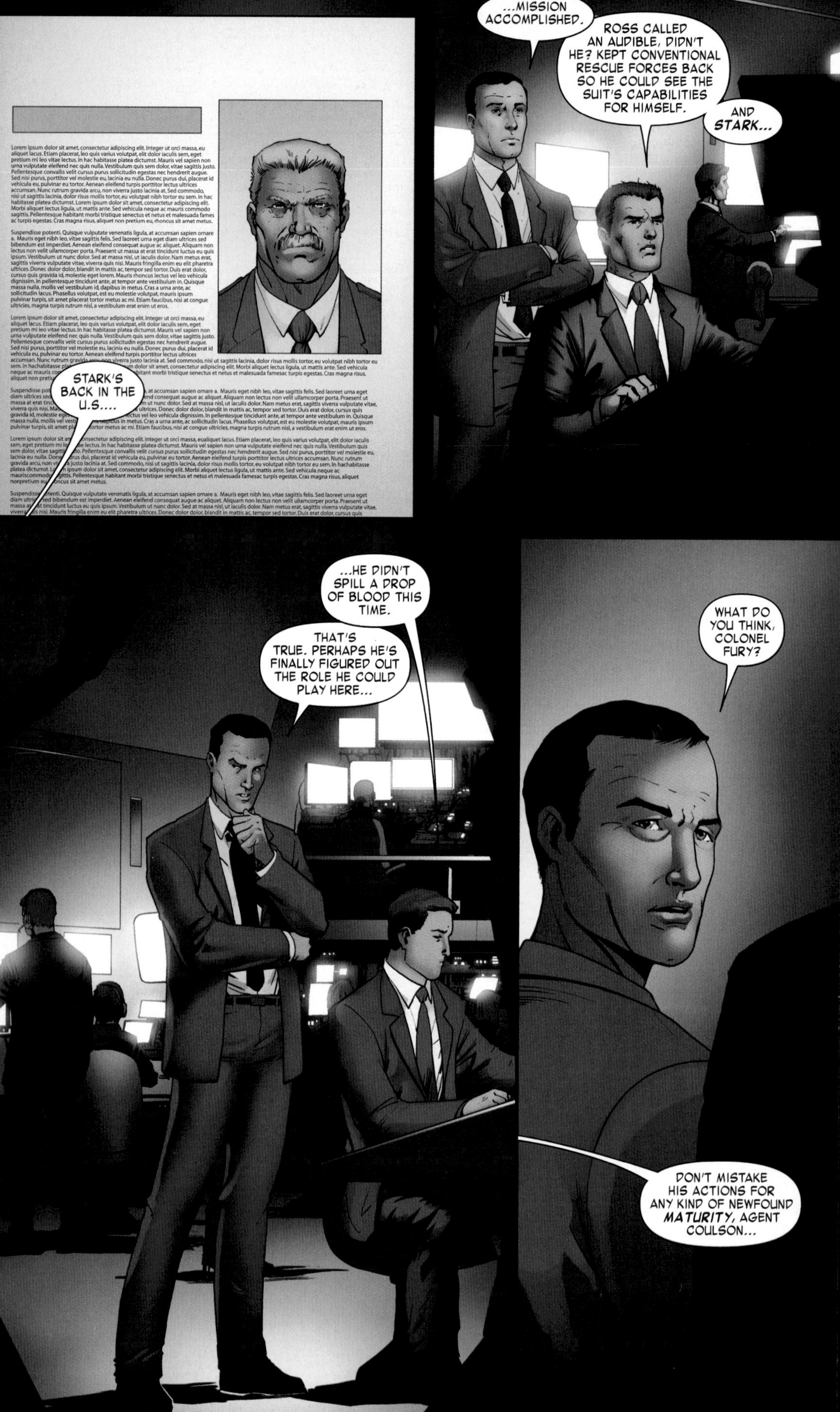
STARK'S BACK IN THE U.S....
...MISSION ACCOMPLISHED.
ROSS CALLED AN AUDIBLE, DIDN'T HE? KEPT CONVENTIONAL RESCUE FORCES BACK SO HE COULD SEE THE SUIT'S CAPABILITIES FOR HIMSELF.
AND *STARK...*
...HE DIDN'T SPILL A DROP OF BLOOD THIS TIME.
THAT'S TRUE. PERHAPS HE'S FINALLY FIGURED OUT THE ROLE HE COULD PLAY HERE...
WHAT DO YOU THINK, COLONEL FURY?
DON'T MISTAKE HIS ACTIONS FOR ANY KIND OF NEWFOUND *MATURITY*, AGENT COULSON...

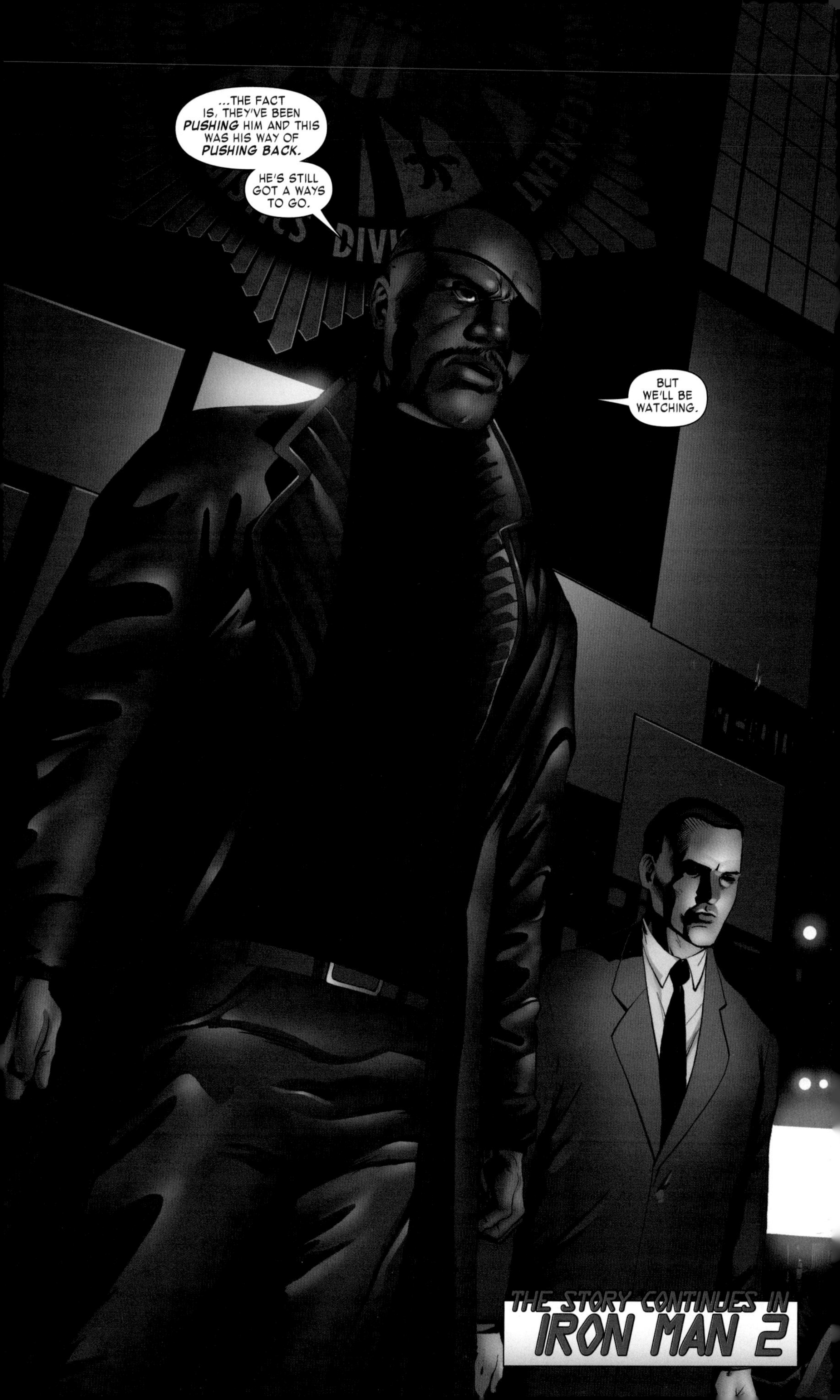
...THE FACT IS, THEY'VE BEEN PUSHING HIM AND THIS WAS HIS WAY OF PUSHING BACK.
HE'S STILL GOT A WAYS TO GO.
BUT WE'LL BE WATCHING.
THE STORY CONTINUES IN
IRON MAN 2

MARVEL STUDIOS

IRON MAN 2

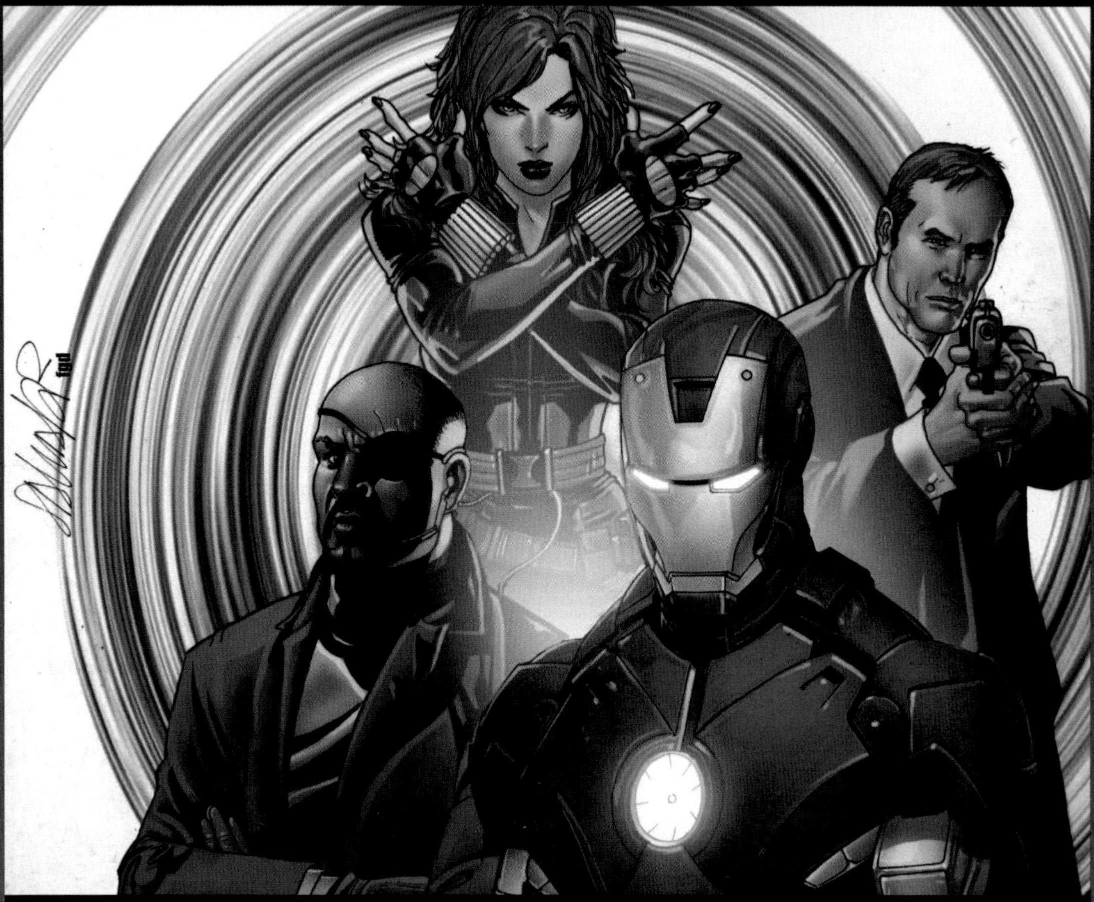

AGENTS OF S.H.I.E.L.D.

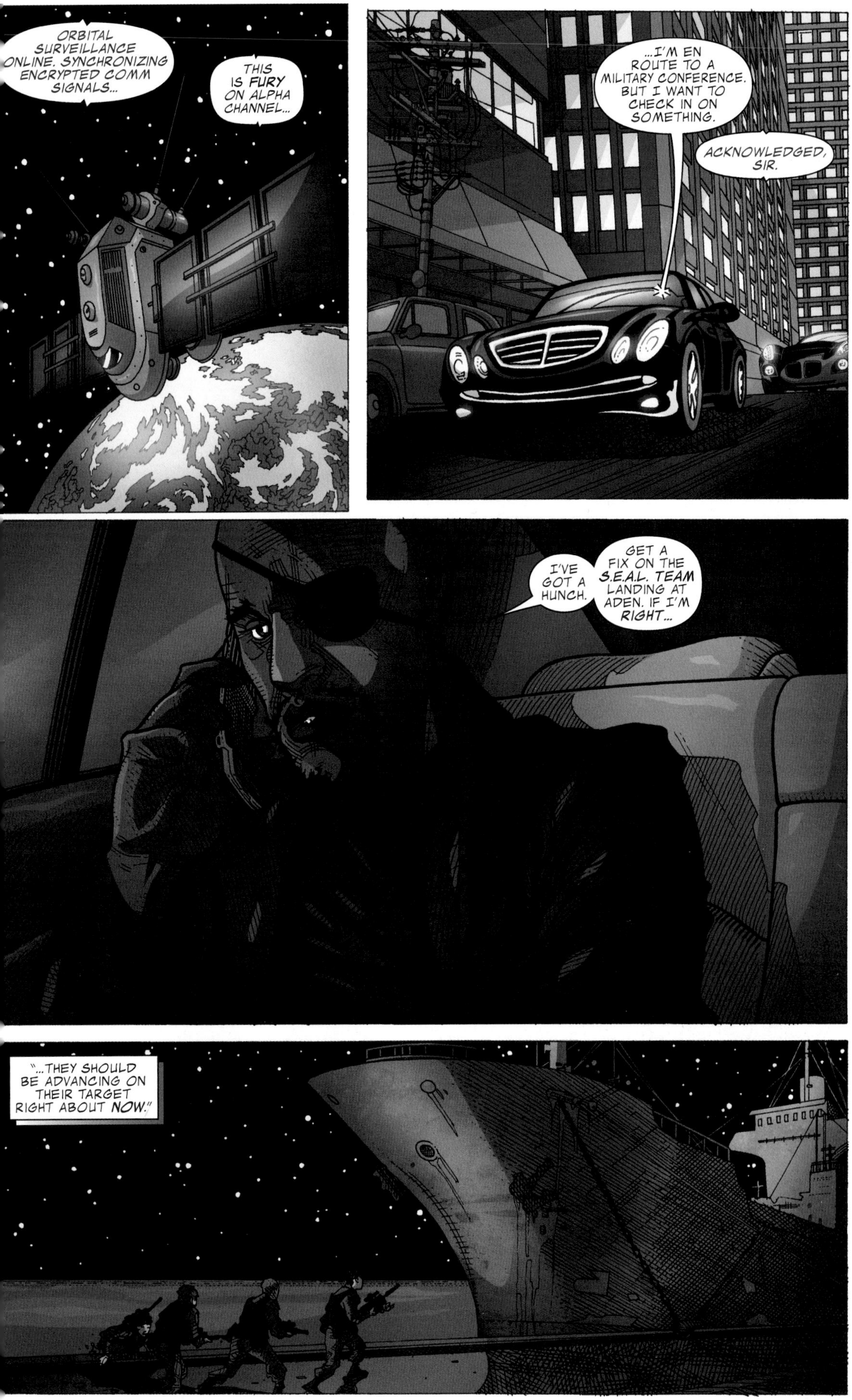
ORBITAL SURVEILLANCE ONLINE. SYNCHRONIZING ENCRYPTED COMM SIGNALS...
THIS IS FURY ON ALPHA CHANNEL...
...I'M EN ROUTE TO A MILITARY CONFERENCE. BUT I WANT TO CHECK IN ON SOMETHING.
ACKNOWLEDGED, SIR.
I'VE GOT A HUNCH.
GET A FIX ON THE S.E.A.L. TEAM LANDING AT ADEN. IF I'M RIGHT...
"...THEY SHOULD BE ADVANCING ON THEIR TARGET RIGHT ABOUT NOW."

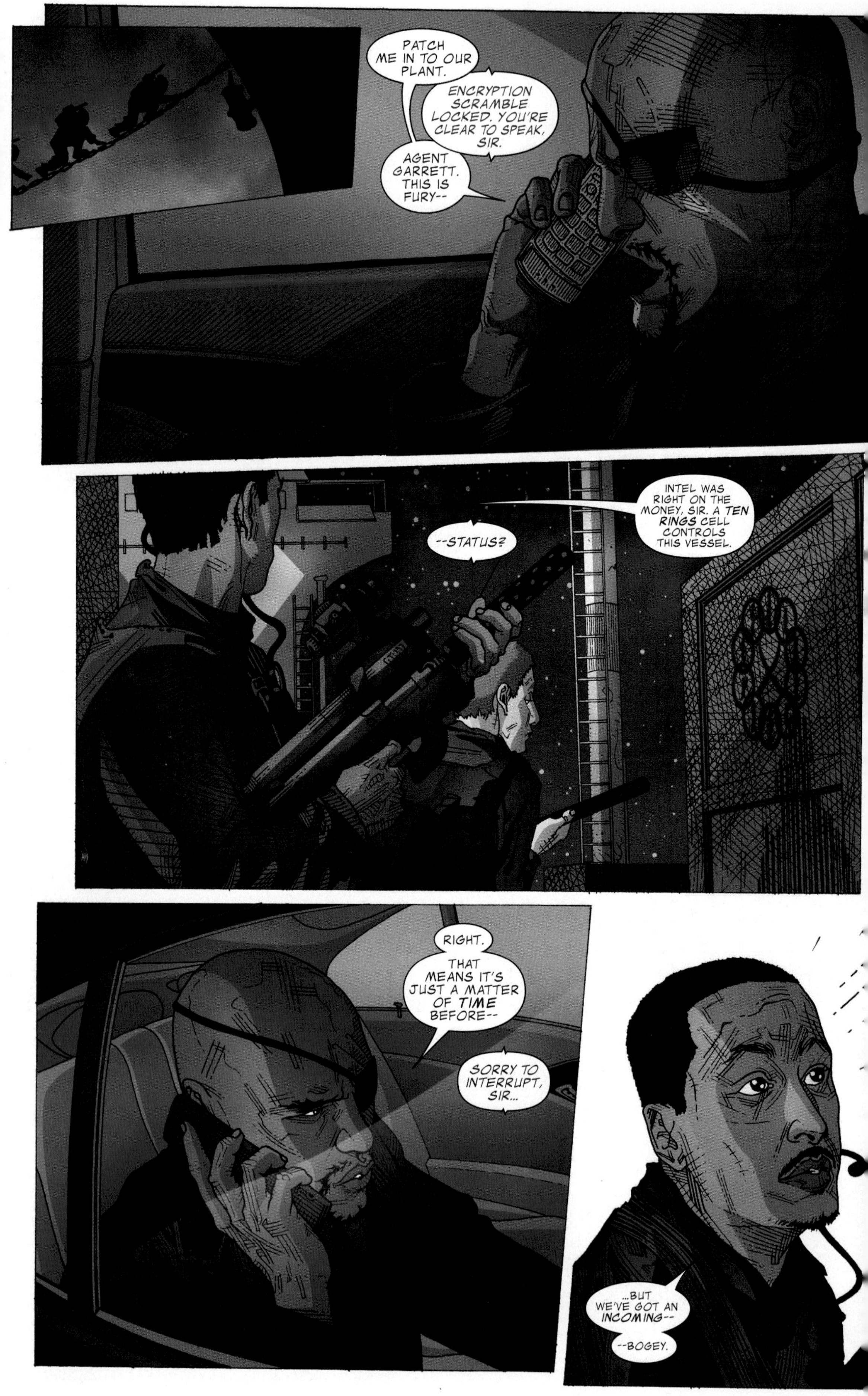

PATCH ME IN TO OUR PLANT.
ENCRYPTION SCRAMBLE LOCKED. YOU'RE CLEAR TO SPEAK, SIR.
AGENT GARRETT. THIS IS FURY--
--STATUS?
INTEL WAS RIGHT ON THE MONEY, SIR. A TEN RINGS CELL CONTROLS THIS VESSEL.
RIGHT.
THAT MEANS IT'S JUST A MATTER OF TIME BEFORE--
SORRY TO INTERRUPT, SIR...
...BUT WE'VE GOT AN INCOMING--
--BOGEY.

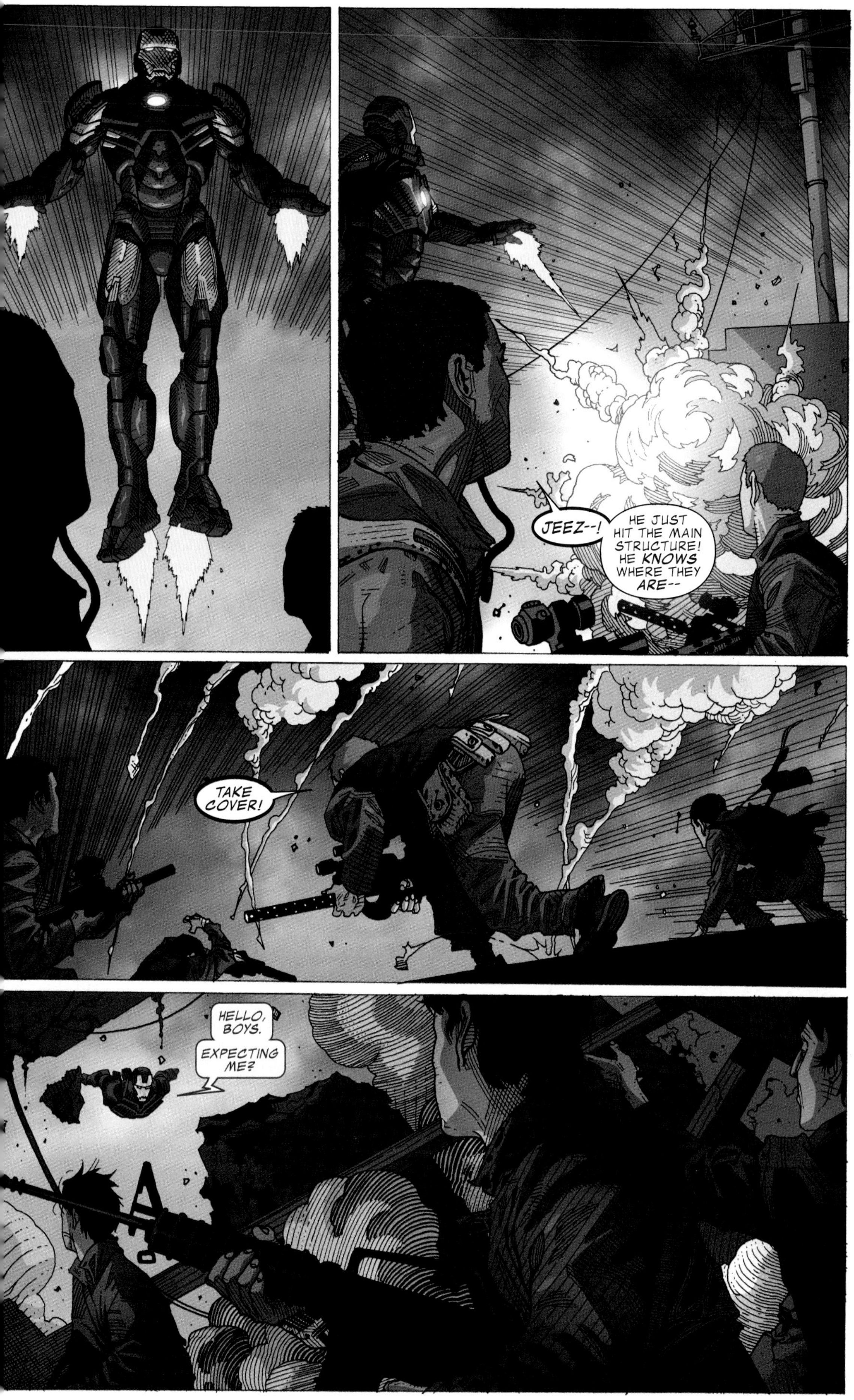
JEEZ--!
HE JUST HIT THE MAIN STRUCTURE! HE KNOWS WHERE THEY ARE--
TAKE COVER!
HELLO, BOYS.
EXPECTING ME?

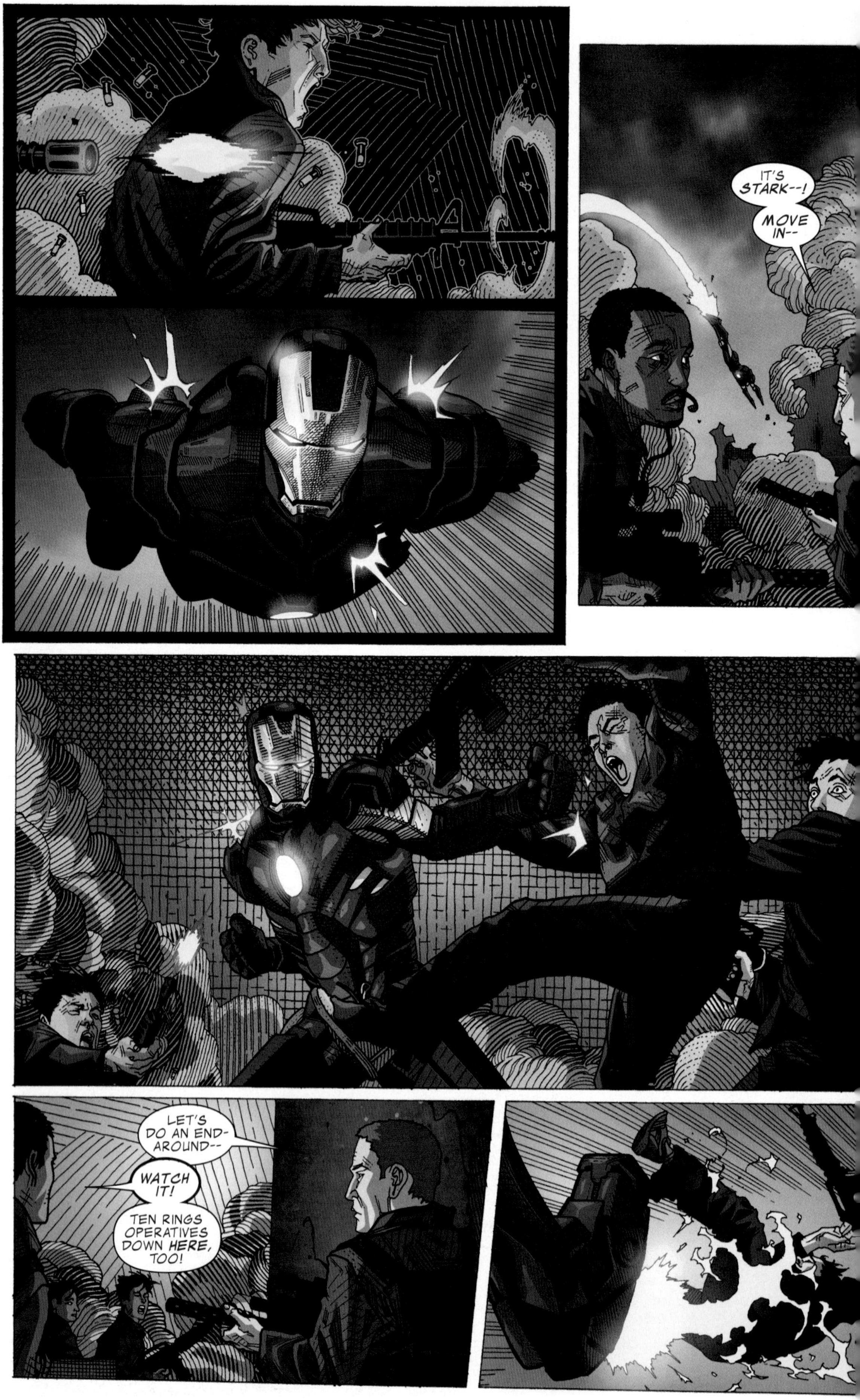
IT'S STARK--!
MOVE IN--
LET'S DO AN END-AROUND--
WATCH IT!
TEN RINGS OPERATIVES DOWN HERE, TOO!

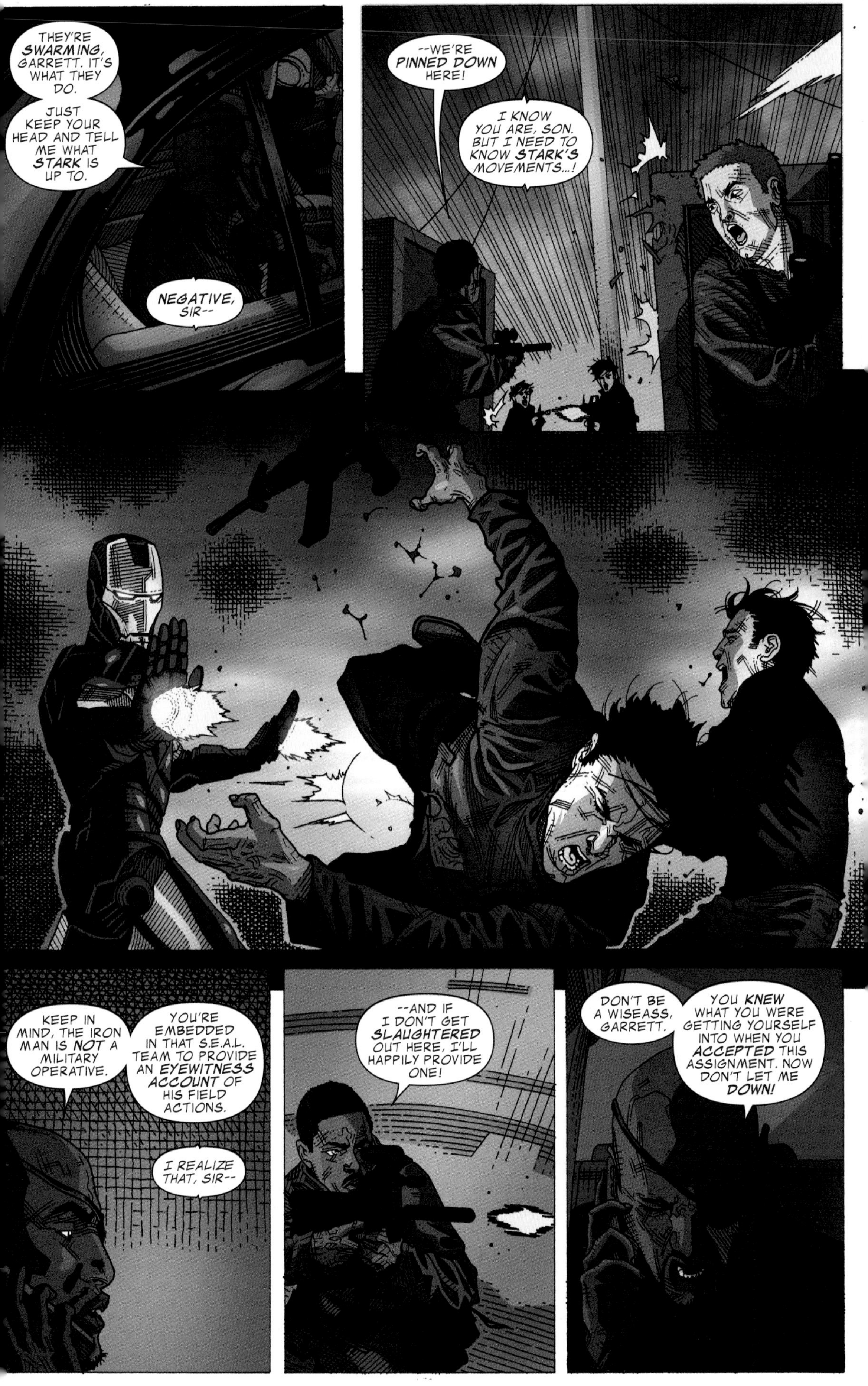
THEY'RE SWARMING, GARRETT. IT'S WHAT THEY DO.
JUST KEEP YOUR HEAD AND TELL ME WHAT STARK IS UP TO.
NEGATIVE, SIR--
--WE'RE PINNED DOWN HERE!
I KNOW YOU ARE, SON. BUT I NEED TO KNOW STARK'S MOVEMENTS...!
KEEP IN MIND, THE IRON MAN IS NOT A MILITARY OPERATIVE.
YOU'RE EMBEDDED IN THAT S.E.A.L. TEAM TO PROVIDE AN EYEWITNESS ACCOUNT OF HIS FIELD ACTIONS.
I REALIZE THAT, SIR--
--AND IF I DON'T GET SLAUGHTERED OUT HERE, I'LL HAPPILY PROVIDE ONE!
DON'T BE A WISEASS, GARRETT.
YOU KNEW WHAT YOU WERE GETTING YOURSELF INTO WHEN YOU ACCEPTED THIS ASSIGNMENT. NOW DON'T LET ME DOWN!

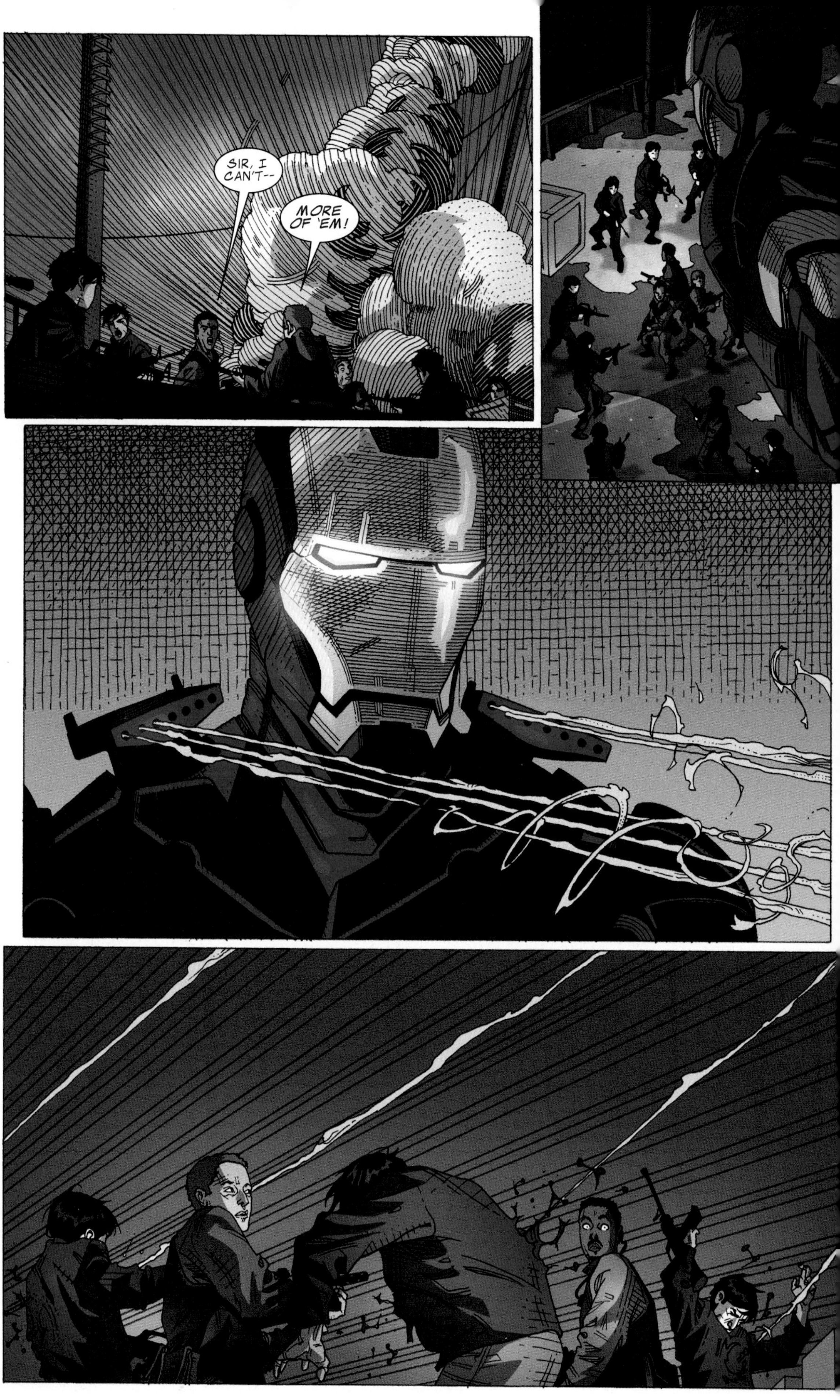
SIR, I CAN'T--
MORE OF 'EM!

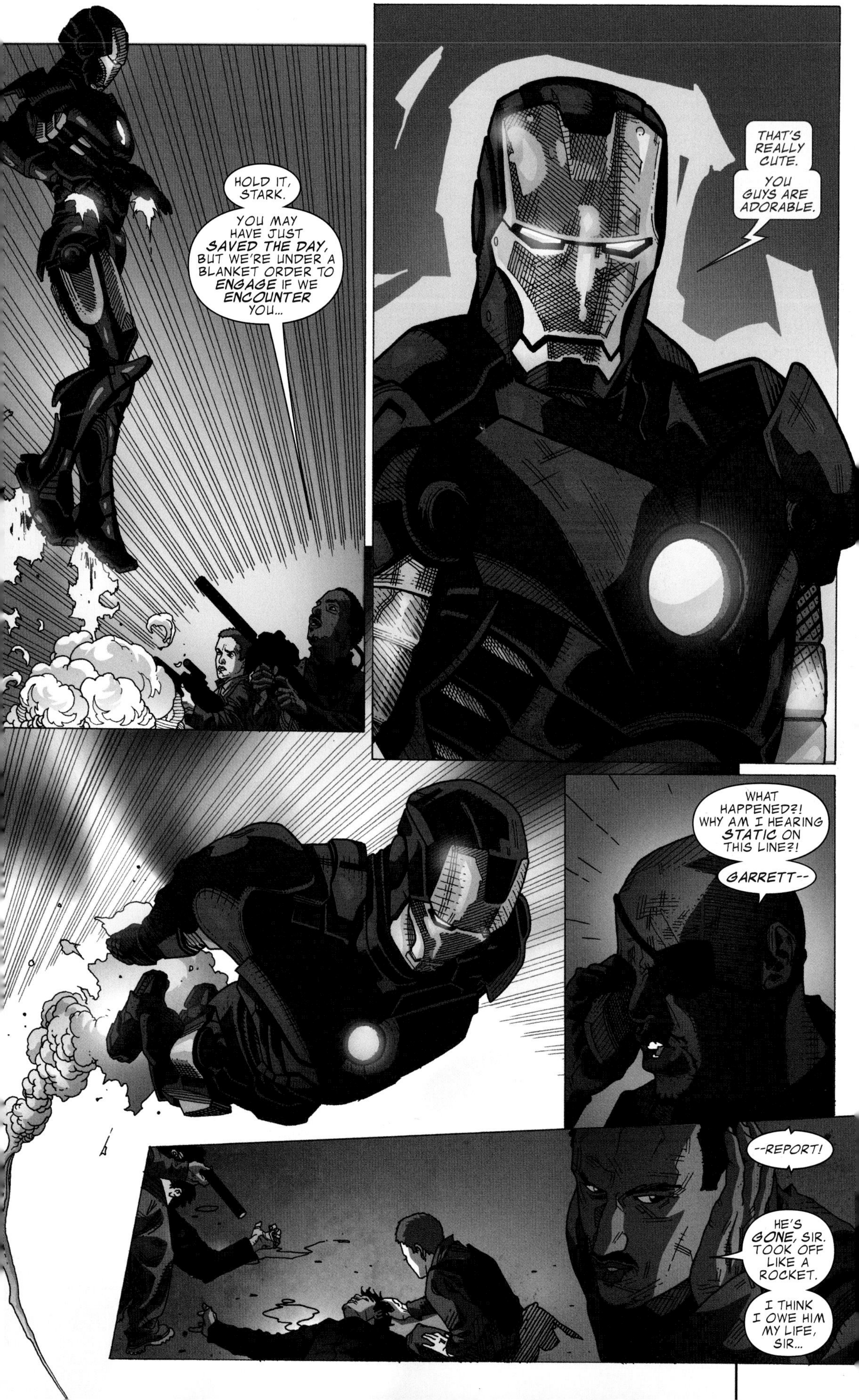
HOLD IT, STARK.
YOU MAY HAVE JUST SAVED THE DAY, BUT WE'RE UNDER A BLANKET ORDER TO ENGAGE IF WE ENCOUNTER YOU...
THAT'S REALLY CUTE.
YOU GUYS ARE ADORABLE.
WHAT HAPPENED?! WHY AM I HEARING STATIC ON THIS LINE?!
GARRETT--
--REPORT!
HE'S GONE, SIR. TOOK OFF LIKE A ROCKET.
I THINK I OWE HIM MY LIFE, SIR...

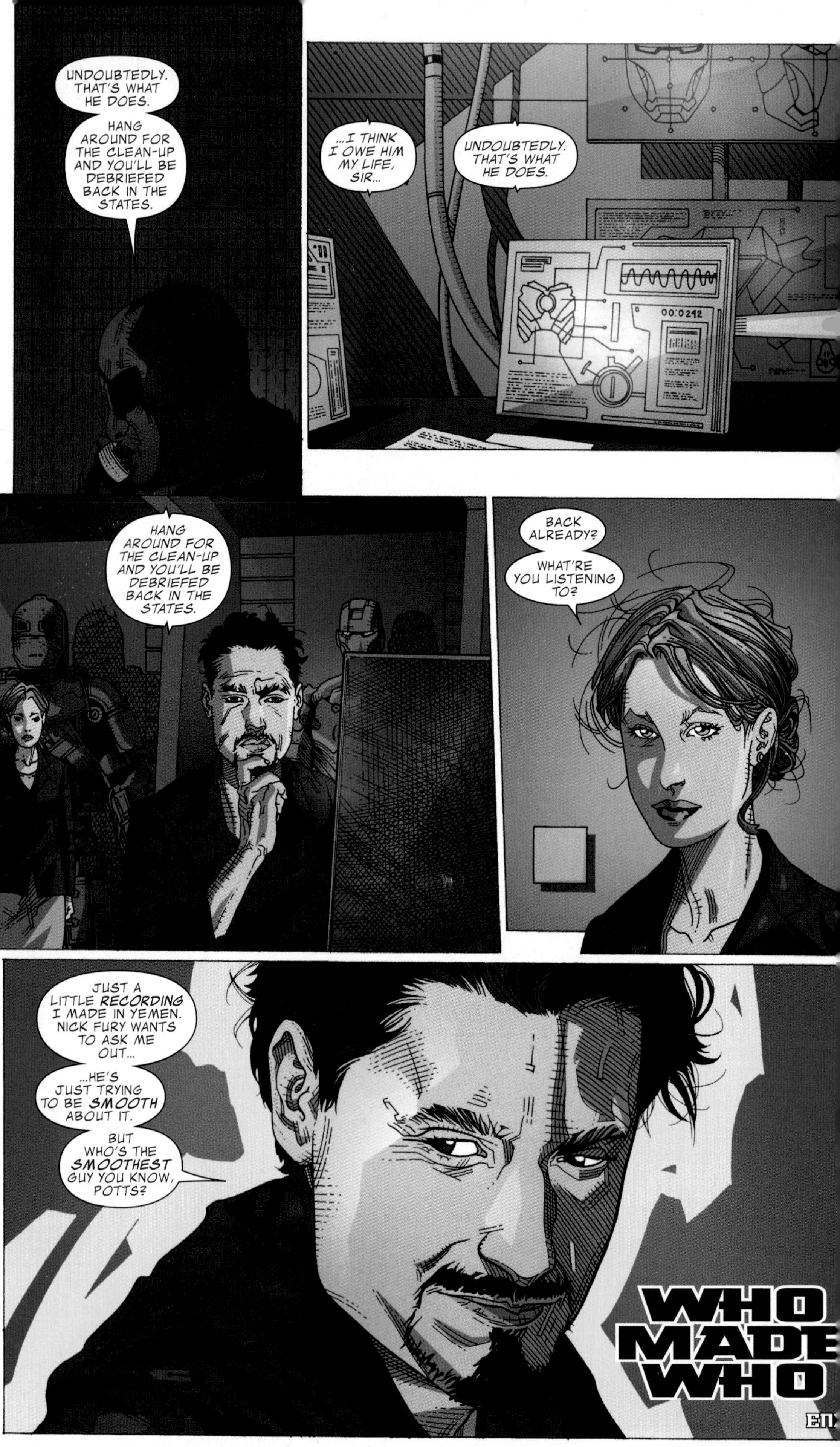
UNDOUBTEDLY. THAT'S WHAT HE DOES.
HANG AROUND FOR THE CLEAN-UP AND YOU'LL BE DEBRIEFED BACK IN THE STATES.
...I THINK I OWE HIM MY LIFE, SIR...
UNDOUBTEDLY. THAT'S WHAT HE DOES.
00:0242
HANG AROUND FOR THE CLEAN-UP AND YOU'LL BE DEBRIEFED BACK IN THE STATES.
BACK ALREADY?
WHAT'RE YOU LISTENING TO?
JUST A LITTLE RECORDING I MADE IN YEMEN. NICK FURY WANTS TO ASK ME OUT...
...HE'S JUST TRYING TO BE SMOOTH ABOUT IT.
BUT WHO'S THE SMOOTHEST GUY YOU KNOW, POTTS?
WHO MADE WHO
END

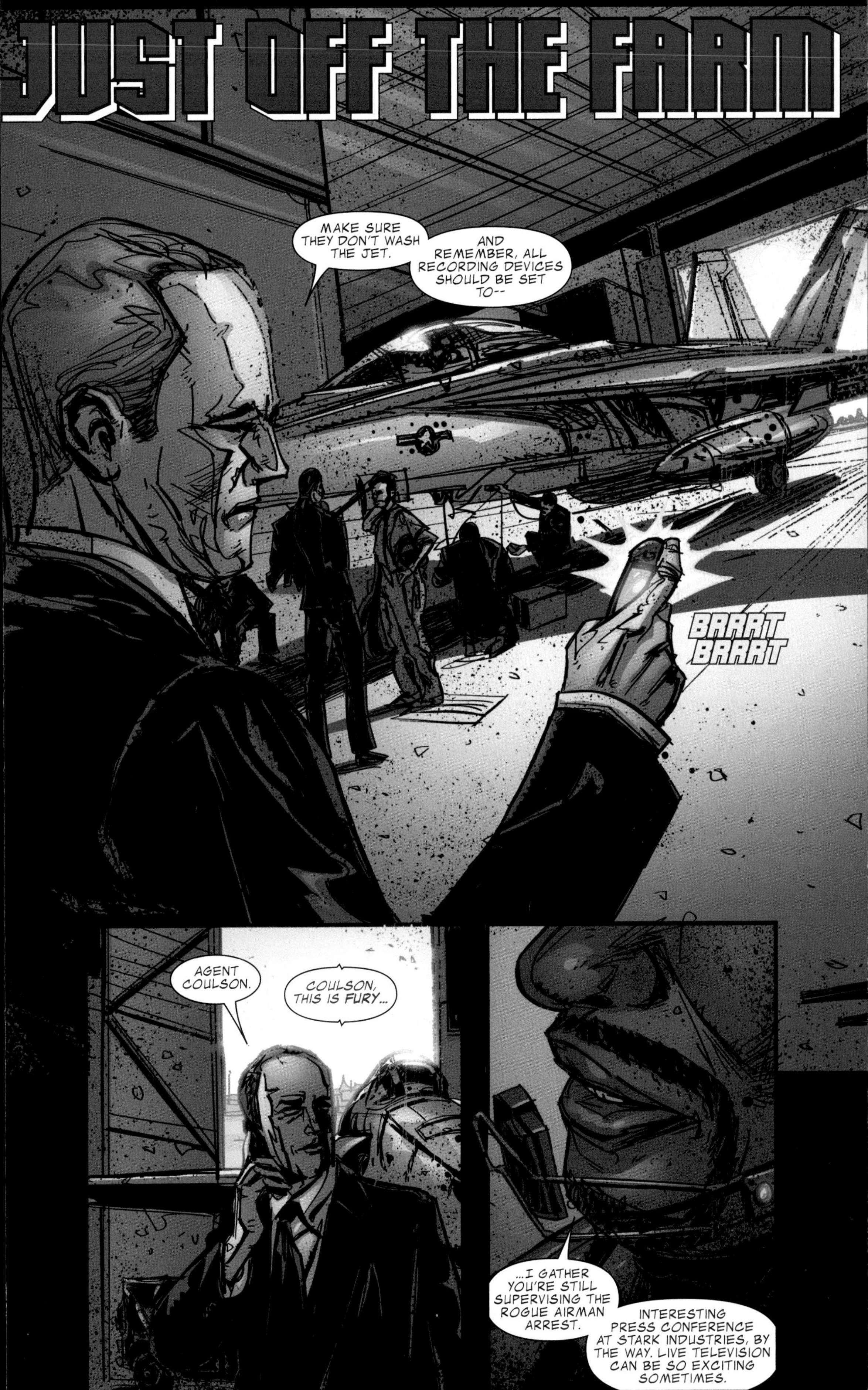
JUST OFF THE FARM
MAKE SURE THEY DON'T WASH THE JET.
AND REMEMBER, ALL RECORDING DEVICES SHOULD BE SET TO--
BRRRT BRRRT
AGENT COULSON.
COULSON, THIS IS FURY...
...I GATHER YOU'RE STILL SUPERVISING THE ROGUE AIRMAN ARREST.
INTERESTING PRESS CONFERENCE AT STARK INDUSTRIES, BY THE WAY. LIVE TELEVISION CAN BE SO EXCITING SOMETIMES.

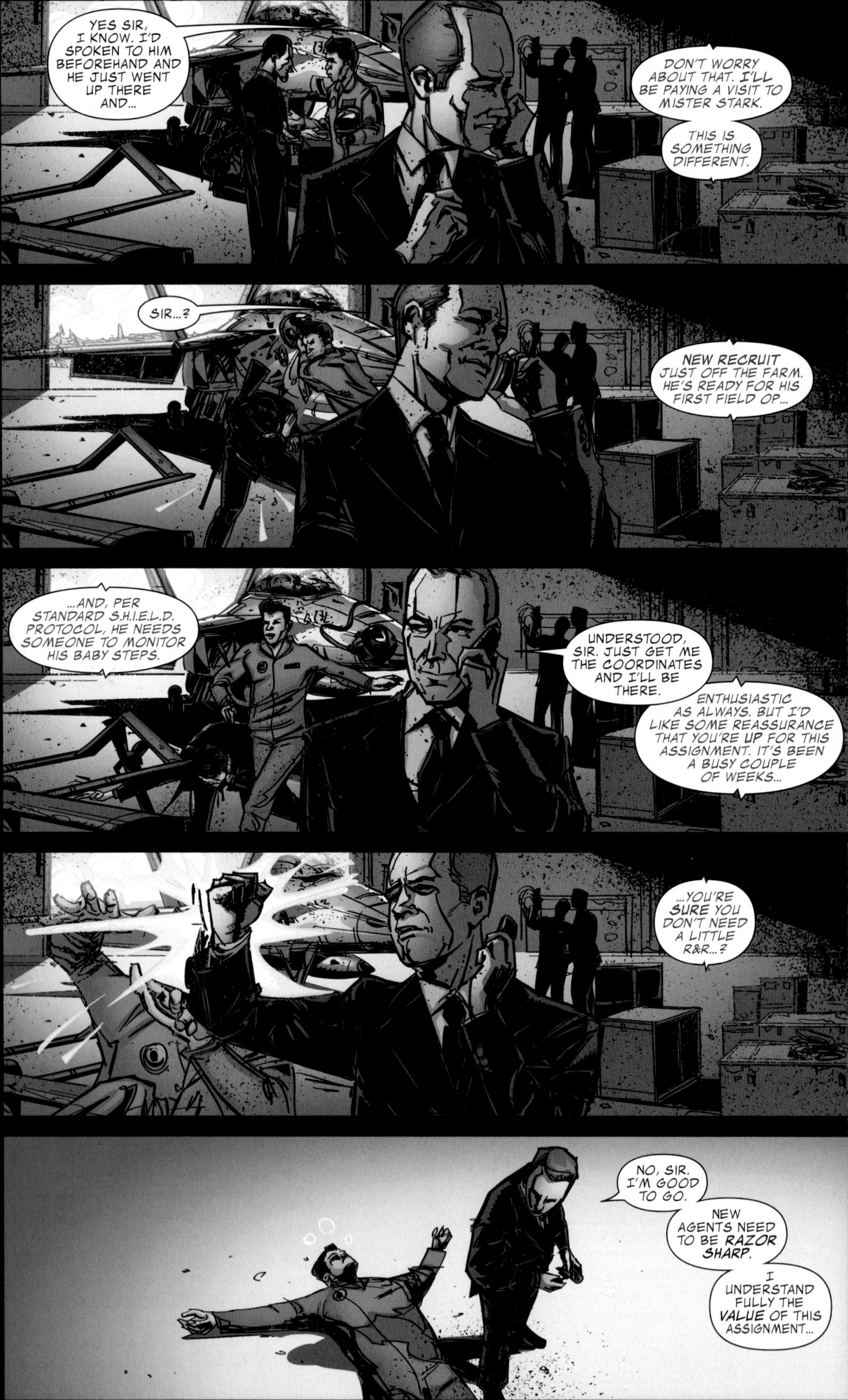
YES SIR, I KNOW. I'D SPOKEN TO HIM BEFOREHAND AND HE JUST WENT UP THERE AND...
DON'T WORRY ABOUT THAT. I'LL BE PAYING A VISIT TO MISTER STARK.
THIS IS SOMETHING DIFFERENT.
SIR...?
NEW RECRUIT JUST OFF THE FARM. HE'S READY FOR HIS FIRST FIELD OP...
...AND, PER STANDARD S.H.I.E.L.D. PROTOCOL, HE NEEDS SOMEONE TO MONITOR HIS BABY STEPS.
UNDERSTOOD, SIR. JUST GET ME THE COORDINATES AND I'LL BE THERE.
ENTHUSIASTIC AS ALWAYS. BUT I'D LIKE SOME REASSURANCE THAT YOU'RE UP FOR THIS ASSIGNMENT. IT'S BEEN A BUSY COUPLE OF WEEKS...
...YOU'RE SURE YOU DON'T NEED A LITTLE R&R...?
NO, SIR. I'M GOOD TO GO.
NEW AGENTS NEED TO BE RAZOR SHARP.
I UNDERSTAND FULLY THE VALUE OF THIS ASSIGNMENT...

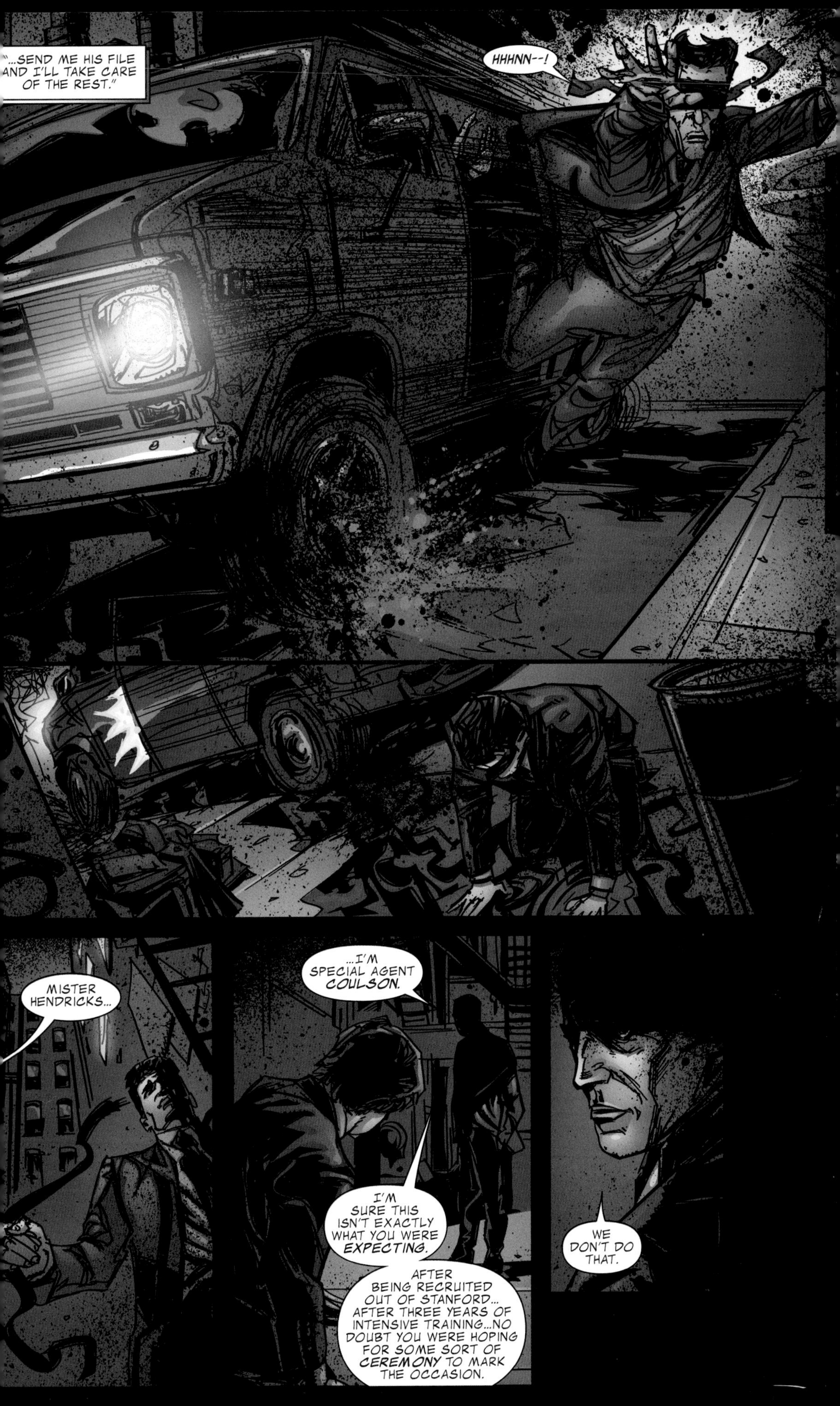

"...SEND ME HIS FILE AND I'LL TAKE CARE OF THE REST."
HHHNN--!
MISTER HENDRICKS...
...I'M SPECIAL AGENT COULSON.
I'M SURE THIS ISN'T EXACTLY WHAT YOU WERE EXPECTING.
AFTER BEING RECRUITED OUT OF STANFORD... AFTER THREE YEARS OF INTENSIVE TRAINING...NO DOUBT YOU WERE HOPING FOR SOME SORT OF CEREMONY TO MARK THE OCCASION.
WE DON'T DO THAT.

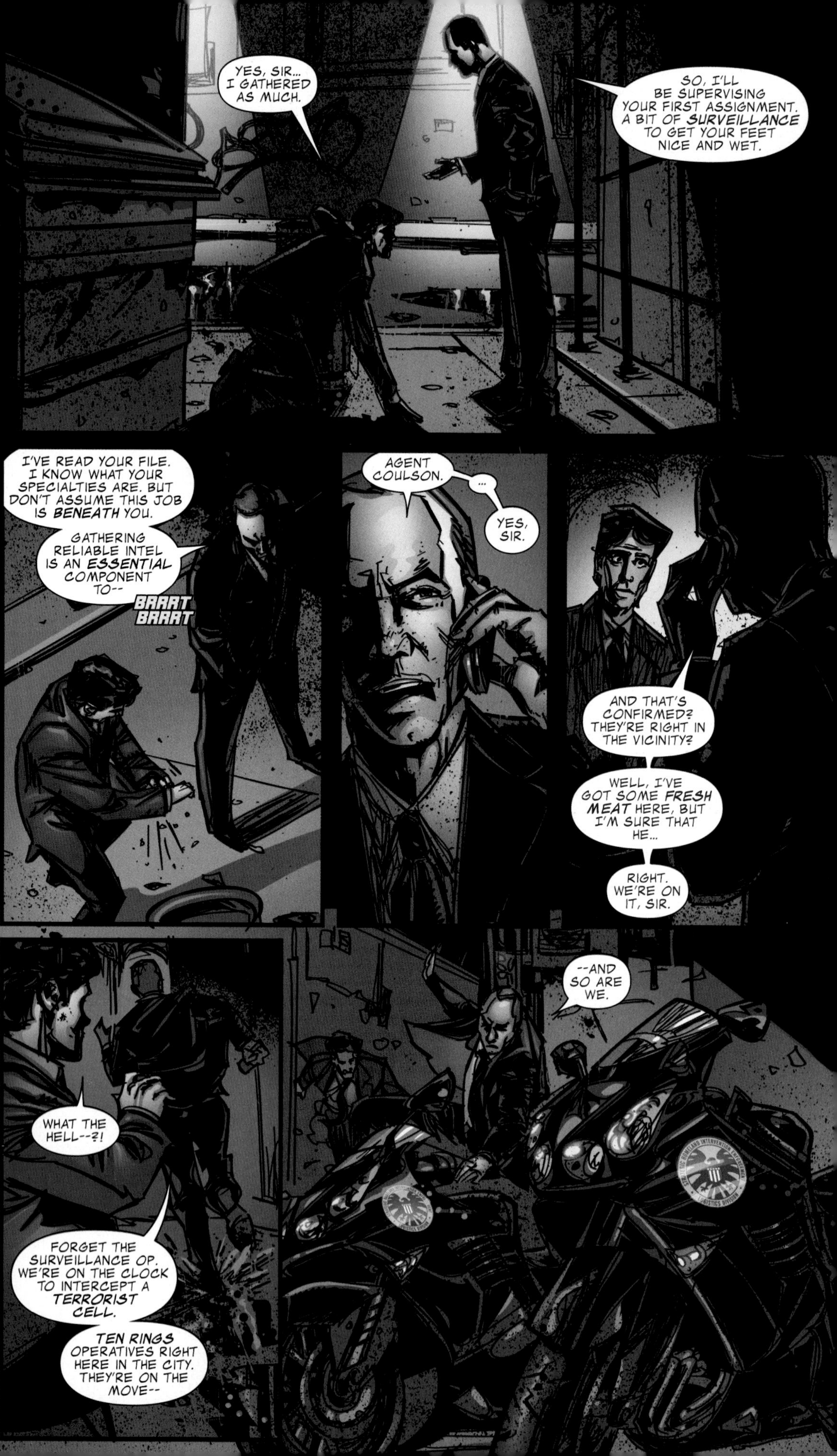

YES, SIR... I GATHERED AS MUCH.
SO, I'LL BE SUPERVISING YOUR FIRST ASSIGNMENT. A BIT OF SURVEILLANCE TO GET YOUR FEET NICE AND WET.
I'VE READ YOUR FILE. I KNOW WHAT YOUR SPECIALTIES ARE. BUT DON'T ASSUME THIS JOB IS BENEATH YOU.
GATHERING RELIABLE INTEL IS AN ESSENTIAL COMPONENT TO--
BRRRT BRRRT
AGENT COULSON.
...
YES, SIR.
AND THAT'S CONFIRMED? THEY'RE RIGHT IN THE VICINITY?
WELL, I'VE GOT SOME FRESH MEAT HERE, BUT I'M SURE THAT HE...
RIGHT. WE'RE ON IT, SIR.
WHAT THE HELL--?!
FORGET THE SURVEILLANCE OP. WE'RE ON THE CLOCK TO INTERCEPT A TERRORIST CELL.
TEN RINGS OPERATIVES RIGHT HERE IN THE CITY. THEY'RE ON THE MOVE--
--AND SO ARE WE.

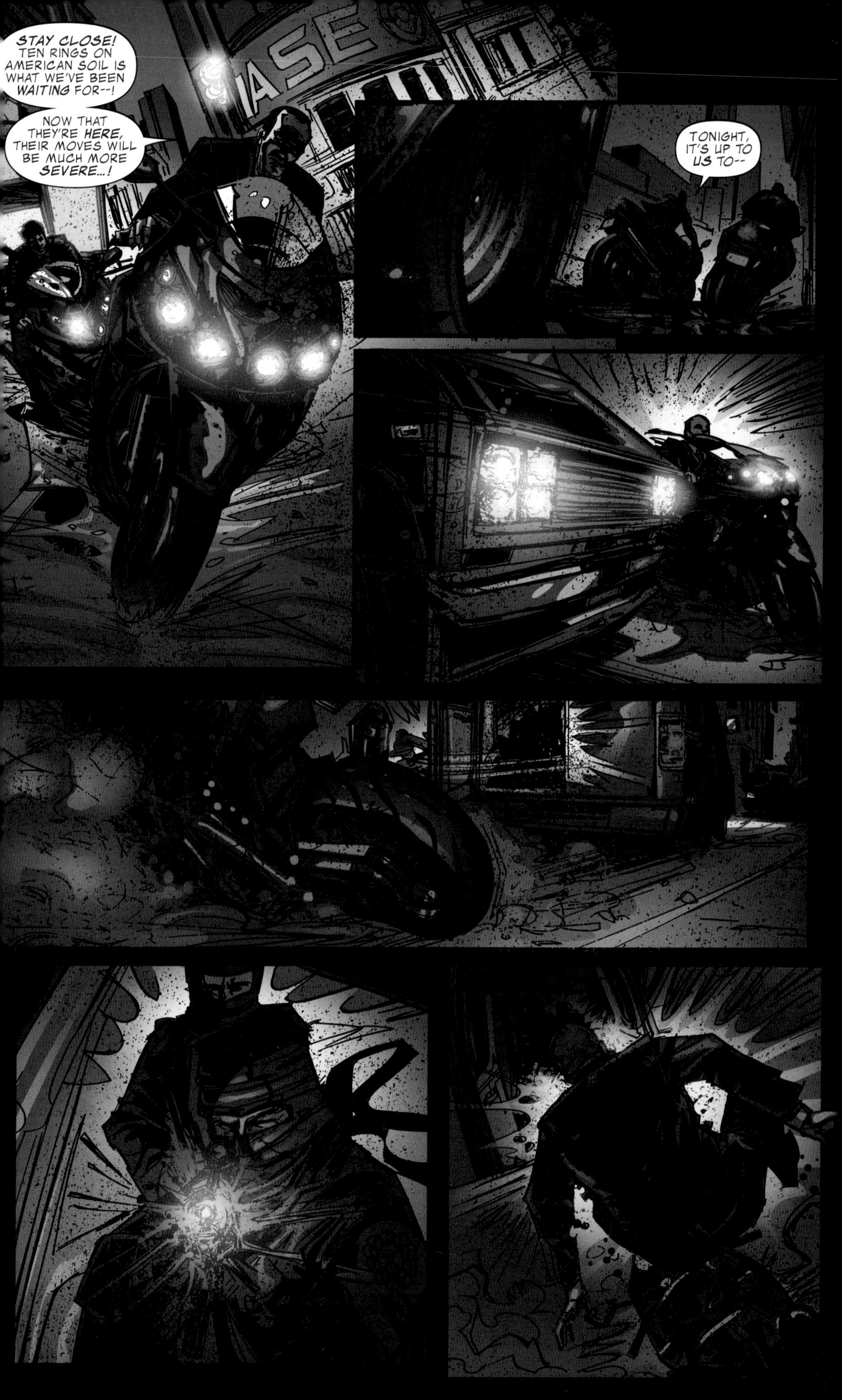
STAY CLOSE! TEN RINGS ON AMERICAN SOIL IS WHAT WE'VE BEEN WAITING FOR--!
NOW THAT THEY'RE HERE, THEIR MOVES WILL BE MUCH MORE SEVERE...!
TONIGHT, IT'S UP TO US TO--

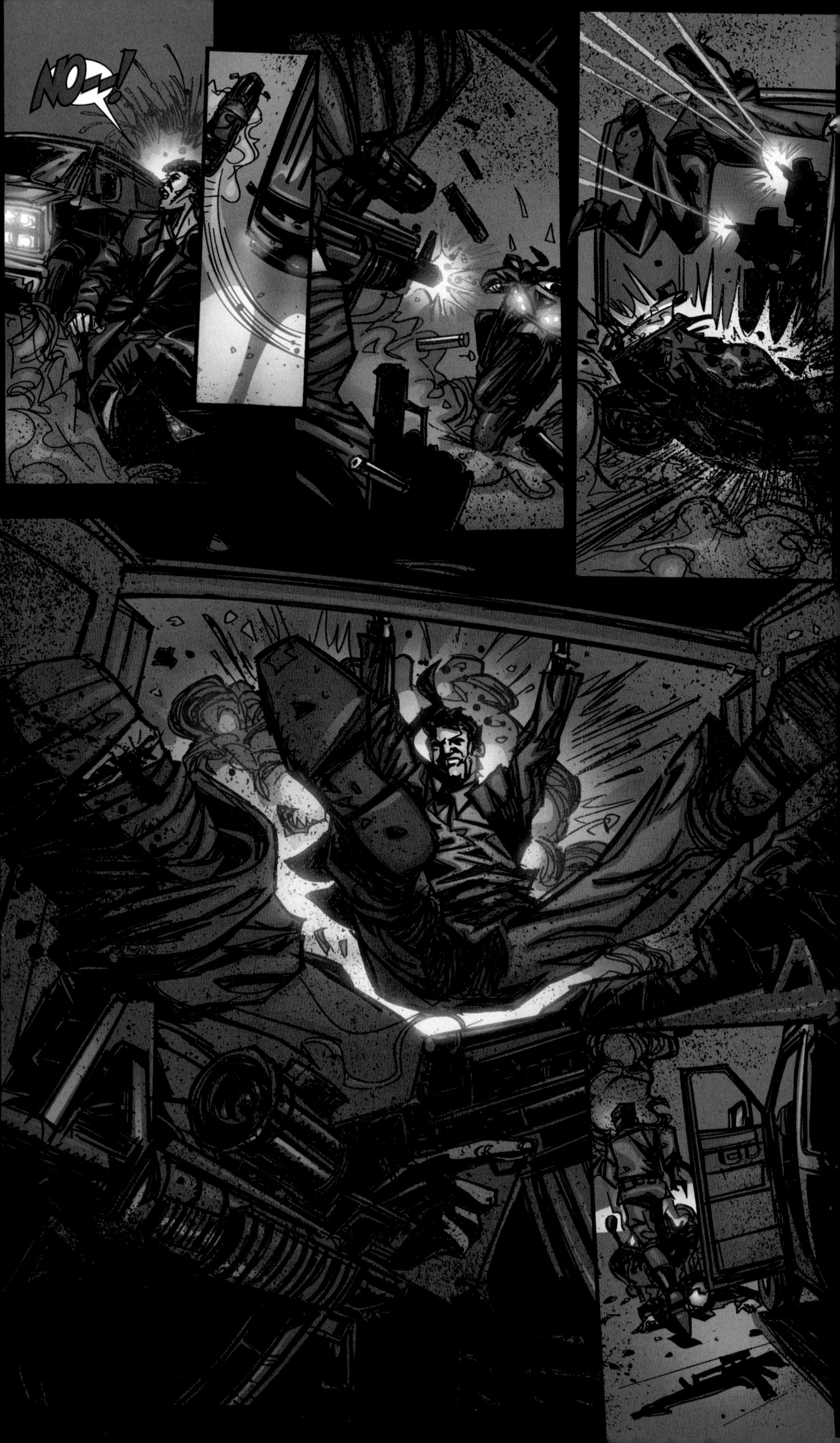
NO--!

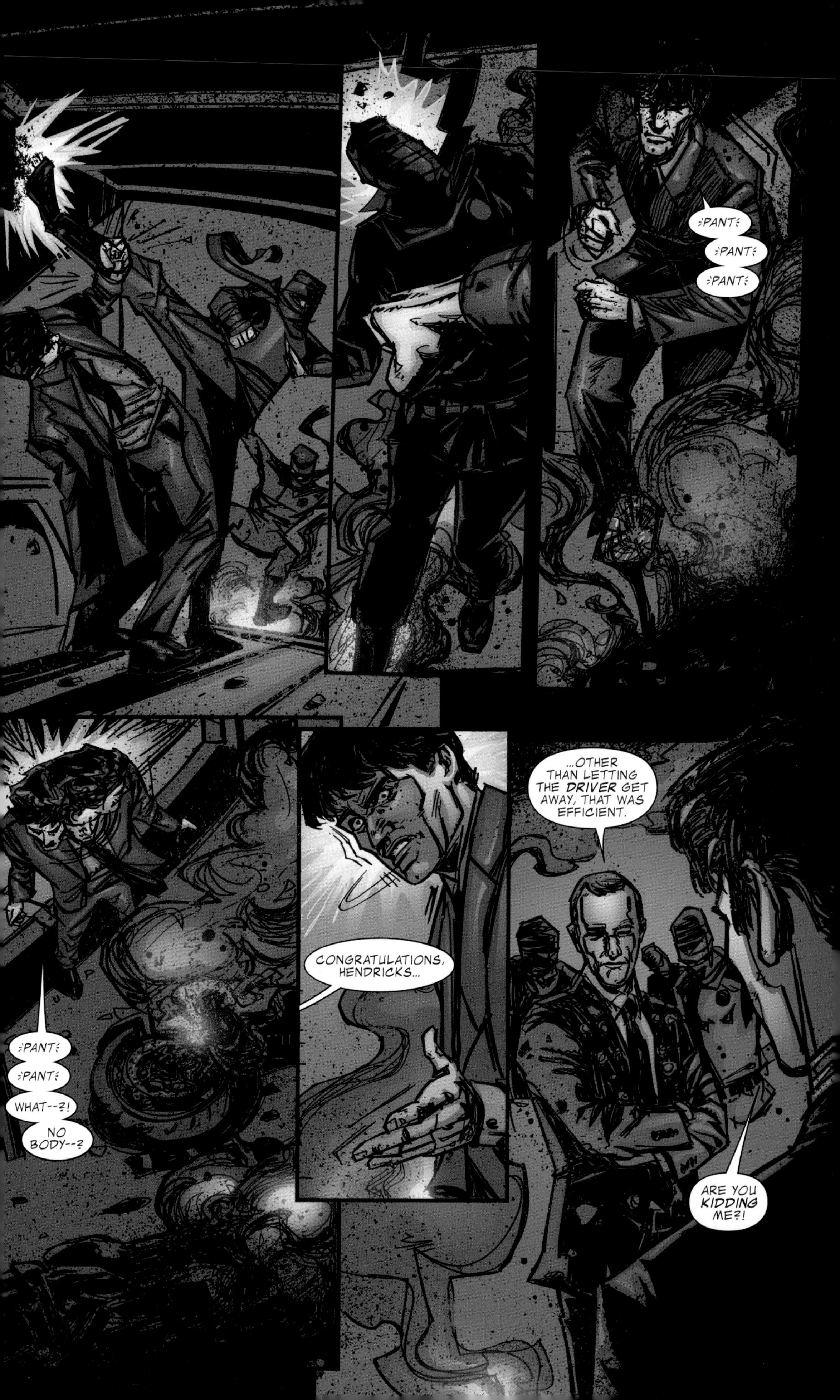

PANT
PANT
PANT
PANT
PANT
WHAT--?!
NO BODY--?
CONGRATULATIONS, HENDRICKS...
...OTHER THAN LETTING THE DRIVER GET AWAY, THAT WAS EFFICIENT.
ARE YOU KIDDING ME?!

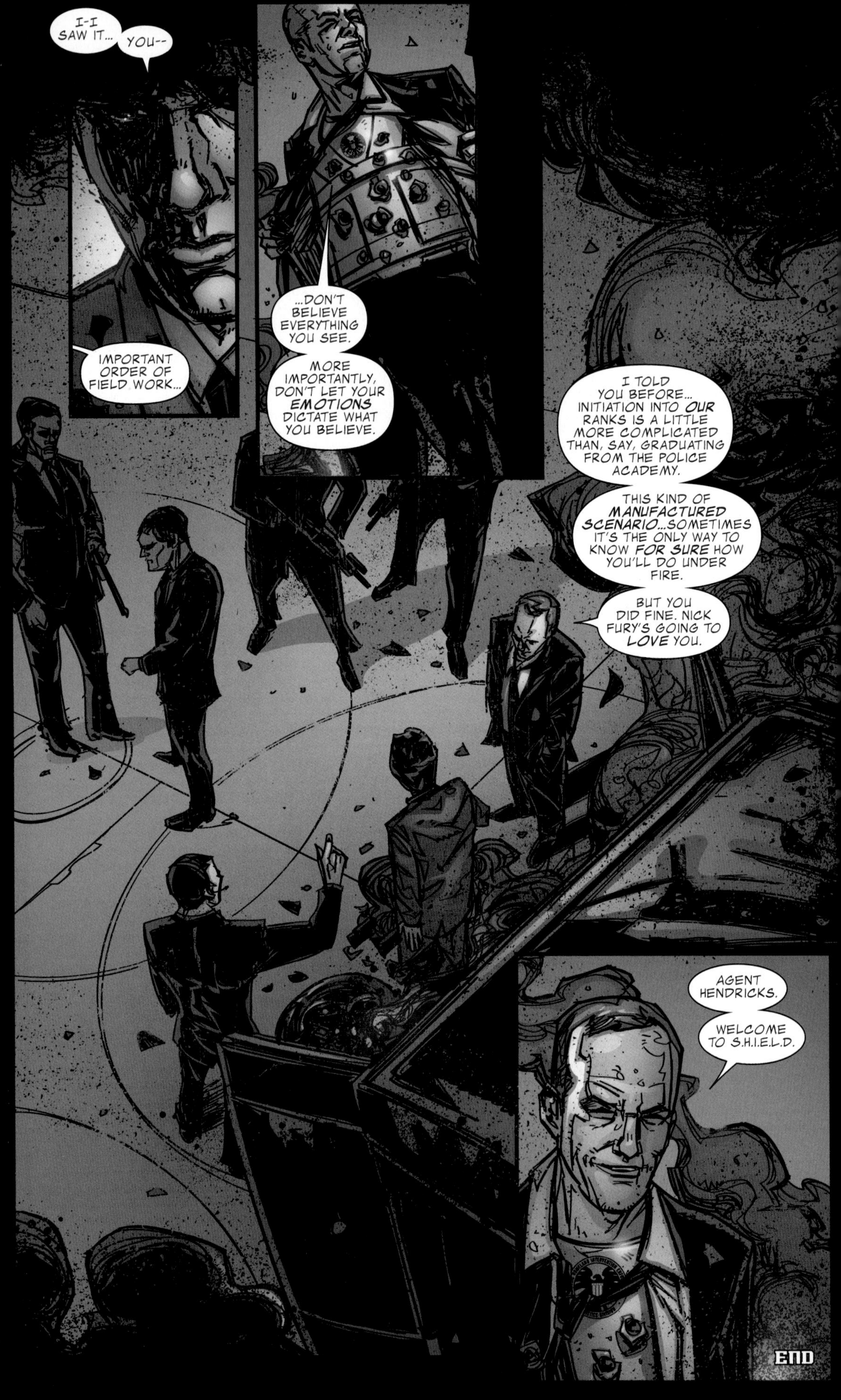
I-I SAW IT...
YOU--
IMPORTANT ORDER OF FIELD WORK...
...DON'T BELIEVE EVERYTHING YOU SEE.
MORE IMPORTANTLY, DON'T LET YOUR EMOTIONS DICTATE WHAT YOU BELIEVE.
I TOLD YOU BEFORE... INITIATION INTO OUR RANKS IS A LITTLE MORE COMPLICATED THAN, SAY, GRADUATING FROM THE POLICE ACADEMY.
THIS KIND OF MANUFACTURED SCENARIO...SOMETIMES IT'S THE ONLY WAY TO KNOW FOR SURE HOW YOU'LL DO UNDER FIRE.
BUT YOU DID FINE. NICK FURY'S GOING TO LOVE YOU.
AGENT HENDRICKS.
WELCOME TO S.H.I.E.L.D.
END

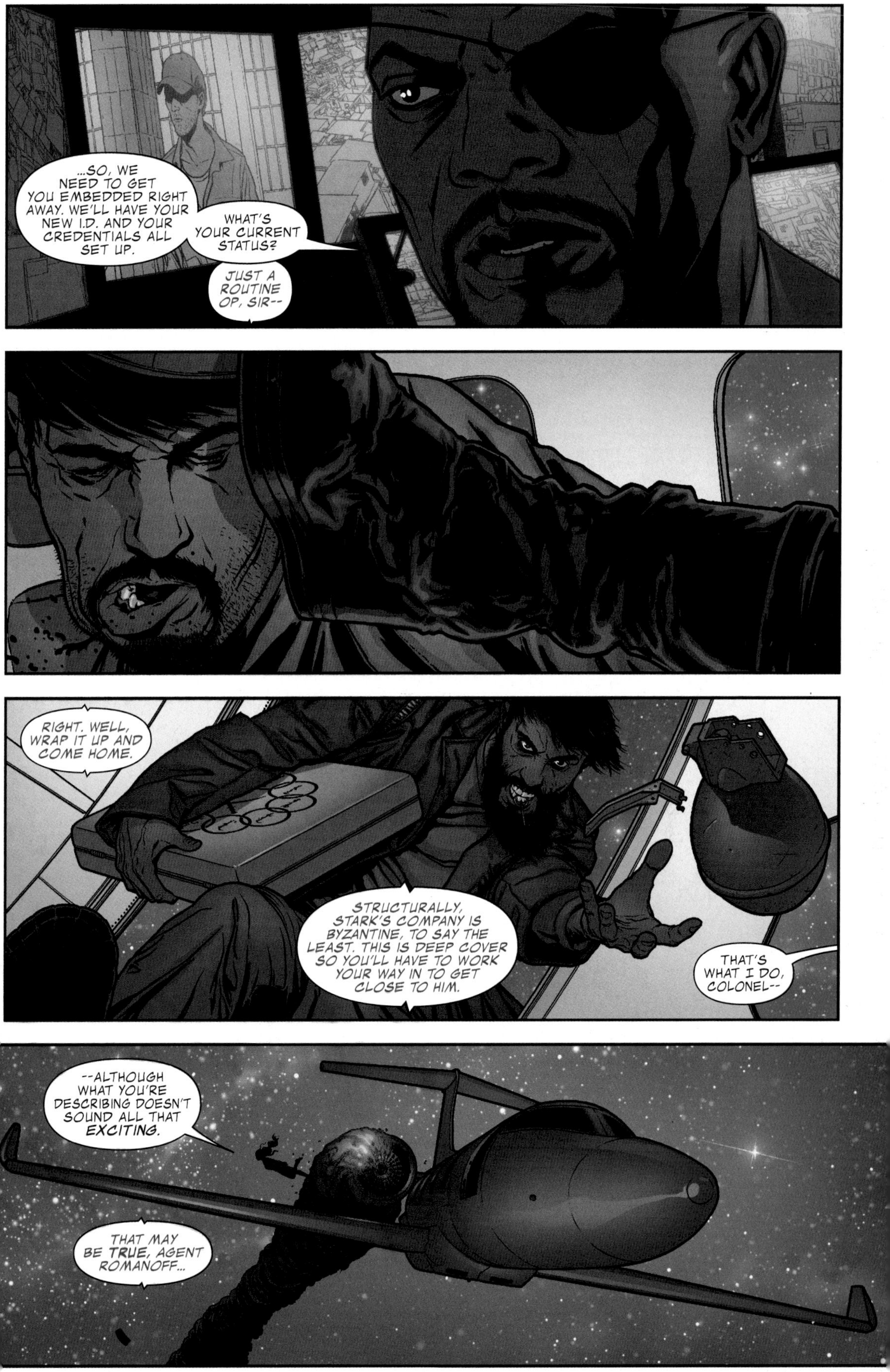

...SO, WE NEED TO GET YOU EMBEDDED RIGHT AWAY. WE'LL HAVE YOUR NEW I.D. AND YOUR CREDENTIALS ALL SET UP.
WHAT'S YOUR CURRENT STATUS?
JUST A ROUTINE OP, SIR--
RIGHT. WELL, WRAP IT UP AND COME HOME.
STRUCTURALLY, STARK'S COMPANY IS BYZANTINE, TO SAY THE LEAST. THIS IS DEEP COVER SO YOU'LL HAVE TO WORK YOUR WAY IN TO GET CLOSE TO HIM.
THAT'S WHAT I DO, COLONEL--
--ALTHOUGH WHAT YOU'RE DESCRIBING DOESN'T SOUND ALL THAT EXCITING.
THAT MAY BE TRUE, AGENT ROMANOFF...

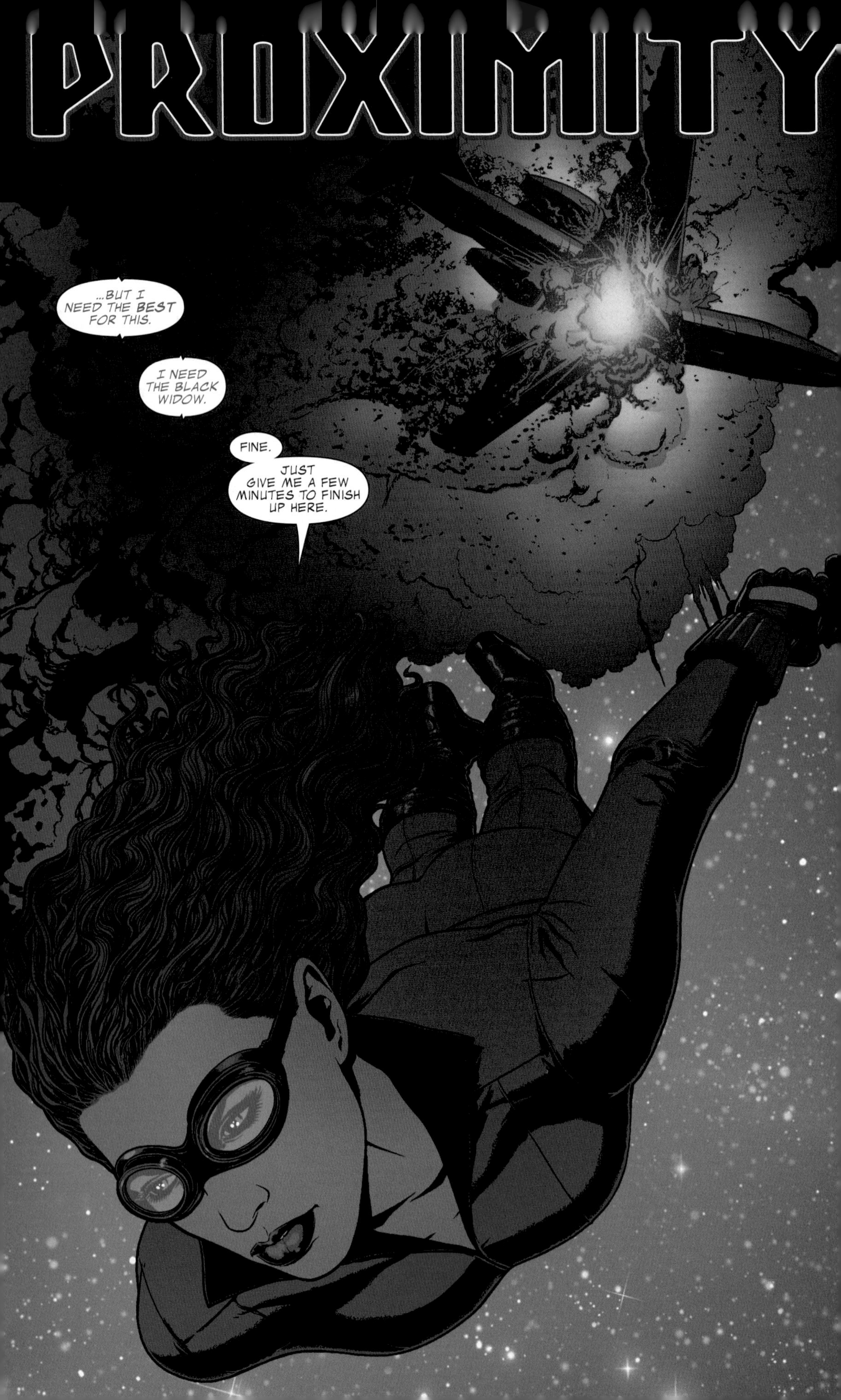
PROXIMITY
...BUT I NEED THE BEST FOR THIS.
I NEED THE BLACK WIDOW.
FINE.
JUST GIVE ME A FEW MINUTES TO FINISH UP HERE.

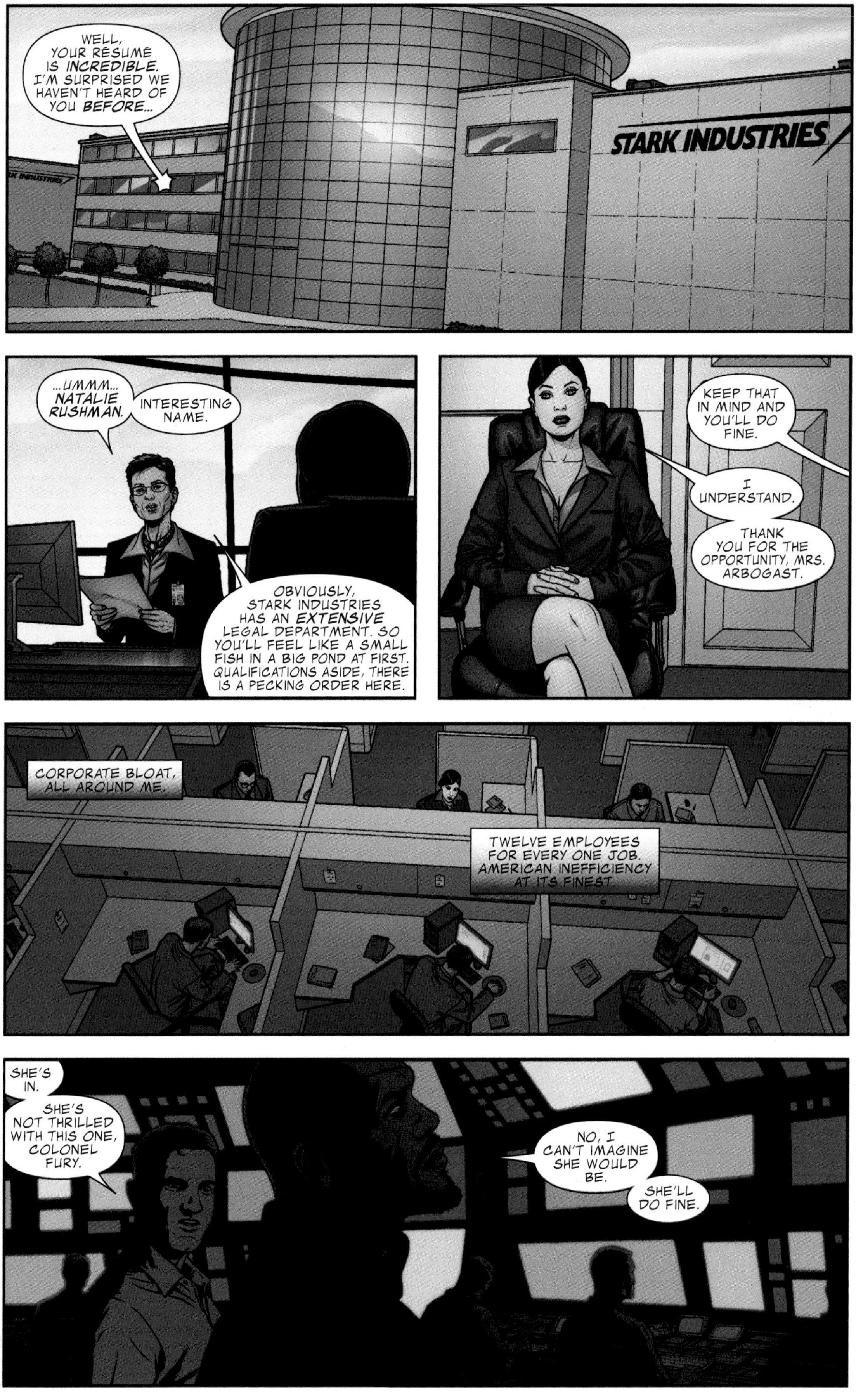

WELL, YOUR RÉSUMÉ IS INCREDIBLE. I'M SURPRISED WE HAVEN'T HEARD OF YOU BEFORE...
STARK INDUSTRIES
...UMMM... NATALIE RUSHMAN.
INTERESTING NAME.
OBVIOUSLY, STARK INDUSTRIES HAS AN EXTENSIVE LEGAL DEPARTMENT. SO YOU'LL FEEL LIKE A SMALL FISH IN A BIG POND AT FIRST. QUALIFICATIONS ASIDE, THERE IS A PECKING ORDER HERE.
KEEP THAT IN MIND AND YOU'LL DO FINE.
I UNDERSTAND.
THANK YOU FOR THE OPPORTUNITY, MRS. ARBOGAST.
CORPORATE BLOAT, ALL AROUND ME.
TWELVE EMPLOYEES FOR EVERY ONE JOB. AMERICAN INEFFICIENCY AT ITS FINEST.
SHE'S IN.
SHE'S NOT THRILLED WITH THIS ONE, COLONEL FURY.
NO, I CAN'T IMAGINE SHE WOULD BE.
SHE'LL DO FINE.

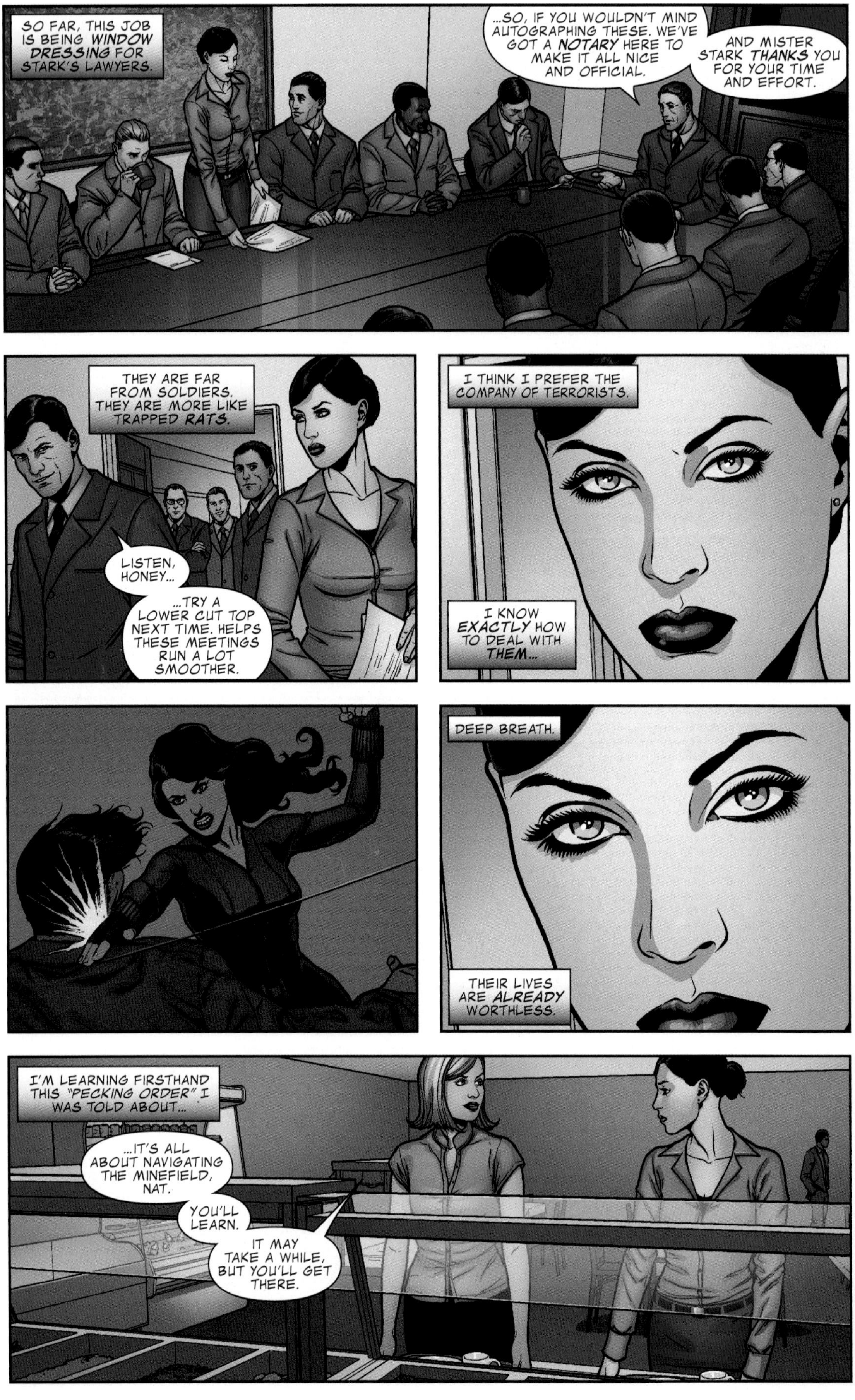
SO FAR, THIS JOB IS BEING WINDOW DRESSING FOR STARK'S LAWYERS.
...SO, IF YOU WOULDN'T MIND AUTOGRAPHING THESE. WE'VE GOT A NOTARY HERE TO MAKE IT ALL NICE AND OFFICIAL.
AND MISTER STARK THANKS YOU FOR YOUR TIME AND EFFORT.
THEY ARE FAR FROM SOLDIERS. THEY ARE MORE LIKE TRAPPED RATS.
LISTEN, HONEY...
...TRY A LOWER CUT TOP NEXT TIME. HELPS THESE MEETINGS RUN A LOT SMOOTHER.
I THINK I PREFER THE COMPANY OF TERRORISTS.
I KNOW EXACTLY HOW TO DEAL WITH THEM...
DEEP BREATH.
THEIR LIVES ARE ALREADY WORTHLESS.
I'M LEARNING FIRSTHAND THIS "PECKING ORDER" I WAS TOLD ABOUT...
...IT'S ALL ABOUT NAVIGATING THE MINEFIELD, NAT.
YOU'LL LEARN.
IT MAY TAKE A WHILE, BUT YOU'LL GET THERE.

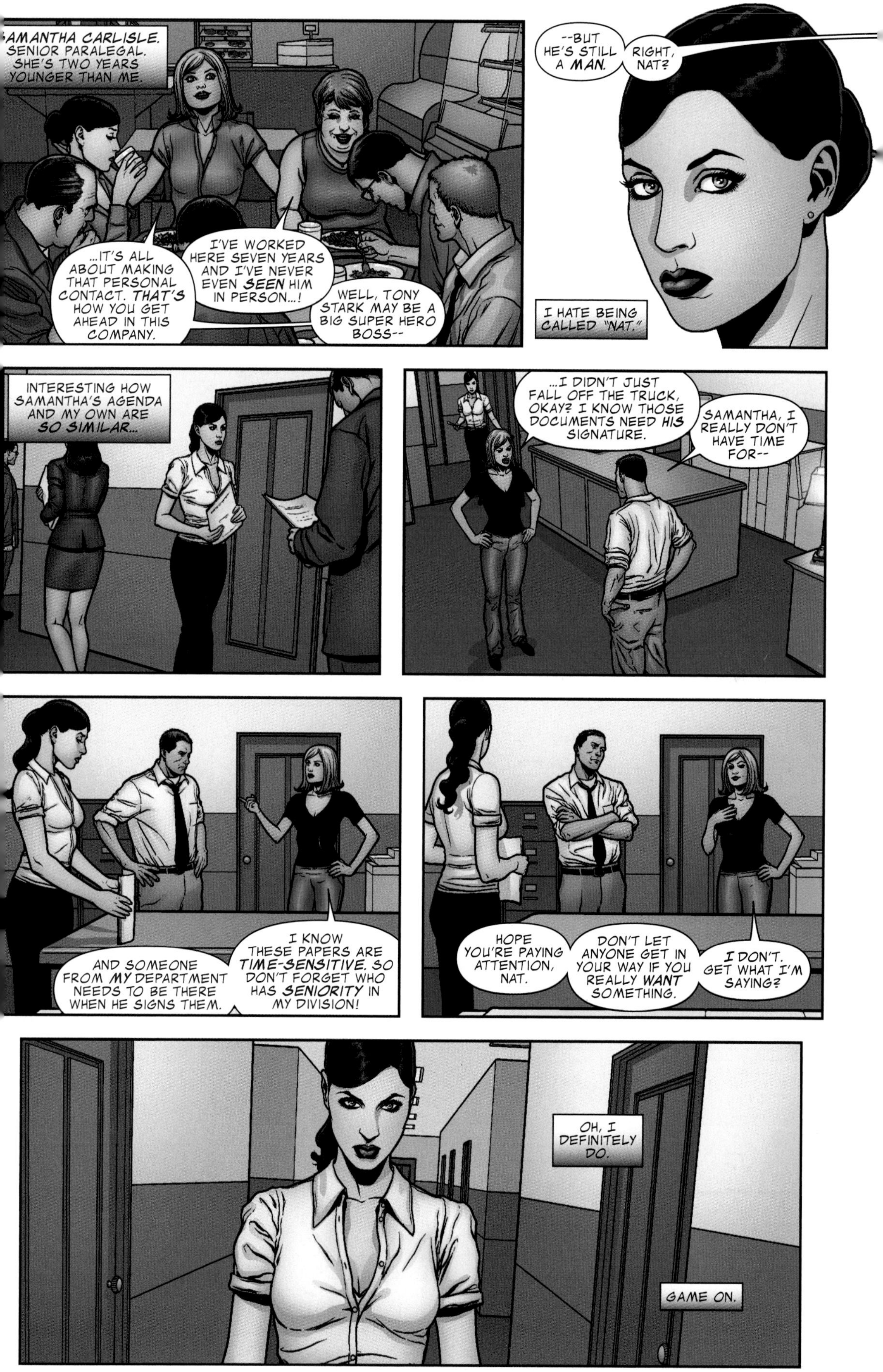
SAMANTHA CARLISLE. SENIOR PARALEGAL. SHE'S TWO YEARS YOUNGER THAN ME.
...IT'S ALL ABOUT MAKING THAT PERSONAL CONTACT. THAT'S HOW YOU GET AHEAD IN THIS COMPANY.
I'VE WORKED HERE SEVEN YEARS AND I'VE NEVER EVEN SEEN HIM IN PERSON...!
WELL, TONY STARK MAY BE A BIG SUPER HERO BOSS--
--BUT HE'S STILL A MAN.
RIGHT, NAT?
I HATE BEING CALLED "NAT."
INTERESTING HOW SAMANTHA'S AGENDA AND MY OWN ARE SO SIMILAR...
...I DIDN'T JUST FALL OFF THE TRUCK, OKAY? I KNOW THOSE DOCUMENTS NEED HIS SIGNATURE.
SAMANTHA, I REALLY DON'T HAVE TIME FOR--
AND SOMEONE FROM MY DEPARTMENT NEEDS TO BE THERE WHEN HE SIGNS THEM.
I KNOW THESE PAPERS ARE TIME-SENSITIVE. SO DON'T FORGET WHO HAS SENIORITY IN MY DIVISION!
HOPE YOU'RE PAYING ATTENTION, NAT.
DON'T LET ANYONE GET IN YOUR WAY IF YOU REALLY WANT SOMETHING.
I DON'T. GET WHAT I'M SAYING?
OH, I DEFINITELY DO.
GAME ON.

TIME TO USE MY *REAL* SKILL SET...

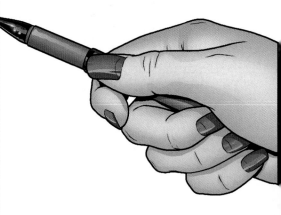

...HEARD SHE STOPPED INTO THE COORDINATOR'S OFFICE AND PRETTY MUCH MARKED HER TERRITORY.

WELL, BE THAT AS IT MAY--

--WE *STILL* NEED SOMEONE TO HEAD OUT TO MALIBU TODAY WITH THOSE PAPERS.

FINE. WE'LL SEND SAMANTHA OVER THERE THIS AFTERNOON.

NICK FURY WANTS ME CLOSE TO TONY STARK. THIS IS MY CHANCE.

SAMANTHA'S ON HER COFFEE BREAK IN THE DINING HALL ON LEVEL FOUR.

IT'S SIX LEVELS DOWN.

SHE'S ONLY THERE FOR ANOTHER THREE MINUTES...

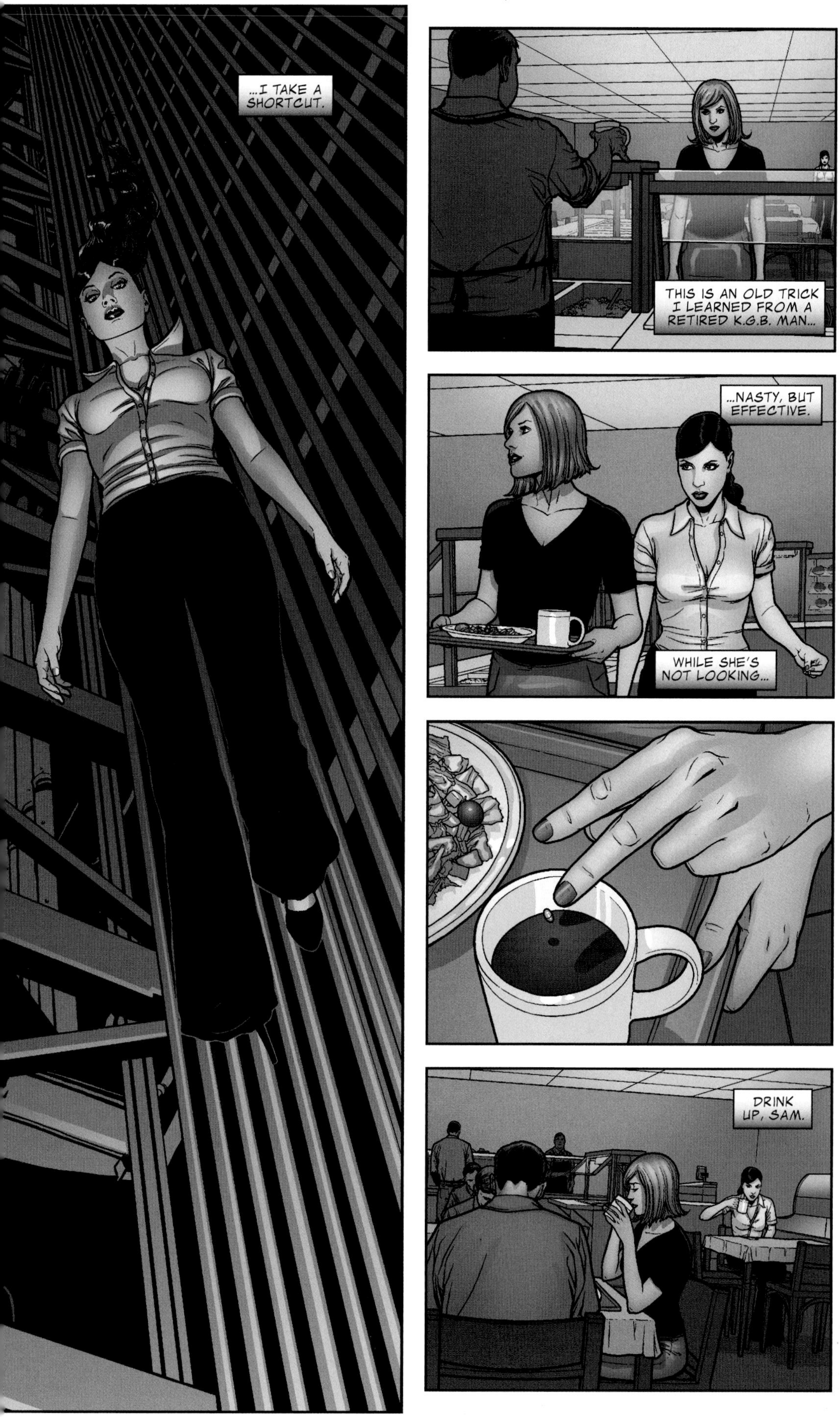
...I TAKE A SHORTCUT.
THIS IS AN OLD TRICK I LEARNED FROM A RETIRED K.G.B. MAN...
...NASTY, BUT EFFECTIVE.
WHILE SHE'S NOT LOOKING...
DRINK UP, SAM.

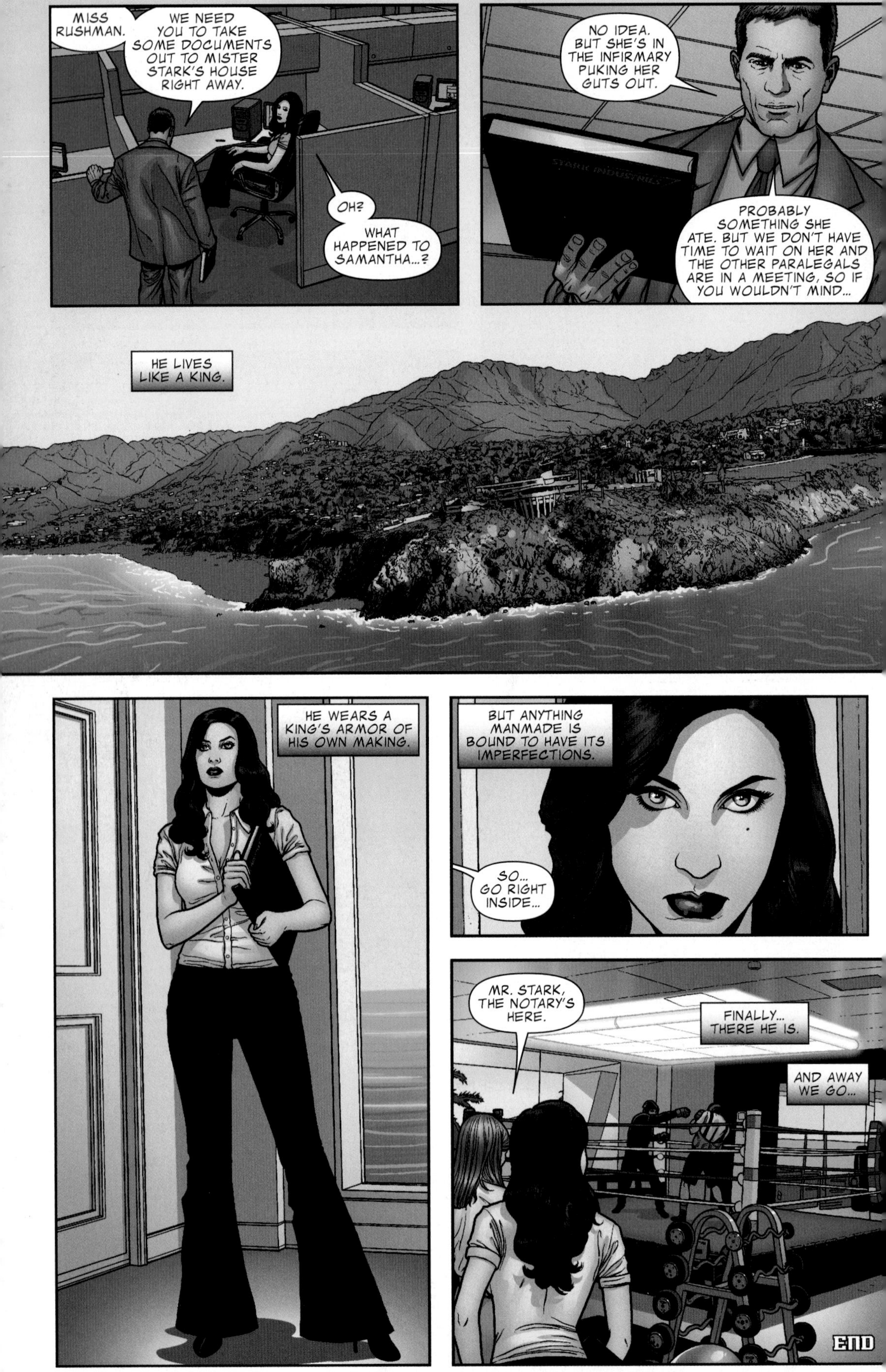

MISS RUSHMAN.
WE NEED YOU TO TAKE SOME DOCUMENTS OUT TO MISTER STARK'S HOUSE RIGHT AWAY.
OH?
WHAT HAPPENED TO SAMANTHA...?
NO IDEA. BUT SHE'S IN THE INFIRMARY PUKING HER GUTS OUT.
STARK INDUSTRIES
PROBABLY SOMETHING SHE ATE. BUT WE DON'T HAVE TIME TO WAIT ON HER AND THE OTHER PARALEGALS ARE IN A MEETING, SO IF YOU WOULDN'T MIND...
HE LIVES LIKE A KING.
HE WEARS A KING'S ARMOR OF HIS OWN MAKING.
BUT ANYTHING MANMADE IS BOUND TO HAVE ITS IMPERFECTIONS.
SO... GO RIGHT INSIDE...
MR. STARK, THE NOTARY'S HERE.
FINALLY... THERE HE IS.
AND AWAY WE GO...
END

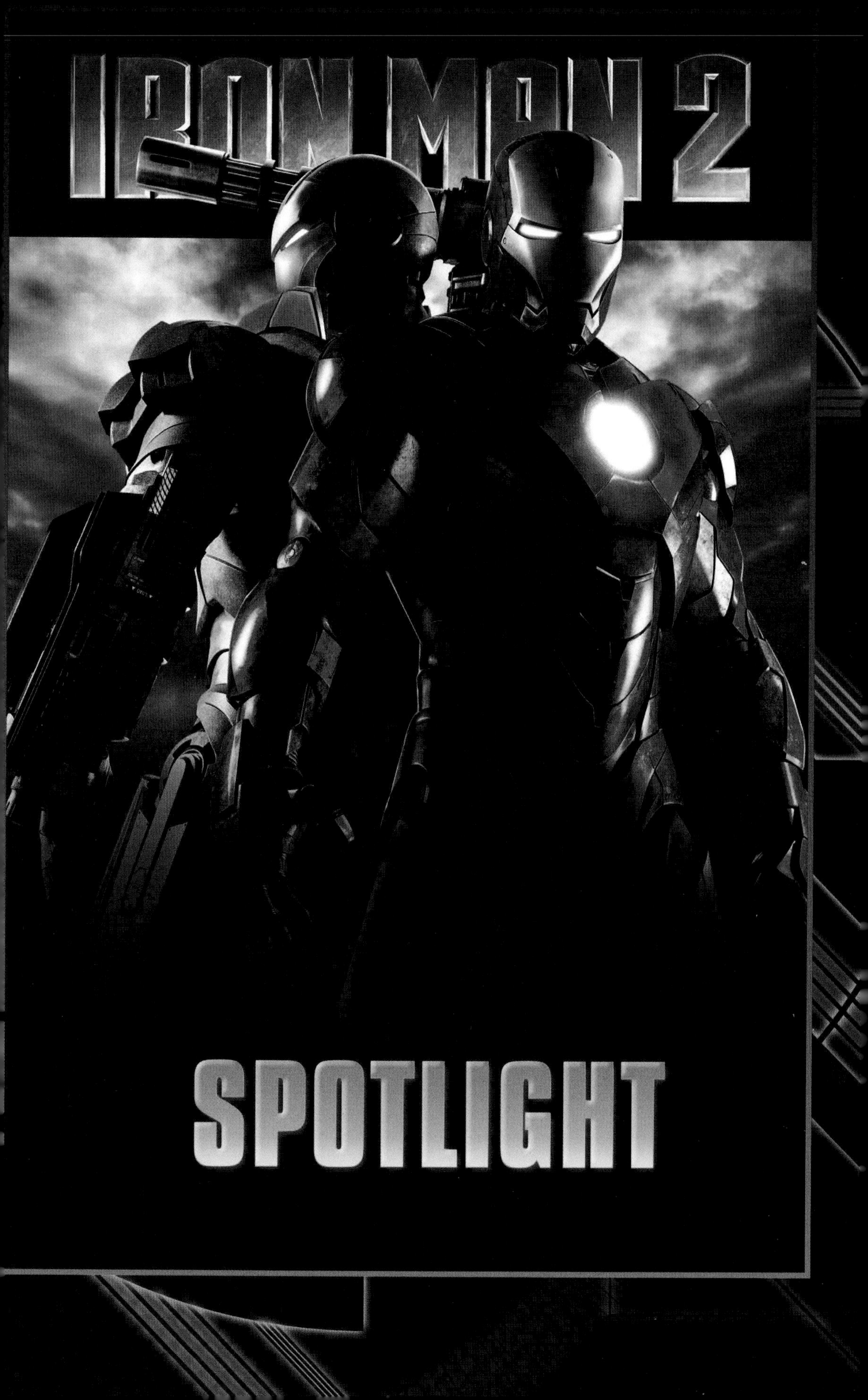
IRON MAN 2
SPOTLIGHT

PLUGGING IN THE SPOTLIGHT!

Welcome to our celebration of all things Shellhead in this extra-special Spotlight on the eve of the release of *Iron Man 2*!

I: Adi Granov's Silver Screen Style

Meet the artist most responsible for the contemporary look and feel of Iron Man on screen and in the pages of Marvel Comics!

II: Iron Man Vs. Whiplash

Writer Marc Guggenheim introduces us to Iron Man's newest and most fierce foe: Anton Vanko, the deadly Whiplash!

III: #1 With A Bullet: Black Widow's Deadly Origin!

There's nobody hotter than Natasha on the Marvel scene! Spotlight checks in with the writers behind her renaissance: Paul Cornell, Paul Tobin and Marjorie Liu!

IV: Iron Man Disassembled: An Interview With Matt Fraction

An in-depth interview with the superstar writer that took Tony Stark to *Invincible* and back again!

V: Armor Wars 2.0: Warren Ellis And Iron Man's Ultimate Future

Warren Ellis is on hand to survey the battle lines drawn in Tony Stark's Ultimate Armor Wars!

VI: The Armored Avenger's Most Memorable Moments

We count down Iron Man's most memorable moments with Earth's Mightiest Heroes!

CREDITS

Head Writer/Editor: **John Rhett Thomas**
Spotlight Bullpen Writers: **Chris Arrant, Jess Harrold** and **Dugan Trodglen**
Special Thanks to **John Barber** and **Jeph York**

Senior Editor, Special Projects: **Jeff Youngquist**
Editors, Special Projects: **Jennifer Grunwald** & **Mark D. Beazley**
Assistant Editor: **Alex Starbuck**
Associate Editor: **John Denning**
Vice President of Sales, Publishing: **David Gabriel**
Book Design: **BLAMMO! Content & Design, Rommel Alama, Lisa Herndon-Baltozer** and **Michael Kronenberg**
Editor in Chief: **Joe Quesada**
Publisher: **Dan Buckley**
Executive Producer: **Alan Fine**

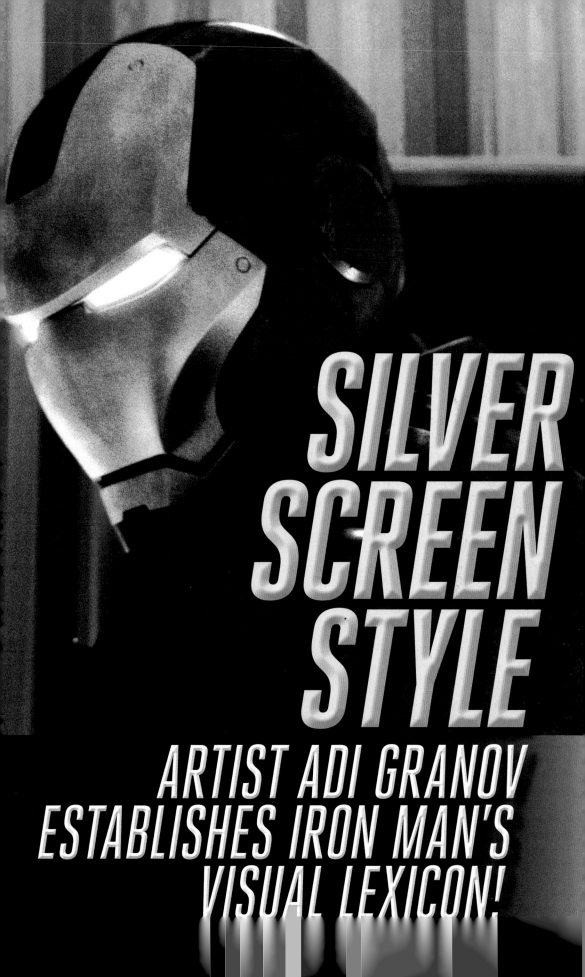

SILVER SCREEN STYLE

ARTIST ADI GRANOV ESTABLISHES IRON MAN'S VISUAL LEXICON!

Not many comic artists see their personal vision of a super hero become recognized the world over. But when the movie *Iron Man* proved an international blockbuster, that's exactly what happened to Adi Granov. The Bosnian artist's revolutionary take on Tony Stark's armor in the Extremis storyline had been so influential on Hollywood producers they hired him as a consultant to help bring Iron Man to the masses. Adi loved seeing his images brought to life so much he went back to work with director and friend Jon Favreau on the sequel - and together they're set to paint the silver screen red and gold all over again, with the movie they could only call *Iron Man 2.* But Tinseltown hasn't seduced Adi away from the day job – in the six years since he was proclaimed one of Marvel's "Young Guns," he's become one of the industry's leading cover artists. From the Agents of Atlas to the X-Men, Adi has delivered a stunning array of eye-catching covers that would grace an art gallery, never mind a comic book store. And, when his schedule permits, Adi has brought his unique style to the interior pages of books including *Dark Reign: The Cabal. Spotlight* caught up with the artist in his adopted home of Leeds, England, to discuss his work.

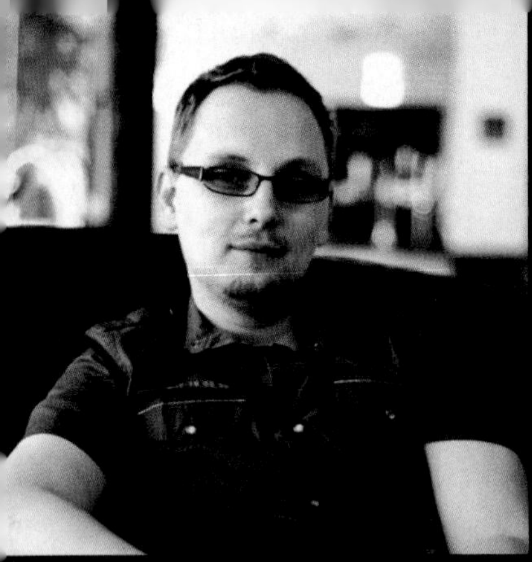

Artist Adi Granov.

SPOTLIGHT: You're a Bosnian boy who's grown up to draw American icons – while living in Britain! What took you on this globetrotting journey? Do you feel like you have triple nationality these days?

ADI: I actually do have triple nationality! Because of the war in Bosnia my family and I moved to the US, where I spent ten years. I started my career with Marvel while in the States. I moved to Britain a few years ago because my wife is English and we decided to move closer to her family. The Internet has really shrunk the world and made it very easy to work with people and companies around the globe. My first published work was in a couple of magazines in Croatia, but it was editorial illustration, not comics. My first comic work was published by a French publisher, but through their American office. It came out in both countries. My first proper job was as a concept designer for Nintendo in the US, where I stayed for a few years. I did a lot of illustration for Wizards of the Coast, primarily for their *Star Wars* projects. The work that directly led me to Marvel was a comic book called *Necrowar* I did for a long defunct publisher, Dreamwave. The guys at Marvel really liked my art in it and reached out to offer me work – which was actually a real miracle of timing, as I was broke and jobless!

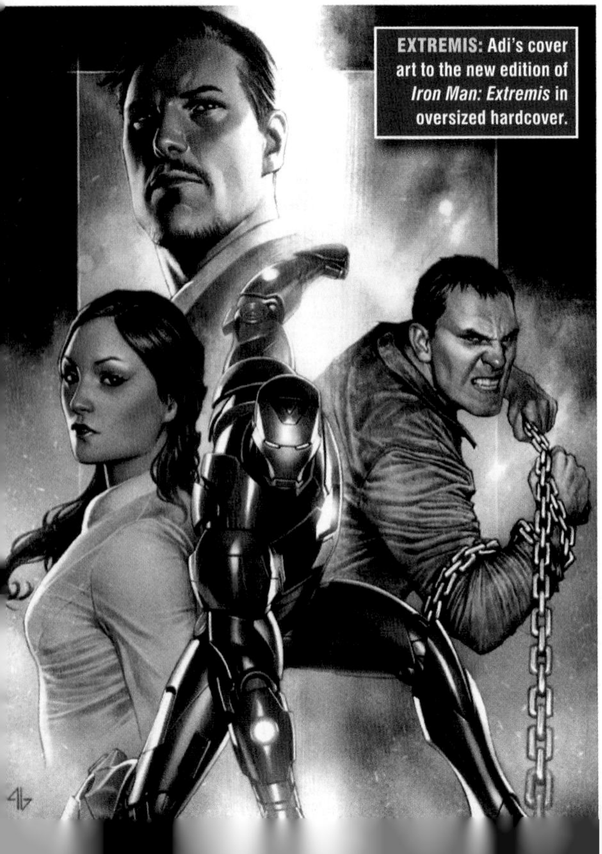

EXTREMIS: Adi's cover art to the new edition of *Iron Man: Extremis* in oversized hardcover.

SPOTLIGHT: And speaking of perfect timing, not long after you arrived you were proclaimed one of Marvel's "Young Guns" (along with Jim Cheung, Olivier Coipel, David Finch, Trevor Hairsine and Steve McNiven). That must have been a wild time for you guys...

ADI: Most of us Young Guns were made so at the Chicago Con back in '04, just about a year after I had started working for Marvel. To be honest, that con was full of crazy moments, which have never since been topped. Unfortunately most of the stuff that went on I really shouldn't put on record as I don't want to have to fear for my life from angry comic book creators. The whole Young Guns promotion was fantastic for our careers and popularity. Most of us involved have really got a huge amount of recognition out of it and have gone to work on some of the biggest projects of the last few years.

SPOTLIGHT: It must have felt like things could barely get any better. But what if someone told you back then that, by 2010, you'd have played such a key part in making Iron Man one of the most famous super heroes on the planet?

ADI: Well, it's a strange thing. I think possibly because of my extreme experiences with the war in Bosnia, and living as a refugee, you could tell me just about anything and I wouldn't discount it being possible. But yes, definitely, working for Marvel was a massive thing because it's such an iconic company with all these amazing characters, and even more so because they were so supportive and open to my art and way of working. From the moment I first started with Marvel it became a ride where things

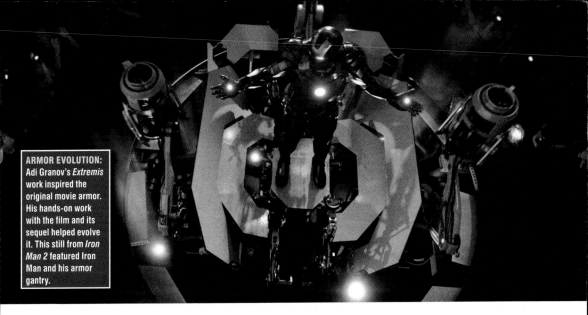

ARMOR EVOLUTION: Adi Granov's *Extremis* work inspired the original movie armor. His hands-on work with the film and its sequel helped evolve it. This still from *Iron Man 2* featured Iron Man and his armor gantry.

just kept happening, so the whole movie thing kind of came up without my ever having much time to pause and reflect. In retrospect it does seem like such a surreal thing to have happened…

SPOTLIGHT: Last time *Spotlight* caught up with you was a day before the *Iron Man* film premiered. Back then you were in no rush to abandon comics for a career in Hollywood. You said that not every project would capture your interest in the same way *Iron Man* did. Luckily another project like that did come your way: *Iron Man 2*! Has working on the sequel changed your view?

ADI: Not at all. I mean, ultimately I am most interested in creating and illustrating exciting images, so any job that will allow me to do that is cool by me. Working on the two *Iron Man* movies has been an outstanding experience, and as interesting as anything in comics. But the reason I like working in comics so much is because there is a real purity of vision, from the writer to the artist without much interference or compromise. Unlike in most other media, where my work is turned into a 3-D or live action model, in comics what I draw is what gets printed. It's both challenging and satisfying. However, after my experience with the first *Iron Man* movie and seeing just how respectful and faithful the film was to my illustrations, I have become a lot more enthusiastic about seeing my designs from the publishing world turned into huge moving images with such amazing mass appeal.

SPOTLIGHT: Was working on the sequel a different challenge, or very much like stepping into comfortable slippers?

ADI: I'd say it was between the two. There wasn't quite as much guesswork as on the first film, and I definitely had a much better

idea of how to work with the producers. But I've always had a very good understanding with Jon Favreau, so from that end it was great to jump back into it, and it was very exciting to meet with him again and Ryan Meinerding, who I met with the first time around as well.

SPOTLIGHT: Is the new armor dramatically different, or is it a case of evolution, not revolution?

ADI: Well, there are things that I really cannot mention yet, but overall I'd say it was definitely evolution, keeping the familiarity and the iconic shape while refining it to convey that it has been made more advanced and exciting. I liken it to car manufacturers updating existing models to either improve them, or make them more exciting after the old shape becomes too familiar. The armors, both in comics and in the movies, are my interpretation of this mental image of what I feel Iron Man should look like. I try to pay respect to what's come before, but without ever being a slave to it.

SPOTLIGHT: Were there any other characters you played a big part in designing this time around?

ADI: Again this is touching on some things I can't discuss yet, but the major one I can is War Machine. Ryan spent as long, if not longer, on designing War Machine than he did Iron Man. It's a design I am very happy with and quite proud to be a part of. It is a monster!

SPOTLIGHT: I've seen you refer to your Iron Man design as "style meets function"…

ADI: My approach to it was to introduce a number of familiar elements to the technology to make it believable in today's world. Making it futuristic and exciting, without pushing it into fantasy.

"IT WAS DEFINITELY EVOLUTION, KEEPING THE FAMILIARITY AND THE ICONIC SHAPE WHILE REFINING IT TO CONVEY THAT IT HAS BEEN MADE MORE ADVANCED AND EXCITING."
– Adi Granov, on Iron Man 2's approach to Tony's armor

"MY APPROACH (WAS) TO INTRODUCE A NUMBER OF FAMILIAR ELEMENTS TO THE TECHNOLOGY TO MAKE IT BELIEVABLE IN TODAY'S WORLD." *–Adi's "style meets function" armor design ethos*

If you think of jet aircraft, most people wouldn't necessarily know how exactly they operate and how the various systems, digital and mechanical, make them fly and handle, but we recognize various elements which give us a basic understanding and acceptance of the technology. So if there is a moving part there is some kind of a piston, or an electric motor that makes it operate. That piston or motor has to have a source of power, which has to come from somewhere and be carried via tubes or wires which have to be able to fit somewhere, and so on. Obviously I am not building a real suit, but introducing some of these familiar elements to what is otherwise a fantasy design makes it more believable. Iron Man technology is already based around a fantastical source of power, the repulsor, which calls for a degree of suspension of disbelief in itself. Combined with him being able to fly, it's making him the most advanced piece of technology in the world. I felt giving him a degree of the familiar would make it not only more believable, but also more appealing. Style without function is fine, but style with function, I feel, is so much better.

SPOTLIGHT: Early on in your Marvel career, you produced one of *the* iconic Shellhead images: that cover from *Iron Man* #76 where he's striking the ground, which went on to become a movie promo image and even a statue. Were you pretty pleased the day you came up with that pose?

ADI: It's been a long time since then, I don't remember exactly what I felt. It was my second ever cover for Marvel so I was probably more nervous about it than anything. I can understand the appeal of the image and the pose, and I am very happy it's become such an icon – they even used it in a *Simpsons* episode! I have done many better images since, but it's impossible to predict which piece of work will become the iconic one. I've had other illustrations of other characters turned into toys, posters, even cakes, but none have had the timing and the exposure that cover has had due to the *Iron Man* movie. I recently did a new cover for the oversize hardcover re-release of *Iron Man: Extremis*, which as its central feature has Iron Man in that very pose. Every time I looked at the original cover it made me want to redo it with my current skill, so I jumped at the opportunity to give it another shot some six years later. It turned out pretty good.

SPOTLIGHT: As you say, there have been quite a few collectibles based on your work. Do you have any at home? Any particular favorites?

ADI: I have a bunch! Most were given to me by the manufacturers or friends. I have the large statue of the ground strike by Sideshow, which is beautiful, and another one, also of the same pose but featuring the movie armor by Attakus. I think one of the most faithful to the design is a standing statue of the movie armor by Kotobukiya. The Minimates figures of all of the movie characters are fantastic! But I think my favorite is a little manga baby Iron Man also striking the ground, which my friend C.B. Cebulski brought for me from Japan. I don't know who made it, but it's absolutely fantastic. I also have really badly made (but really fantastic) knock-off figures bought for me from Hong Kong. Countless other things: figures, posters, stickers, and so on. Too much!

SPOTLIGHT: Moving away from ol' Shellhead, and taking a look at your cover work, another character that you really have created a stunningly fresh take on is Spider-Man – somehow at the same time both incredibly reverential and innovative...

ADI: Ah, thank you. I think I was very inspired by the work of Lee Bermejo in my take of Spider-Man. Lee is one of those guys whose art really pushes me to work harder on my own stuff. But my main aim with Spidey was to give some angular aggression to his demeanor, which I feel he usually lacks. He's often depicted as very fluid, almost rubbery, which fits his character well, but not my own style. Again, I take the same approach as with my take on technology, introducing some familiar elements into the fantastic, in order to give the character more "weight" in the viewer's eye. So things like folds in the costume, shadows revealing that there is a human face under the mask and restrictions of the human anatomy are all things that the viewer will, even subconsciously, pick up on, which will make this fantasy character and his powers appear that much more striking.

SPOTLIGHT: Your Spidey really shows how that spandex body stocking costume could really work and look cool in the real world. With the recent news that Spider-Man is all set for a movie reboot, is that one project that could capture your imagination like the *Iron Man* films did?

ADI: I don't see that there could be much freedom in re-designing Spider-Man, aside from detail changes. He's too much of an icon. My take on him is mostly stylistic; the design is pretty faithful to the classic costume. But villains offer a lot of potential, so depending in which direction they end up taking the films there could be a lot of interesting possibilities.

SPOTLIGHT: Another character your style fits well is Nova, you give his costume real texture...

ADI: Again, I just did my take on the design Marvel showed me. When I look at a design someone else has done sometimes there are things that are a bit confusing, or unclear, so I try to stay faithful to it while sorting those elements so they make sense to me. If I were forced to stick 100% to a given design I would find it very difficult, and not fun at all. Luckily, I can usually adjust

STATUE IMAGE PROVIDED BY RANDY BOWEN.

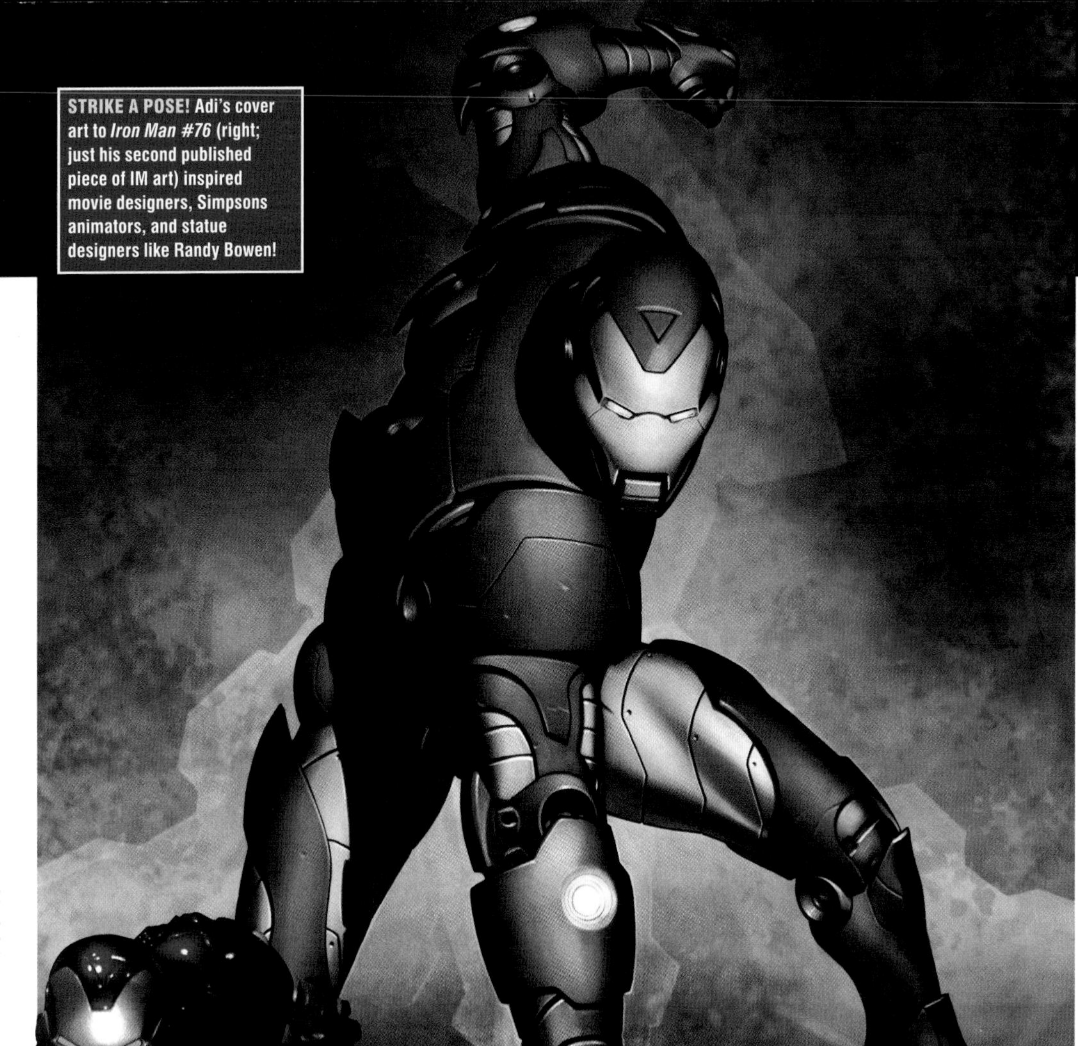

STRIKE A POSE! Adi's cover art to *Iron Man #76* (right; just his second published piece of IM art) inspired movie designers, Simpsons animators, and statue designers like Randy Bowen!

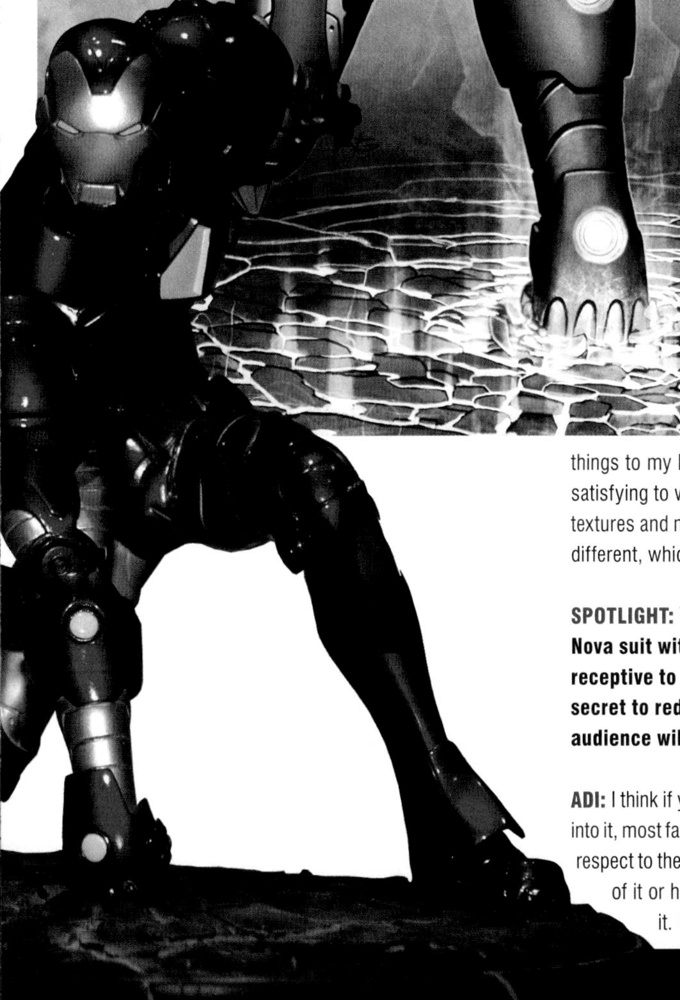

things to my liking which helps make most characters fun and satisfying to work on. As you point out, I really like playing with textures and materials. It's a challenge to make surfaces appear different, which is very satisfying.

SPOTLIGHT: Your covers arguably helped cement the new Nova suit with comics fans, who traditionally aren't so receptive to costume redesigns. What do you think is the secret to redesigning a popular character in a way the audience will embrace?

ADI: I think if you do anything well, put a lot of care and attention into it, most fans will respond to it. If a redesign is thoughtful, pays respect to the character and its fans, it's not done just for the hell of it or half-heartedly, then most people tend to be open to it. Of course, there are always those who will never

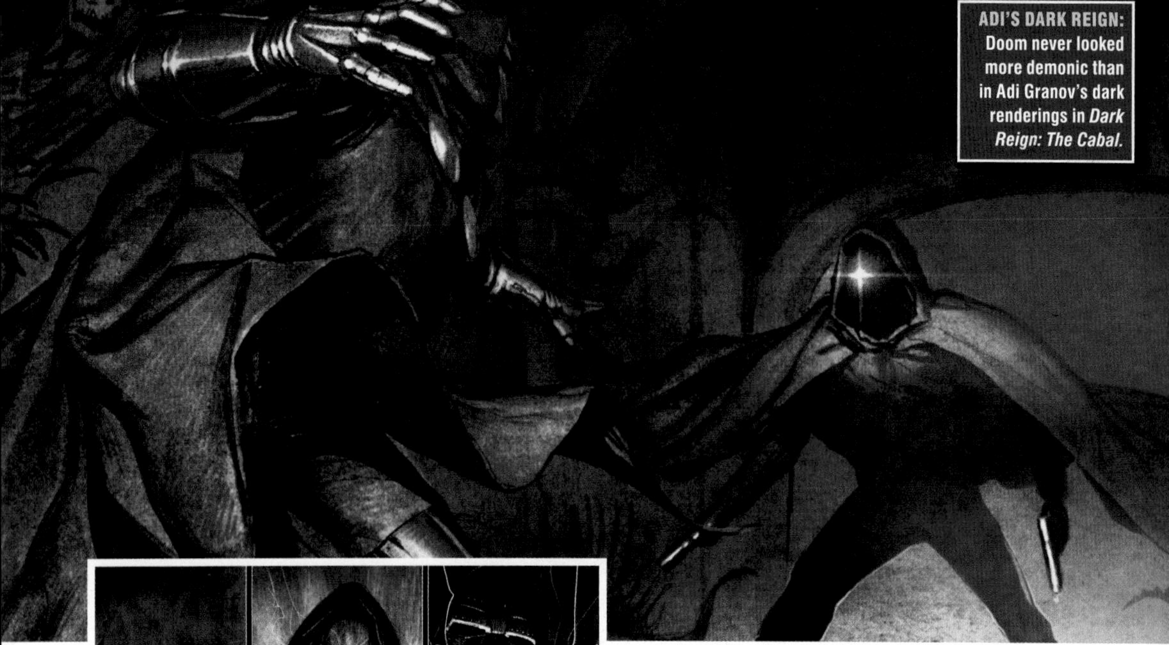

ADI'S DARK REIGN: Doom never looked more demonic than in Adi Granov's dark renderings in *Dark Reign: The Cabal.*

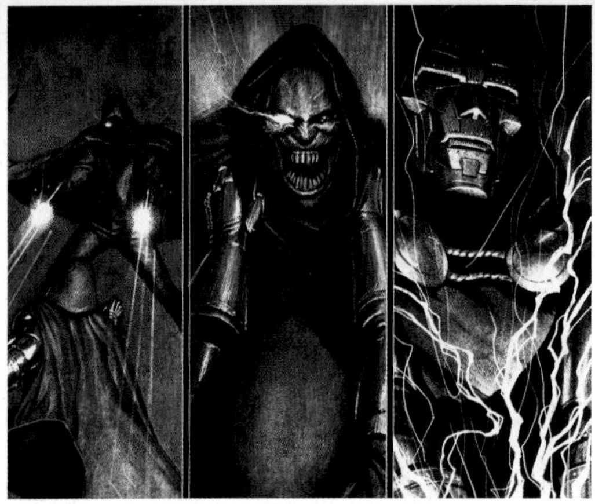

be receptive to change, or who will dislike a particular take on a character, and definitely, sometimes a redesign just plain misfires. Obviously, presenting a new design in a well-painted illustration also helps a lot as it shows the character in his or her element as opposed to just a standing pose, or something like that.

SPOTLIGHT: Your work isn't all about the guys though. You've delivered some beautiful covers featuring powerful women including She-Hulk and, recently, Black Widow. Your women are attractive, without being exaggerated physically or gratuitously posed. Is that important to you as a creator?

ADI: Definitely. It's one of the most important things to me in fact. As I mentioned, I try to be respectful and thoughtful to the subject matter and characters I draw. Comic book art tends to be seen by the general public as overly macho, even sexist, because of the way women have been drawn in some books, especially during the '90s, which pushes a lot of the female audience away and gives our industry the stereotypical image it has struggled with. A lot of this has changed drastically as new blood has come into the industry and I think I am just a part of that wave. My wife is a big comic book fan and I want to do the kind of work that will be as attractive to her as it would be to any guy reading it. Not to say I don't try to draw the most attractive women I can, it's just that absurd anatomy in impossible clothes isn't my vision of beauty.

SPOTLIGHT: Both your men and women look very natural and real. Do you use real life models at all?

ADI: I used to a lot more than I do now. It's one of those things I've naturally moved away from as I've gotten more skilled and knowledgeable. My goal is to create believable, realistic, but not photorealistic characters. I still use reference to inform my work, but while I used to shoot specific photos, I now use bits and pieces I need based on the sketches that are drawn without any reference to keep them dynamic and fresh. But it's taken years to get comfortable enough with my own skill to be able to cheat realism and bend the rules.

SPOTLIGHT: One of my favorite covers you've done was for the *Iron Man Omnibus*, showing your take on the *Tales of Suspense* #39 cover and the original armor. It's one of a number of homage covers you've done; is that a process you enjoy?

ADI: I really enjoyed doing the *Tales of Suspense* cover, but the homage covers are always requested by editors. It's usually not my first choice.

SPOTLIGHT: Your extensive list of covers has seen you

"MY GOAL IS TO CREATE BELIEVABLE, REALISTIC, BUT NOT PHOTOREALISTIC CHARACTERS." *-Adi Granov*

draw a huge range of Marvel characters. Are there any we haven't mentioned that stand out as favorites? Any you're still itching to draw?

ADI: I'm doing a number of X-Men covers at the moment, which I'm finding hugely enjoyable. So many different characters and possibilities! I did a couple of Silver Surfer covers many years ago and I'd really love to do more as he's been one of my favorite characters since I was a kid. Unfortunately he seems a bit dormant in the Marvel Universe at the moment... I'd also love to do something with Thor.

SPOTLIGHT: It strikes me that a collected edition of your covers would be a big seller. Has there been any mention of that as a possibility down the line?

ADI: I'm really glad you think so! I'd love to do it. It's been mentioned, but nothing more than that. Books like that are hugely popular in Europe, but I think for Marvel to do it they'd need to make a case for it in the US.

SPOTLIGHT: You're known for your distinctive artistic approach, which involves you penciling, inking and digitally painting your own work. Do people wrongly assume that your art is either completely or mostly done on computer? I was lucky enough to watch you sketching a while back, and I was struck by the quality of your unembellished pencils. Are you ever tempted to collaborate with other creators?

ADI: People often do assume that the work is digital, when in fact only the color is added that way. All of the hard work is done on paper. I don't really do any inking in the traditional sense. Any ink I use is incorporated into the drawing process, so it would be impossible to separate it. As for coloring, I tried a long time ago to have it done by someone else, but it just didn't work for either of us. My wife, Tamsin, often assists with the technical part of the coloring, which helps speed the process a lot but leaves me to take care of the stylistic part of the job and maintain full creative control. I am probably too controlling and selfish, but I don't like handing off the work and relinquishing control over the final product.

SPOTLIGHT: The inevitable time constraints of that process mean we haven't seen as much interior art from you outside of the *Iron Man* work on *Extremis* and *Viva Las Vegas*.

One standout for me, though, is the great little tale in *Dark Reign: The Cabal*. Best. Doom. Story. Ever.

ADI: Haha, thank you! I love Doom, so it was a real pleasure to do that. It was a character I've always wanted to draw.

SPOTLIGHT: Now that the movie work is out of the way again, do you have any plans for more interior work? Any cool projects you can tantalize us with?

ADI: There should be quite a bit of sequential stuff this year. I've been half done with a short story for a while, but all these covers have kept me from finishing it. After that I'm doing a really cool one-shot loosely based on one of my ideas and written by one of my very favorite writers. I really wanted to work with him so I inquired if he'd want to write it, and he did! The script is done, I just need some free time. After that there is a much larger project, but it's still in its infancy and too early to even mention really. ●

SECOND COMING: Adi brings his distinctive art style to the X-Universe in this cover to *X-Force #26*.

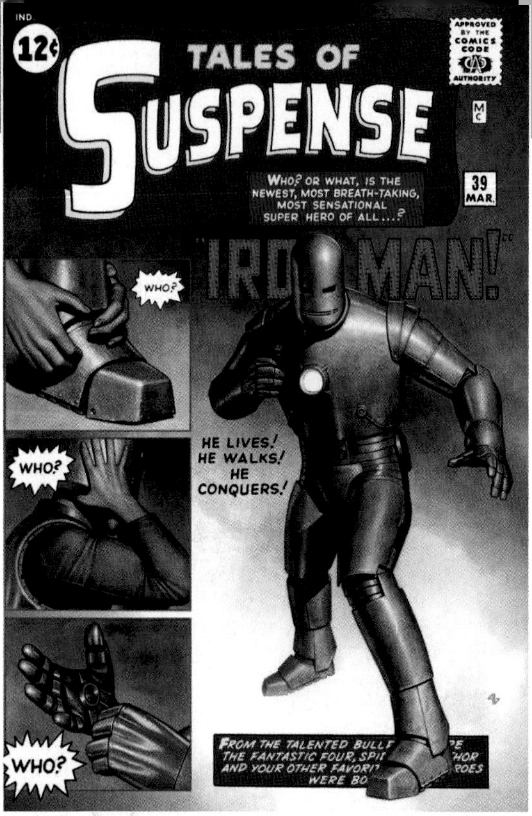
IND.
12¢
TALES OF
SUSPENSE
APPROVED BY THE COMICS CODE AUTHORITY
MC
39
MAR.
WHO? OR WHAT, IS THE NEWEST, MOST BREATH-TAKING, MOST SENSATIONAL SUPER HERO OF ALL...?
MAN!
WHO?
WHO?
WHO?
HE LIVES! HE WALKS! HE CONQUERS!

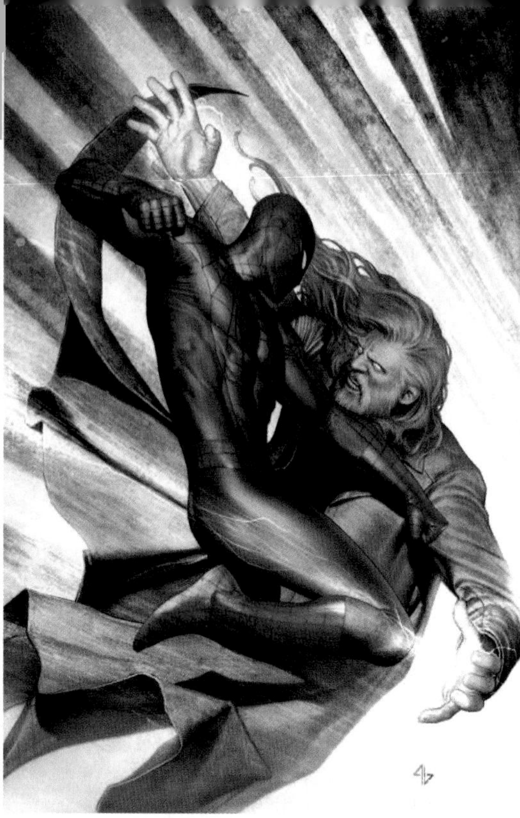

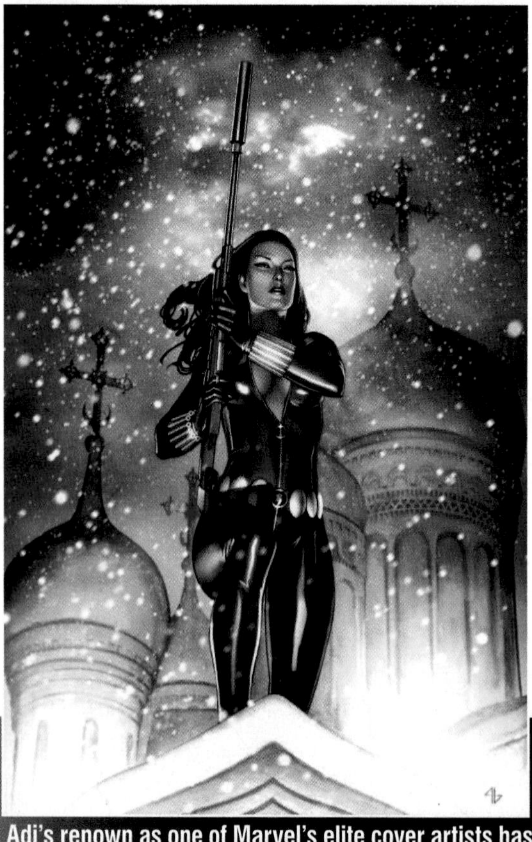

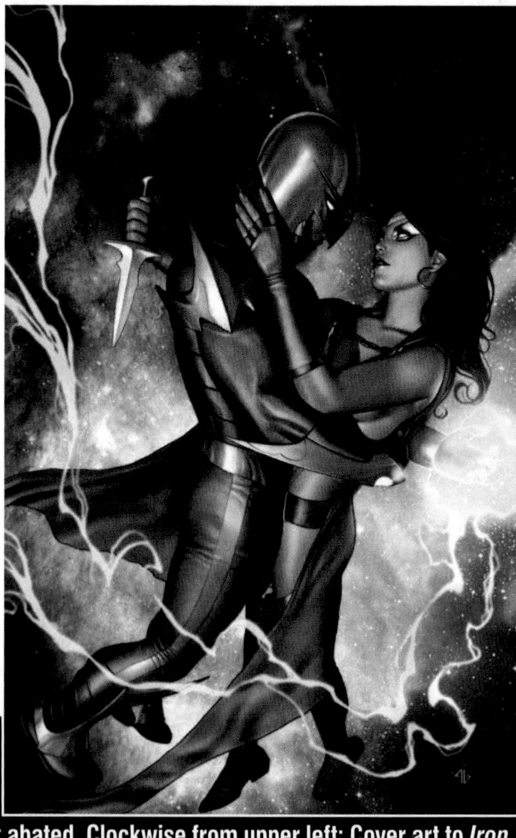

Adi's renown as one of Marvel's elite cover artists has not abated. Clockwise from upper left: Cover art to *Iron Man Omnibus Vol. 1* hardcover, *Amazing Spider-Man #610*, *Nova #10* and *Black Widow: Deadly Origin #2*.

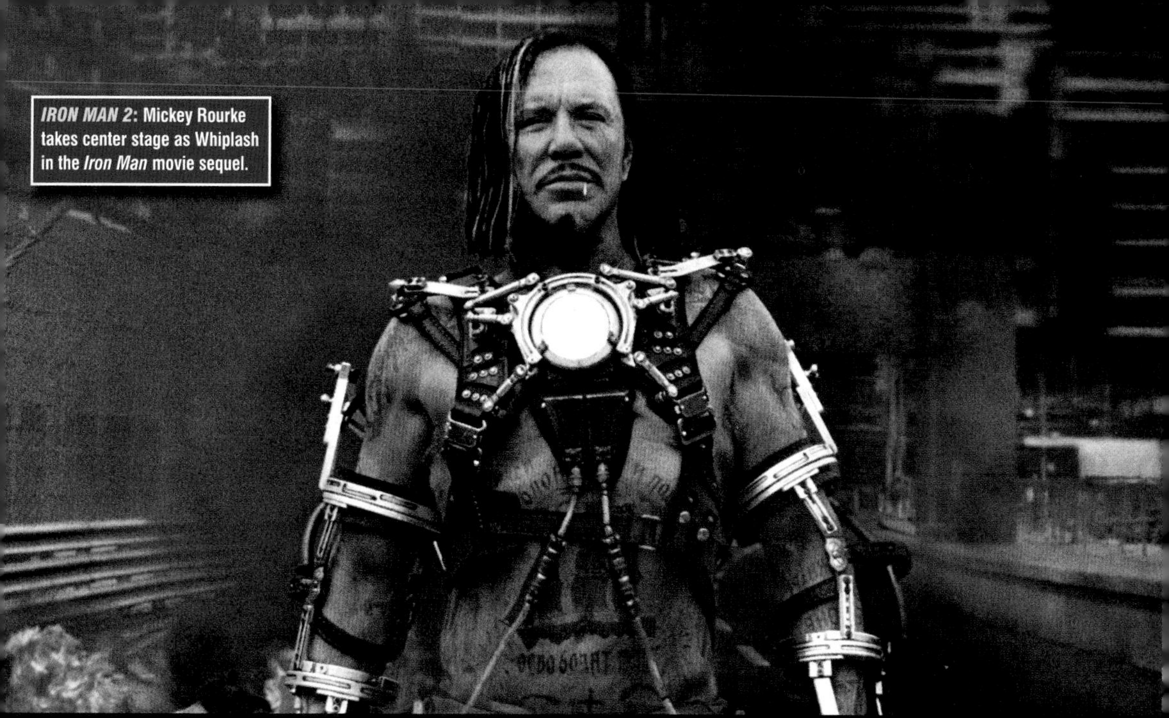

***IRON MAN 2*: Mickey Rourke takes center stage as Whiplash in the *Iron Man* movie sequel.**

IRON MAN VS. WHIPLASH

WRITERS MARC GUGGENHEIM AND BRANNON BRAGA WHIP UP A FIERCE NEW IRON MAN FOE BY CHRIS ARRANT

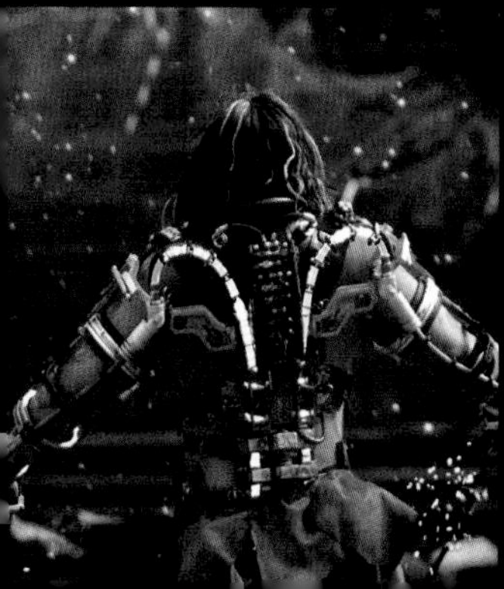

It takes a lot to pose a real threat to Tony Stark. Besides being an unparalleled genius and a wealthy businessman, he has the bleeding edge technology of the Iron Man armor. But a new threat named Whiplash is giving him a run for his money – both in the upcoming movie and the recent comic book miniseries *Iron Man vs. Whiplash.* ● All roads lead to *Iron Man vs. Whiplash.* For fans of the first (or second) Iron Man movie the collected edition comes out just one week after the sequel's release. And for comic fans, it's an introduction to an all-new Whiplash that exalts the C-list character to a viable and violent threat for the Armored Avenger. ● *Vs. Whiplash* writers Marc Guggenheim and Brannon Braga are long time television writers and producers with credits on shows such as *FlashForward*, *Eli Stone* and *24,* and while this is Braga's first time in comics, it's a well-traveled road for Guggenheim, who's worked for years at Marvel, most notably on *Amazing Spider-Man.* We talked with Marc not only about this book, but bringing in Brannon Braga, as well as the movie series.

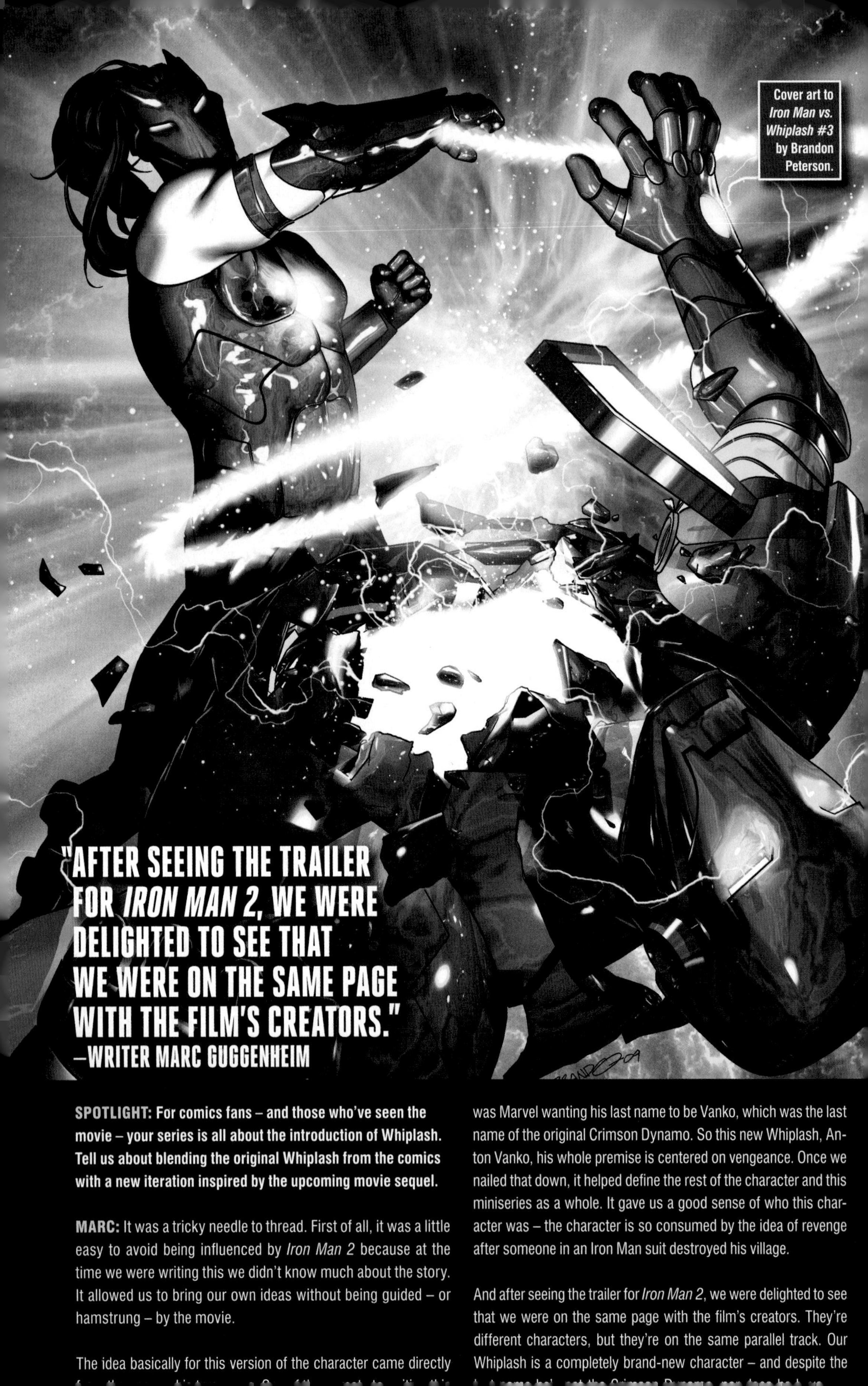

Cover art to *Iron Man vs. Whiplash #3* by Brandon Peterson.

"AFTER SEEING THE TRAILER FOR *IRON MAN 2*, WE WERE DELIGHTED TO SEE THAT WE WERE ON THE SAME PAGE WITH THE FILM'S CREATORS."
—WRITER MARC GUGGENHEIM

SPOTLIGHT: For comics fans – and those who've seen the movie – your series is all about the introduction of Whiplash. Tell us about blending the original Whiplash from the comics with a new iteration inspired by the upcoming movie sequel.

MARC: It was a tricky needle to thread. First of all, it was a little easy to avoid being influenced by *Iron Man 2* because at the time we were writing this we didn't know much about the story. It allowed us to bring our own ideas without being guided – or hamstrung – by the movie.

The idea basically for this version of the character came directly

was Marvel wanting his last name to be Vanko, which was the last name of the original Crimson Dynamo. So this new Whiplash, Anton Vanko, his whole premise is centered on vengeance. Once we nailed that down, it helped define the rest of the character and this miniseries as a whole. It gave us a good sense of who this character was – the character is so consumed by the idea of revenge after someone in an Iron Man suit destroyed his village.

And after seeing the trailer for *Iron Man 2*, we were delighted to see that we were on the same page with the film's creators. They're different characters, but they're on the same parallel track. Our Whiplash is a completely brand-new character – and despite the

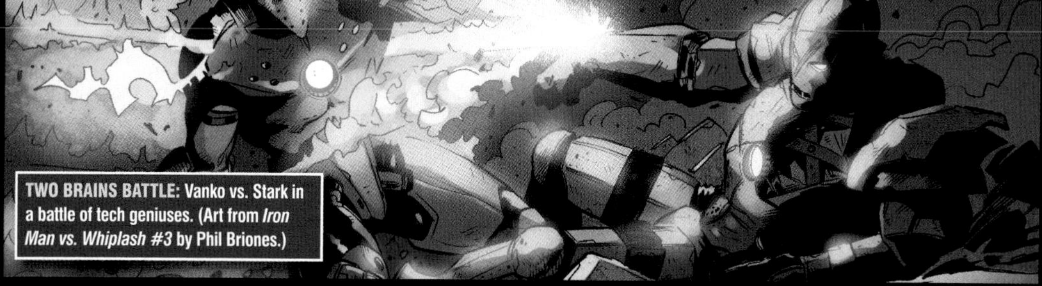

TWO BRAINS BATTLE: Vanko vs. Stark in a battle of tech geniuses. (Art from *Iron Man vs. Whiplash #3* by Phil Briones.)

relation to the old Whiplash.... but the origins of the armor he uses in this miniseries is one of the main subjects of this story.

SPOTLIGHT: How does Anton measure up to Tony Stark?

MARC: Anton's a brilliant technical and mechanical genius – on the level of Tony. In Whiplash, Iron Man is facing someone every bit as inventive as him. A big part of this is how the armor he builds – the Whiplash armor – becomes his weapon of ultimate vengeance. The series opens with the destruction of Vanko's hometown by someone in the Iron Man armor, and while Vanko can't stop the massacre he does manage to shoot off a piece of the Iron Man tech in the conflict. He takes that tech and adapts it for his own purposes.

SPOTLIGHT: That armor looks nothing like Tony's – what are the big adjustments?

MARC: The most visible are the electric lashes – Anton took the monofilament wire that's a regular part of the interior of the Iron Man armor and turns it outside to become these lashes. He's taking Tony's tech – turning it on its head – and giving it right back to him.

I have to give a lot of credit for that – and the series itself – to my co-writer Brannon Braga. He came up with the idea of monofilament becoming the basis for Whiplash. He also came up with the opening scene with Iron Man attacking Vanko's village of Volstok. Starting out with such a surprising scene really puts readers on their heels asking why Iron Man would do this, and how.

When we start out, we don't give those answers – and that's why Tony's put on trial because everyone knows he's Iron Man and from the reports, Iron Man did it. I give Brannon a lot of credit for thinking outside of the box.

SPOTLIGHT: I really like the idea of Iron Man in a mystery – a high-tech mystery, but mystery none the less. Iron Man's stories are traditionally big battles between two big brains. How'd this concept of a mystery come into it?

MARC: I'm a sucker for mysteries, and not knowing where things are going. The notion that Iron Man might've attacked a village and all evidence points to him; even though you know Iron Man won't turn into mass murderer, the mystery is how Tony can extricate himself from this dilemma.

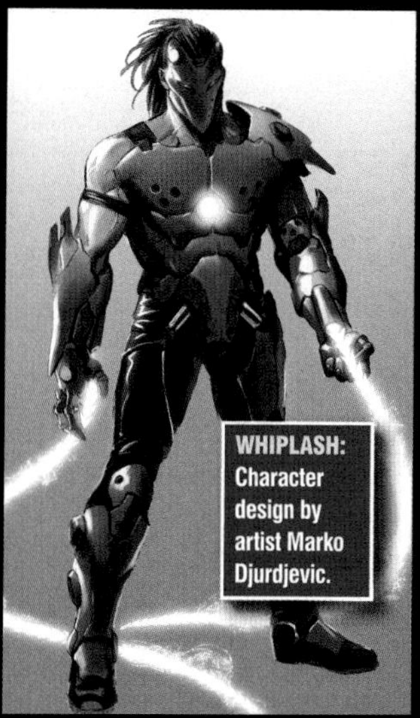

WHIPLASH: Character design by artist Marko Djurdjevic.

And that whole mystery is thanks to Brannon. Brannon is the biggest Iron Man fan ever. When I brought him onto this project, he made it clear he wanted to do an Iron Man project that he'd never seen. I was coming into this project from the perspective of wanting to appeal to people coming in from the movie as well as hard-core Shellhead fans who want to see something new.

SPOTLIGHT: Speaking of Brannon – how did he get involved with this project? This is his first comics gig.

MARC: Basically, the original editor for this series at Marvel, John Barber, called me to pitch the concept of bringing a new Whiplash into regular Marvel continuity to lay the track for the upcoming second *Iron Man* movie. When he said that to me, I got to thinking about Brannon, who I had been working with on *FlashForward*. He co-created it and we're both executive producers, but aside from that Brannon is such a big Iron Man fan. I loved the idea of writing this with him – and luckily so did he!

In television, I'm very used to working with other writers, but comics is primarily a solo job. But working on this with someone who's not only a talented writer and a die-hard fan was great. I've been reading *Iron Man* since I was a kid, but Brannon owns every issue going back to his debut in *Tales of Suspense*.

SPOTLIGHT: You've been working steadily in Hollywood for years – writing for *Law & Order*, *Eli Stone* and you've had a hand in writing the screenplay for DC's *Green Lantern* movie. First off – does Robert Downey Jr.'s turn as Tony Stark influence the way writers like you write the character in comics?

MARC: There's a funny gag in issue 3 where Tony checks into a hotel; he's on the run from the law, so he gives an alias of 'Robert Downey Jr.' since – hey – he looks just like him! (*Laughter.*) I thought that was a fun tip of the hat to Robert and the amazing job he's done. I mean, that movie – that franchise – is amazing. Not since Christopher Reeve's role as Superman has someone just come in and become the character in every identifiable way.

If you want to identify with Whiplash before the movie, give Marc and Brannon's series a shot. With stunning artwork by the great Phil Briones, the last issue of the four-issue mini should be on stands right about now. Or look for IRON MAN VS. WHIPLASH in trade paperback in April!

#1 WITH A BULLET

After Key Supporting Slots In *Captain America* and *Invincible Iron Man*, The Widow Will Be At Her Peak In A Brand New Series And *Iron Man 2*!

By Dugan Trodglen

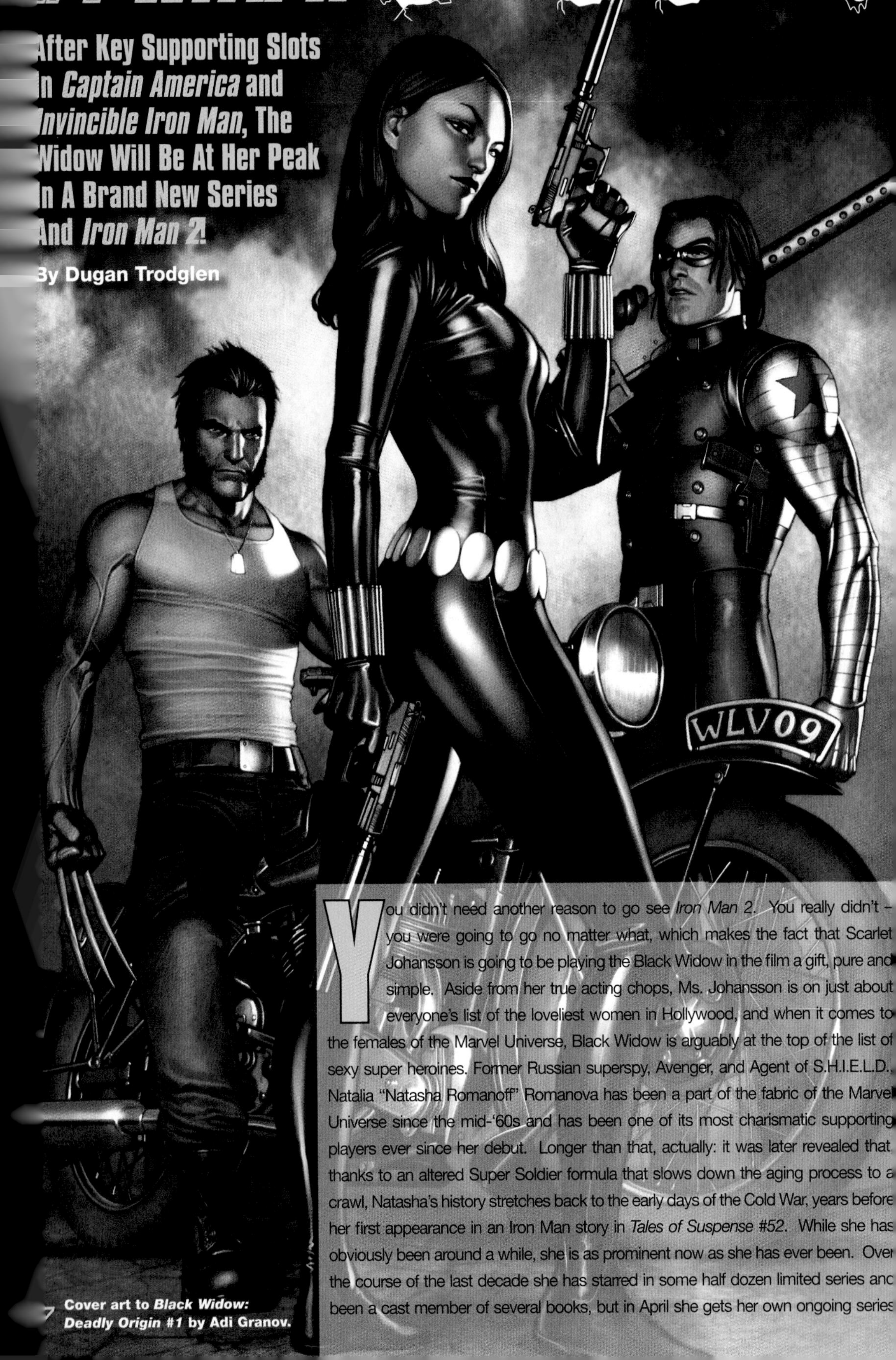
WLV09

***Cover art to Black Widow: Deadly Origin #1* by Adi Granov.**

You didn't need another reason to go see *Iron Man 2*. You really didn't – you were going to go no matter what, which makes the fact that Scarlet Johansson is going to be playing the Black Widow in the film a gift, pure and simple. Aside from her true acting chops, Ms. Johansson is on just about everyone's list of the loveliest women in Hollywood, and when it comes to the females of the Marvel Universe, Black Widow is arguably at the top of the list of sexy super heroines. Former Russian superspy, Avenger, and Agent of S.H.I.E.L.D., Natalia "Natasha Romanoff" Romanova has been a part of the fabric of the Marvel Universe since the mid-'60s and has been one of its most charismatic supporting players ever since her debut. Longer than that, actually: it was later revealed that thanks to an altered Super Soldier formula that slows down the aging process to a crawl, Natasha's history stretches back to the early days of the Cold War, years before her first appearance in an Iron Man story in *Tales of Suspense #52*. While she has obviously been around a while, she is as prominent now as she has ever been. Over the course of the last decade she has starred in some half dozen limited series and been a cast member of several books, but in April she gets her own ongoing series

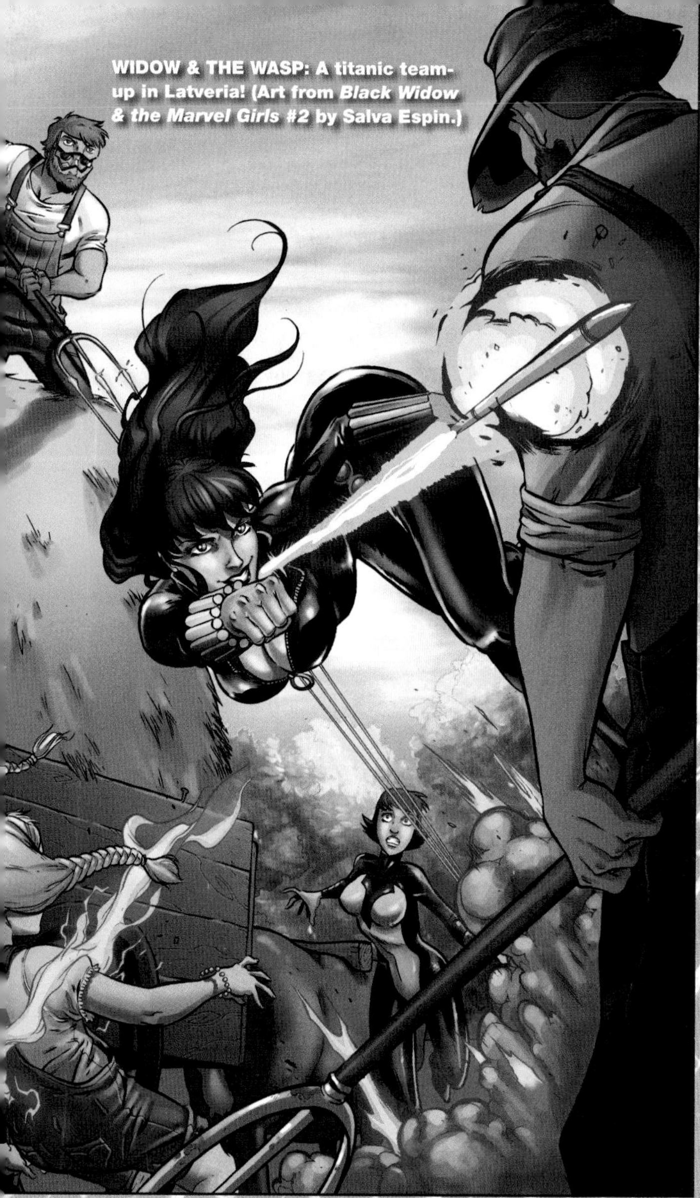

WIDOW & THE WASP: A titanic team-up in Latveria! (Art from *Black Widow & the Marvel Girls* #2 by Salva Espin.)

for the first time.

It doesn't take a genius to figure out that the timing of this book has everything to do with *Iron Man 2* (not to mention Marvel's 2010 celebration of the Women of Marvel), but it is more than just marketing synergy that has brought the Black Widow to prominence in the last few years. Today's top writers simply love writing Natasha. She was a member of Brian Michael Bendis' *Mighty Avengers*, and she has been a key cast member of Matt Fraction's *Invincible Iron Man* and Ed Brubaker's *Captain America*. (Oh yeah, she gets around.) Throughout her history, she has been "associated" with a who's who of Marvel's leading men: the list includes Iron Man, Nick Fury, Hawkeye, Daredevil, Wolverine, Hercules, and her latest flame, Bucky Barnes (the current Captain America).

One needs look no further than the recent limited series *Black Widow: Deadly Origin*, by writer Paul Cornell and artists Tom Raney and John Paul Leon. In the series, it is revealed that in her younger days in Russia's espionage community, Natasha was infected with deadly nanites that she would pass on to people she was close to throughout her life. In the series, the nanites were activated in something called the "Icepick Protocols," putting the lives of everyone she has been close to in danger. This puts Natasha on a mission to locate these loved ones and "cure" them via counter-nanites. This mission serves to illustrate the Black Widow's rich history in the Marvel Universe, as she goes from character to character, each encounter illuminating another side of Natasha. Although the relationships vary, "I think every one of them demonstrates that unbending strength of hers," explains Cornell.

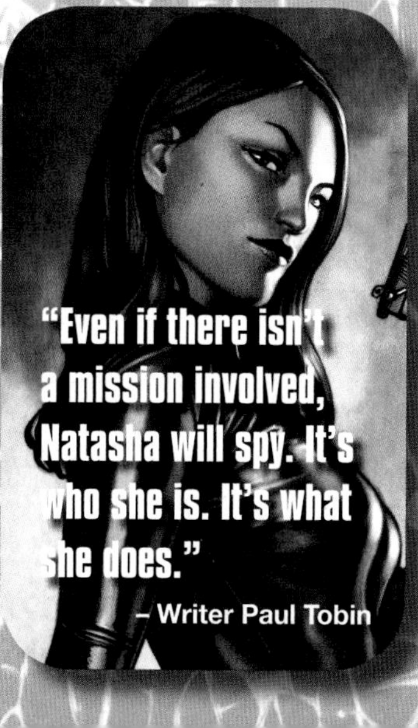

"Even if there isn't a mission involved, Natasha will spy. It's who she is. It's what she does."
– Writer Paul Tobin

Mulling over her various relationships, Cornell fills us in on love Black Widow style. "Hercules, the son of Zeus, felt comfortable taking orders from her. The happy-go-lucky adventurer that Daredevil was back then made her the sensible one of that partnership, but also let her relax and find herself. Tony Stark was only ever a target for her mixed-up mind back then, and she used Clint Barton horribly while she was being used

LOVE REMEMBERED: Black Widow's love affairs with Hawkeye and Daredevil sensitively explored in flashback sequences by artist John Paul Leon. (Art from *BW:DO* #2 and 3.)

And she's seen too much suffering not to be grateful."

While *Black Widow: Deadly Origin*, among other things, examines Natasha's relationship with various men of the Marvel Universe, another recent limited series, *Black Widow & the Marvel Girls*, looks at, well, you can figure that one out. Written by Paul Tobin, the series consists of four "done in one" issues progressing through Black Widow's history, and looking at her through the eyes of the Enchantress, the Wasp, Ms. Marvel, and Storm. The catch is that none of these women know much about Black Widow going into the story, but coming out, have learned much about her along with the reader. In particular, we learn of her heroic nature and steely reserve, as well as the necessity that she not open herself up too much to her peers: Knowledge is power and can be deadly in her world of espionage, and the more she can withhold about herself, the more power she has.

In each story, her co-star sees a different side of her. "That was one aspect of the series that I really enjoyed: devising (and ultimately watching) how Natasha felt around others," Tobin explains. "We all have different sets of friends where we act somewhat differently... work friends and old friends and family friends and so on... and with each of them we develop and maintain different personas. If I go out clubbing with Wolverine, I'm going to act a whole lot different than if I'm with... oh, let's say Aunt May. Natasha was even more complex, because along with everything else, she has the dual sides of wanting to do the right thing, and then never giving a piece of herself away. Those sides are in conflict, and the presence of others further shakes them up."

The thread through it all, however, is that even if Natasha is running around with Avengers, mutants, or goddesses, she is at heart a spy. When asked if

in turn, but both Tony and Clint came to respect her. I think she's great with Bucky: the equal pairing, people who've both been through far too much, and who both combine a certain wry humor with that weight."

The Black Widow has been around for decades, and experienced a lot cultural and political change over the years. She shares this with characters like Wolverine and both Captain Americas, Steve Rogers and Bucky Barnes. She definitely has a different perspective than the others, Cornell explains: "I think she's slightly better adjusted than Logan, who couldn't remember a lot of his past for a long time, and Steve and Bucky, who both missed long stretches." While there is an intensity to some of the memories, and the regrets than anyone might have over the course of a life, she's not tortured by her past. "She's really lived it, and she's comfortable with that," says Paul. "Maybe because she's had sanity and freedom only in relatively recent decades, but she's kind of relaxed into her long lifespan.

establishing this was a goal of *Black Widow & the Marvel Girls*, Tobin replied, "Bingo. Even if there isn't a mission involved, Natasha will spy. When she walks into a room, she *needs* to know every last thing about every person in the room. Even if she's never going to use the information, even if she would die before revealing some secrets, she needs those secrets. It's who she is. It's what she does." This as much as anything explains Black Widow's unique position in the Marvel Universe, and much of her appeal (okay, the skintight black bodysuit doesn't hurt either).

All of this brings us to *Black Widow*, Natasha's first ongoing series of her own, from writer Marjorie Liu and artist Daniel Acuna. Liu is very excited to be

"She's relentless. Totally in control. But that doesn't mean she's cold, either…"
– Writer Marjorie Liu

she's cold, either," Liu explains. For Liu, her history on the other side of the fence makes her all the more heroic: "She's fighting with the good guys, even though she didn't start out that way. The Black Widow could have had any life she wanted, but that's the one she chose. And that choice, the reasons behind it, add another layer to her character that I'm eager to explore." How she views herself is another rich topic as well. When asked about her affiliations in the series, Liu reveals, "Natasha is a difficult woman to tie down under any circumstance – and I suspect that deep inside, she's always considered herself to be a free agent, despite her close associations with the Avengers and Nick Fury."

DEADLY DAMSEL: Be careful when a Black Widow crosses your path! (Art from *BWMG #1* by Salva Espin.)

One thing important to making this new series work is to not get overly involved with the character's past. Liu's job is to keep the character fresh. "I don't plan to dwell on her past, though I'm not going to ignore it, either," Liu says. "This first arc – and the series, in general – focuses on the present and future of the Black Widow, and her place within the super-hero community. This is partly an attempt to keep the book accessible to readers who might be new to her character – but also, quite honestly, Natasha's history has already been explored and fleshed out by some incredible writers. There's no need to rehash what's been done so well already."

tackling the character. "There's so many things that make her a joy to write," she says. She is especially enjoying Natasha's ability to hold her own in a world of super heroes: "Black Widow has no powers, and yet she manages to stand and fight alongside all these super heroes who are intimidated by her, and who respect her. And they do so because she's cunning, ruthless – and staggeringly intelligent.

"On top of that? She never gives up. She's relentless. Totally in control. But that doesn't mean

Look for BLACK WIDOW: DEADLY ORIGIN in Premiere Hardcover to hit store shelves in March, and BLACK WIDOW & THE MARVEL GIRLS to be available in Marvel's cool new Graphic Novel/Trade Paperback format in April. And Marjorie Liu and Daniel Acuna's BLACK WIDOW #1 is all set for release in April as well, so make sure to reserve your copy of the debut issues of the hottest character in comics now! •

IRON MAN DISASSEMBLED

Superstar Writer Matt Fraction Has Arrived And Is Getting Ready For His Close Up!

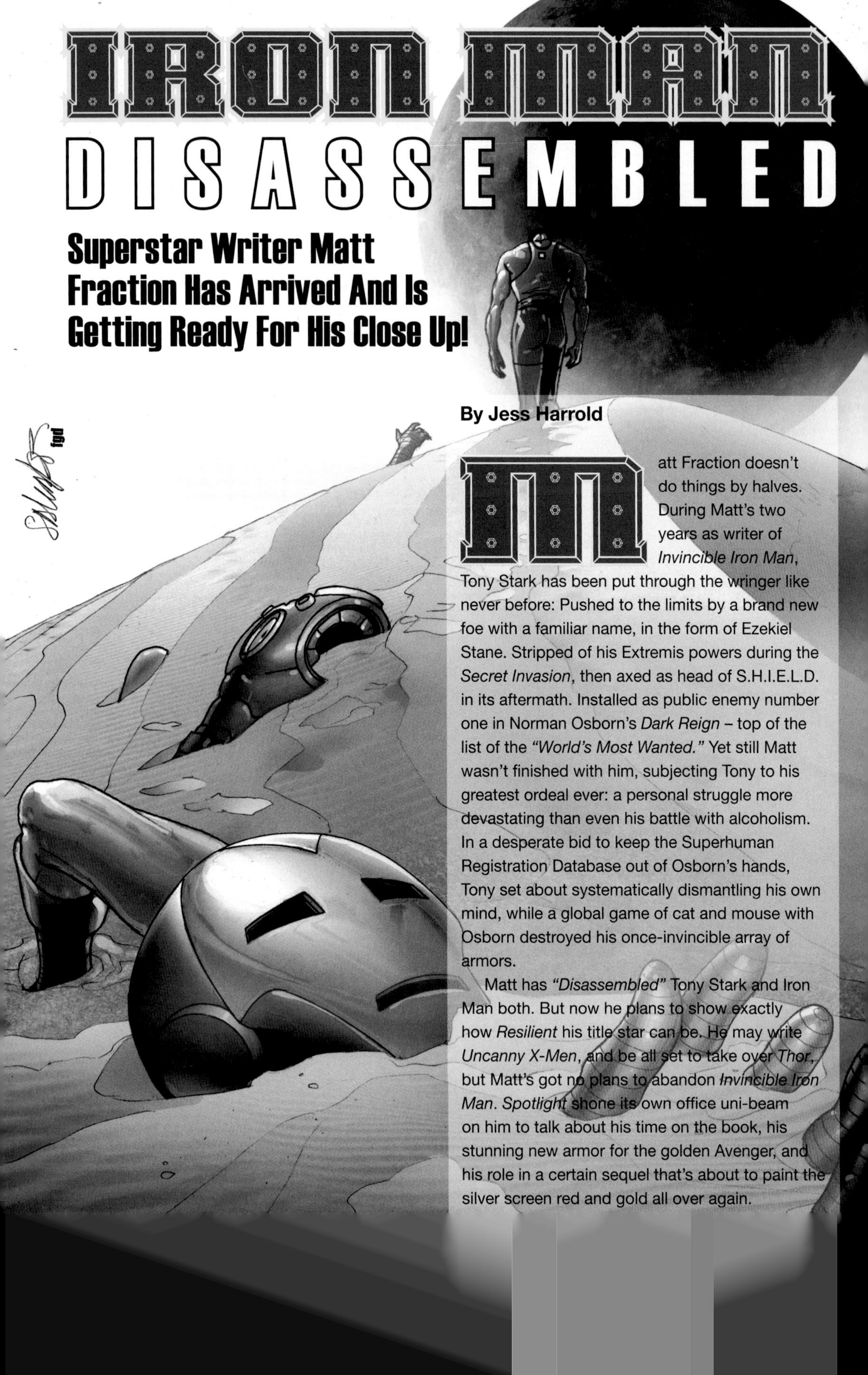

By Jess Harrold

Matt Fraction doesn't do things by halves. During Matt's two years as writer of *Invincible Iron Man*, Tony Stark has been put through the wringer like never before: Pushed to the limits by a brand new foe with a familiar name, in the form of Ezekiel Stane. Stripped of his Extremis powers during the *Secret Invasion*, then axed as head of S.H.I.E.L.D. in its aftermath. Installed as public enemy number one in Norman Osborn's *Dark Reign* – top of the list of the *"World's Most Wanted."* Yet still Matt wasn't finished with him, subjecting Tony to his greatest ordeal ever: a personal struggle more devastating than even his battle with alcoholism. In a desperate bid to keep the Superhuman Registration Database out of Osborn's hands, Tony set about systematically dismantling his own mind, while a global game of cat and mouse with Osborn destroyed his once-invincible array of armors.

Matt has *"Disassembled"* Tony Stark and Iron Man both. But now he plans to show exactly how *Resilient* his title star can be. He may write *Uncanny X-Men*, and be all set to take over *Thor*, but Matt's got no plans to abandon *Invincible Iron Man*. *Spotlight* shone its own office uni-beam on him to talk about his time on the book, his stunning new armor for the golden Avenger, and his role in a certain sequel that's about to paint the silver screen red and gold all over again.

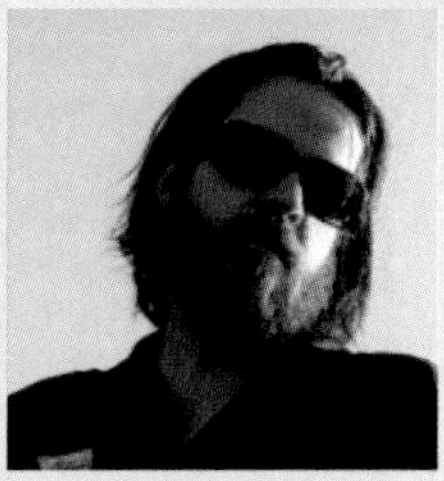

Writer Matt Fraction.

SPOTLIGHT: Last time you spoke with us, in early 2008, you delivered a note-perfect guide to Tony Stark ahead of the launch of *Invincible Iron Man*. After two years of writing the character, have you learned anything new about him you didn't know then?

MATT: Oh, sure. I have no idea how to *quantify* it, but, yeah. It's an organic, evolving, learning experience.

SPOTLIGHT: One thing's for sure: With you in charge, Tony has certainly been taught some hard lessons about himself and his legacy. Taking his encounter with Ezekiel Stane in *"The Five Nightmares"* first, what impact do you think that had on Tony?

MATT: Stane was Tony's own worst-case scenario – the bad ending to the movie, the *sturm und drang* that started with Stark and never ends. Stane is the unending inevitable – the bad idea you can't shake, the itching sense of dread you'll never be free of. He is the face of war in the 21st century. Post-national, post-religious. Asymmetrical chaos. The real degree of impact he had on Tony – and on STARK – is something we're going to keep exploring, especially post-Disassembled.

SPOTLIGHT: One particularly great scene during that first arc was Tony beating Reed Richards at chess. It was a great way of showing the differences between two of the Marvel Universe's most brilliant minds.

MATT: Thanks. I wanted to show Tony's lateral thinking in action before tipping our hand with the big Stane fight. A little game of chess with Reed seemed like a fun bit of business.

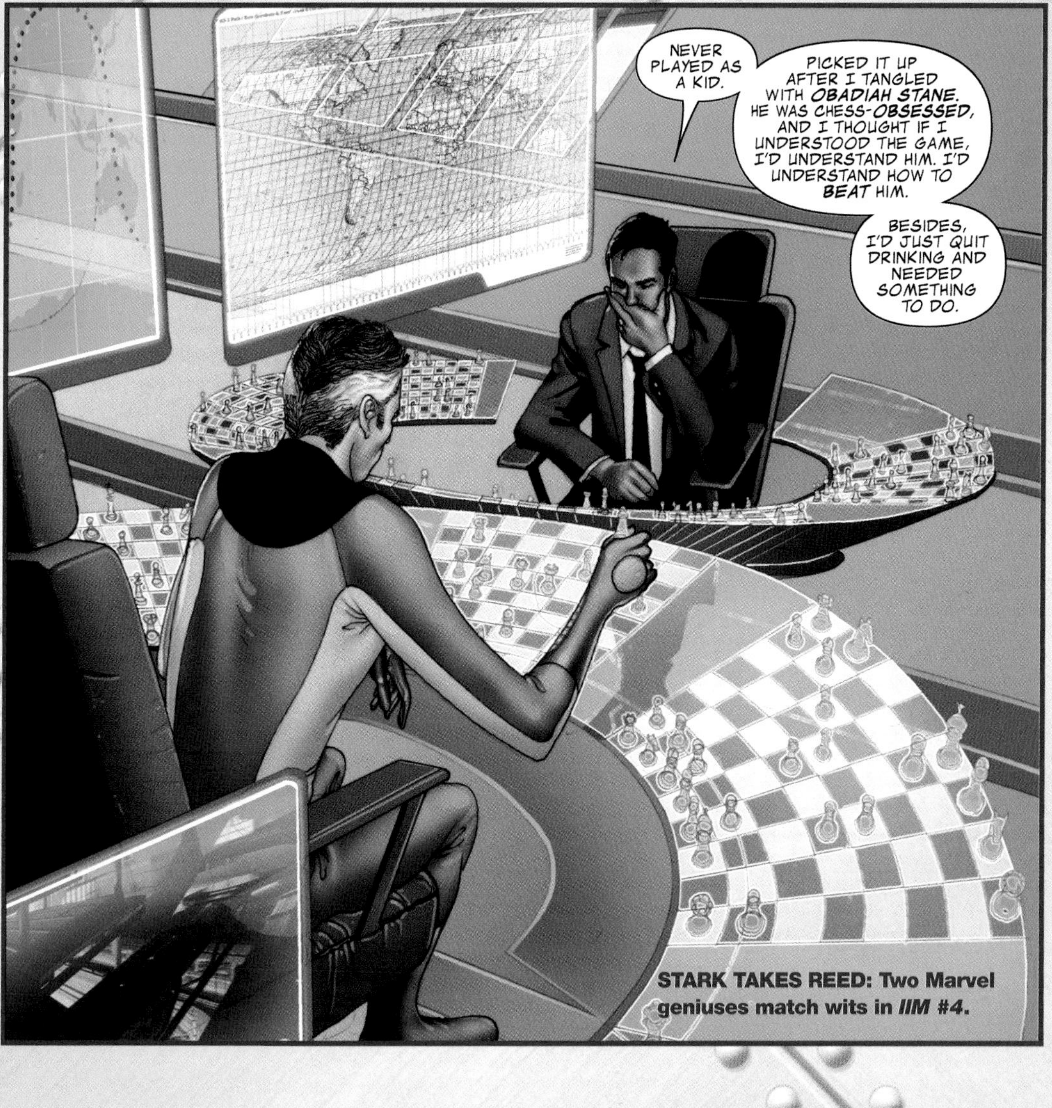
NEVER PLAYED AS A KID.
PICKED IT UP AFTER I TANGLED WITH OBADIAH STANE. HE WAS CHESS-OBSESSED, AND I THOUGHT IF I UNDERSTOOD THE GAME, I'D UNDERSTAND HIM. I'D UNDERSTAND HOW TO BEAT HIM.
BESIDES, I'D JUST QUIT DRINKING AND NEEDED SOMETHING TO DO.

STARK TAKES REED: Two Marvel geniuses match wits in *IIM* #4.

VIGIL: Tony Stark fights for his life surrounded by his closest comrades, Maria Hill, Black Widow, Captain America (Bucky Barnes), Doctor Don Blake (Thor) and Pepper Potts (Rescue). (Art from *IIM #20*.)

SPOTLIGHT: And when it came down to that big fight, it was Stark the man that defeated Stane. It's important for Iron Man writers, be they comic writers or, these days, screenwriters, to remember that the guy inside the suit is the greatest weapon of all, right?

MATT: Absolutely. No one could, or should, be able to do what Tony does. Tony's mind is his power, and it's his power that defines his character, and it's his character that ultimately shows him to be a hero. For me, getting Tony dialed back a few notches after the mythos had grown some was critical. It's not about dialing back the mythos, I don't want to dial the mythos back at all – I want to grow it, enhance it, make it bigger, make it better, make it unmissable. That was the job from day one. But if there are dozens of armors, and dozens of pilots, Tony's not so special.

> "Tony's mind is his power, and it's his power that defines his character, and it's his character that ultimately shows him to be a hero."
> — Writer Matt Fraction

SPOTLIGHT: Was deactivating Tony's Extremis powers important in dialing him back a little? Is that gone forever, as far as you are concerned?

MATT: The Extremis-barfing was already on the board when I came in; I know it had been written and I suspect even drawn, at that point, but I could be wrong. Anyway it was already a horse on the carousel, as it were. And yeah, as far as I'm concerned it's gone forever – at least in the way that the MK 0 is gone forever, that the silver centurion is gone forever. That is to say, it's a tool in the armory that's not getting used anymore. But it was essential in leading Tony, and Iron Man, down the road they're on.

SPOTLIGHT: And what a road… During *Dark Reign*, Norman Osborn may have taken his job, his Avengers Tower, and his armors, but he still declared Stark the "World's Most Wanted." That certainly gave you a unique opportunity to tell a markedly different Iron Man tale.

MATT: I hope so, anyway. *World's Most Wanted* was about stripping away all the special effects and putting a time bomb on Tony's superpower – his own mind – to see what he was capable of at his core. Stripping away the tech and the glamour and getting to see the man inside it all.

SPOTLIGHT: You told us before that, after the last few turbulent years, Tony was going to be faced with a reckoning and then, with hope, a redemption. *World's Most Wanted* brought Tony to his knees, but also showed the extent of his heroism, and the personal sacrifices he would make to keep vital information out of Osborn's hands. Did you accomplish everything you set out to achieve with the story?

> "I knew World's Most Wanted was a valedictory long before anyone else did."
> – Fraction, on saying goodbye to Extremis

MATT: Oh, gosh, I don't know. I don't think we're done with my ultimate mission for Tony yet, and I know for a *fact* he's a long way from redeemed. I think we definitely brought a reckoning...

SPOTLIGHT: So this was the first step in a lengthy process?

MATT: I'm not sure there's a magic bullet solution to redemption. Somebody might just need to hear him say he's sorry; somebody else might want to spit in his face; somebody else might want him dead. All Tony can do is keep his side of the street clean and, for the first time in a long while, I feel like that is what he's starting to do.

SPOTLIGHT: How much of a blast was it to take a nostalgic tour back through Tony's old wardrobe as his intellect diminished? To what extent did that idea come from just wanting to see how cool Salvador would make his old armor look?

MATT: It was great but, at the same time, it was a bummer, because I knew we were blowing them all up! Part of *World's Most Wanted* was about reducing all those spare suits and getting down to just the one prime Iron Man for Tony to pilot. So... it was great, as a fan, but I knew *World's Most Wanted* was a valedictory long before anyone else did. And Salva just makes everything look cool, so I knew that, going in, he'd be bringing the pyrotechnics.

SPOTLIGHT: At the start of your run, Tony Stark had recently lost two of his very best friends, Steve Rogers and Happy Hogan, Rhodey was off doing his own thing and then the subsequent events of *Secret Invasion* cost him his S.H.I.E.L.D. support network and place in the Avengers. That all gave you the opportunity to develop two of his remaining allies, Pepper Potts and Maria Hill. What

MOST WANTED...And not just by Osborn! Tony's love triangle with Maria Hill and Pepper Potts is another plot thread heading for trouble!
(Art from *IIM #10* and *#16*.)

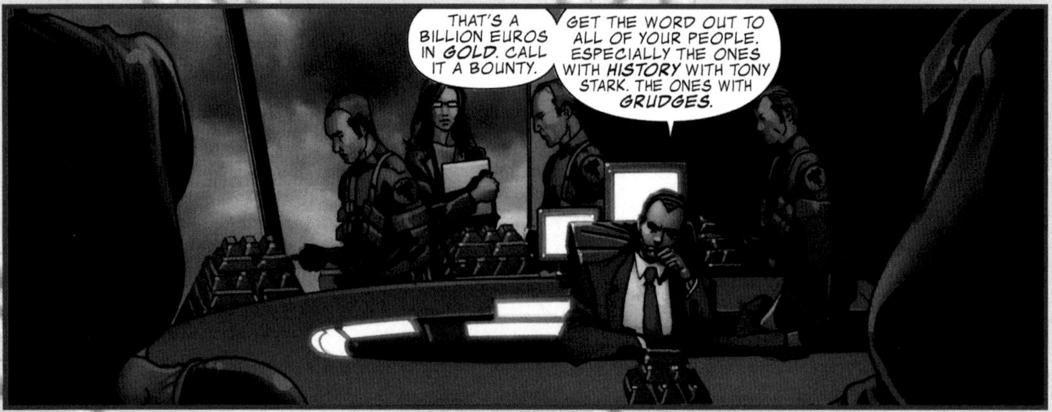
THAT'S A BILLION EUROS IN GOLD. CALL IT A BOUNTY.
GET THE WORD OUT TO ALL OF YOUR PEOPLE. ESPECIALLY THE ONES WITH HISTORY WITH TONY STARK. THE ONES WITH GRUDGES.

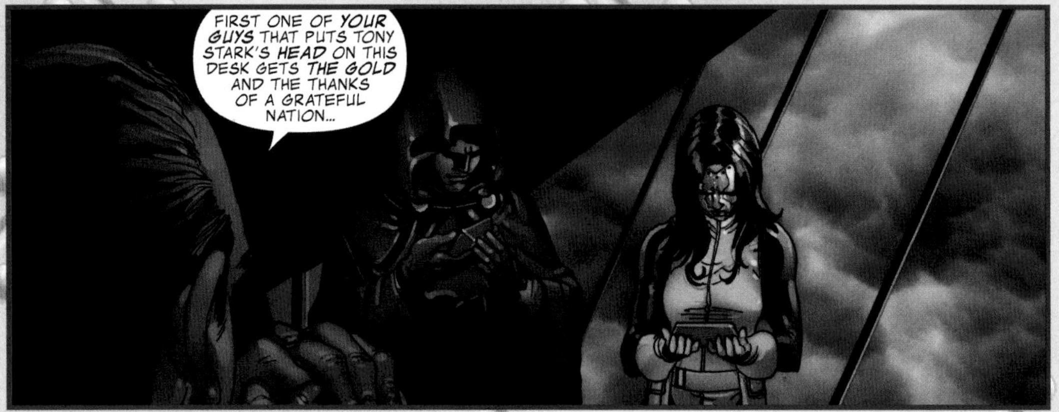
FIRST ONE OF YOUR GUYS THAT PUTS TONY STARK'S HEAD ON THIS DESK GETS THE GOLD AND THE THANKS OF A GRATEFUL NATION...

EXECUTIVE ORDER: The manhunt for Stark is handed to the Hood and Madam Masque! (Art from *IIM* #12.)

particularly appealed to you about Pepper and Maria?

MATT: They were women. They were strong, ferocious, independent women and comics, as the Godfather of Soul sang, is a man's world. Pepper had been a long process. When I started writing *The Order* my wife was pregnant with our first child and we didn't know if it was a boy or girl. And I realized that if it was a girl I would have a lot of explaining to do for my chosen field one day. Anyway it became a pet mission to start equalizing the sexes in my books somewhat and Pepper was on the trajectory for a suit of armor ever since *The Order* was a notion in my notebook, and long before I knew I was getting *Iron Man*. And Hill I just loved. I loved her in *New Avengers* and didn't want her to go away because S.H.I.E.L.D. was going away. Anyway it all just made sense with what I wanted to do; Tony would be dead without these two. And he owes them everything. You can introduce romantic subplots, too, which are always fun to pluck at. Tony *did* kind of sleep with them both... And that's just one of many things he'll have to deal with going forward...

SPOTLIGHT: Is Pepper's armored persona Rescue a big part of your plans moving forward with the title?

MATT: Yes. Absolutely.

SPOTLIGHT: Turning to the *"Stark: Disassembled"* arc, Tony's carefully woven plan to reboot himself finally reunited some staunch allies: *Siege* might get the fanfare, but *Invincible Iron Man* #21 was the place to see Tony, Steve Rogers and Thor in a room together for the first time in years. Already a collector's item classic?

MATT: Um... yes. You should buy fifty and put your kids – and mine – through college.

SPOTLIGHT: That complex relationship between the big three Avengers must be something you're hoping to explore further...

MATT: Yeah, no doubt. Especially now that I get to write *Thor*, too, the interplay between Tony and Thor is a big deal going forward. The destinies of Stark and of Asgard are intertwined.

SPOTLIGHT: The relationship between Thor and Tony should make for some very interesting reading. Steve Rogers, you figure, is the forgiving kind. He and Tony have patched up

I BELIEVE MS. POTTS GAVE YOU A DIRECT ORDER. SOLAR RESERVES AT 3%.

MASQUE ATTACK: Pepper and the Rescue armor put Whitney Frost in her place. (Art from *IIM #16*.)

major differences before. But with the recent offense of Tony's involvement with cloning Thor, Thor arguably has even more to forgive. Possibly too much?

MATT: We'll see. Forever is a long, long time.

SPOTLIGHT: Thor did however play his part in "reassembling" Stark, a complex process that required the additional aid of Stephen Strange and set Tony on one of his most personal struggles. Where does it leave Tony, and what is different about him going forward?

MATT: You should be sure to check out *"Resilient,"* our new story arc!

SPOTLIGHT: What can you tell us about it? Will it even be Tony in the armor?

MATT: Have you read *Invincible Iron Man #24* yet? Have you? I'll wait…
La dee da dee da.
Deedle deedle deedle dee.
You done? Okay. So. Yes. *Resilient* will see a

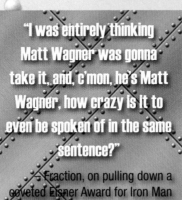

"I was entirely thinking Matt Wagner was gonna take it, and, c'mon, he's Matt Wagner, how crazy is it to even be spoken of in the same sentence?"

— Fraction, on pulling down a coveted Eisner Award for Iron Man

new story, new threats, new loves, a new *Stark*, a new Tony, and new armor. Whew!

SPOTLIGHT: Wow. And, oh yeah, that spiffy new suit, co-created by Iron Man and Thor movie designer Ryan Meinerding and a certain Mr. Matt Fraction! Talk us through the design process and your role in it. Are you pretty nifty with a pencil?

MATT: Oh, no, not at all… All I did was talk about what it *did*, and what I wanted it to look like. I know how it works, and could just do my best to describe it, and give Tony's thinking about its design. There was lots of good input from Joe Quesada, Tom Brevoort, Ralph Macchio and Alejandro Arbona as well as Ryan. It was cool because we started with asking, "What does it do?", and I got to write a couple pages about the state of Stark and where he was going… and why the suit would have to follow.

SPOTLIGHT: And you must be itching to put it through its paces against the villains! So far

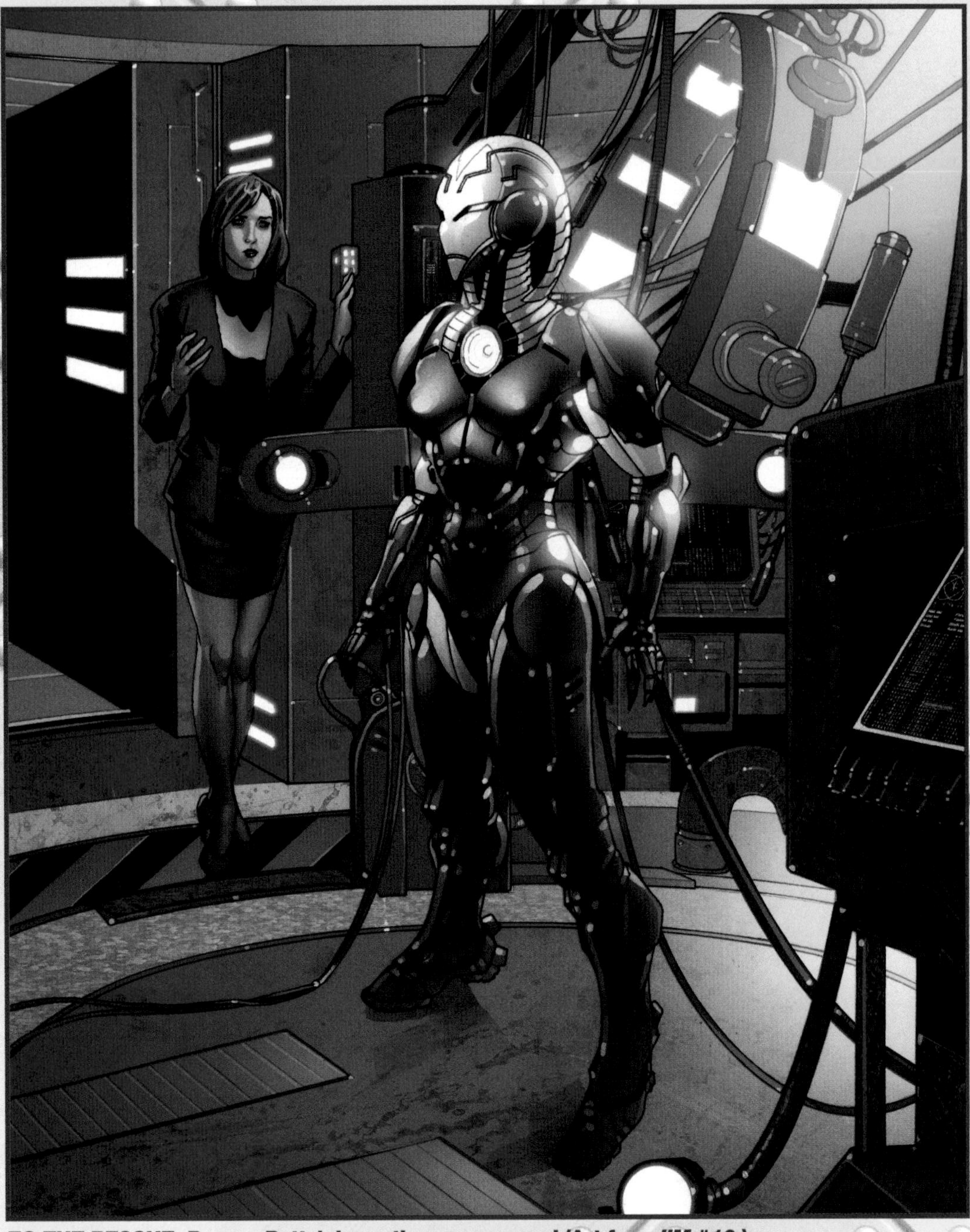

TO THE RESCUE: Pepper Potts' dramatic new persona! (Art from *IIM #10*.)

you've delivered a deadly new Stane, a fresh and sinister take on the Controller and got to play with Madame Masque and the revamped Ghost. Are there any other classic Iron Man rogues you're planning to put your stamp on?

MATT: Yes. That "rings" a bell. Get it? I said "rings" because the Mandarin has all those rings.

SPOTLIGHT: We've got to "hand" it to you on that one! [*Okay, enough with the bad puns!* – Ed.] Now, *Invincible Iron Man* launched alongside the existing *Iron Man: Director of S.H.I.E.L.D.*, before events made your book Shellhead's one true flagship title. So have you done the math yet for the next big anniversary issue that might see the title renumbered? Any big plans for it?

MATT: Wow, no, I haven't. I haven't even thought about it until just now. Have you? I've got lots of big plans but no idea if we're getting renumbered or not.

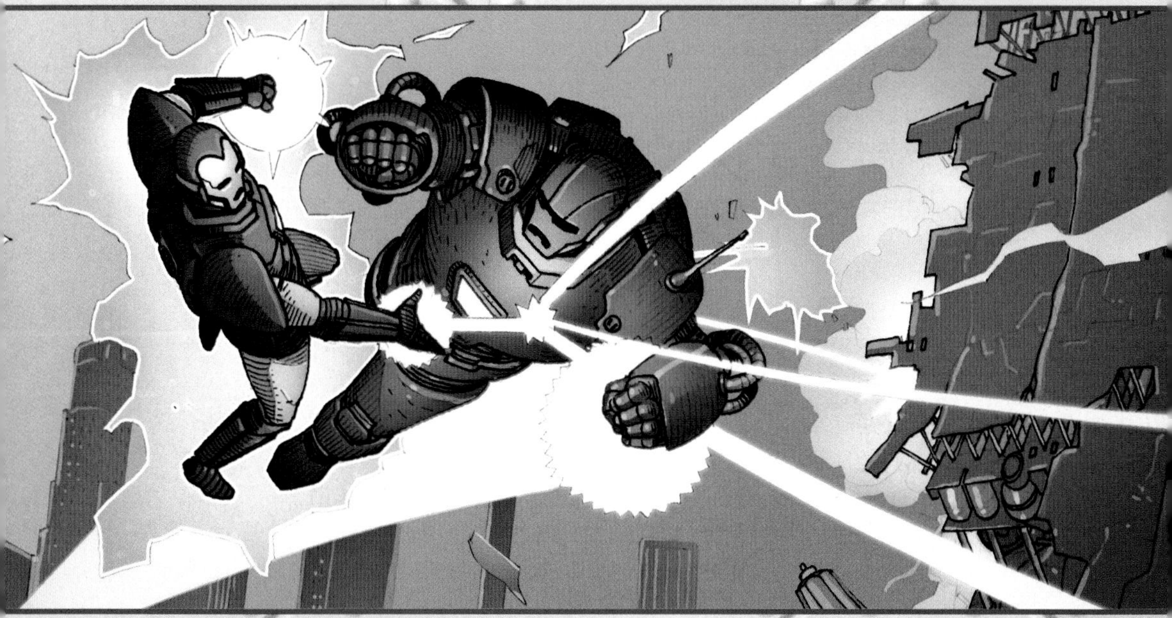

SILVER CENTURION: Classic armor (in a flashback battle against Iron-Monger) is a favorite of Fraction's! (Art from *IIM #3*.)

SPOTLIGHT: It's certainly not a calculation to be undertaken lightly! But speaking of momentous occasions, last year *Invincible Iron Man* deservedly took the Eisner for Best New Series. For those that don't know, talk us through the Eisner process. Is there a ceremony? Speeches? Honestly, did you think you'd win?

MATT: Oh, God no. In fact, I was talking with Steve Wacker (Spider-editor extraordinaire) and Alejandro Arbona on our way to the ceremony and we were all laughing about how amazing it was that a book like *Invincible Iron Man* was even nominated. Like, that alone is a victory, you know? First off – it's freakin' *Iron Man*. How crazy is that? Second, none of us were wholly sure how a book that ostensibly started in 1968 was even *eligible*, but we weren't going to point that out. Anyway so I was entirely thinking Matt Wagner (of *Mage* and *Grendel* fame) was gonna take it, and, c'mon, he's Matt Wagner, how crazy is it to even be spoken of in the same sentence? You go to a big ballroom and you sit at a big round table and slog through an endless drink line and then the show starts on a big stage. There's a host and guest presenters and slides and speeches and then they say the name of your book and you kind of *freak out!* I tried to thank everyone involved with the book and get off stage as quickly as possible. Because it feels as though the whole of the comics industry is staring at you. It was a thrilling, crazy, honor. Oh! And there was no wi-fi, or cell reception, and I didn't want to be rude and leave so we had to wait until it was all done to get word out. Which meant waking people up at 4a.m. on the East Coast. But what the heck, we were happy. And Salva found out on his birthday, so that was pretty great.

SPOTLIGHT: Very cool. Iron Man is such a central figure in the Marvel Universe these days, to the extent that his title has been dramatically affected by the events like *Civil War, Secret Invasion* and *Siege*. There are writers who don't like having to fit their plans in with major crossovers but I'm guessing that, working on books like *Iron Man* and *Uncanny X-Men*, you aren't one of them. Is it part of the job you find particularly enjoyable? Particularly challenging?

MATT: Working with everyone to tell what we hope are big, satisfying, engaging events is always fun. It can be a pain in that waiting for anything you want to do can be a pain – like, say, the questions people will be *screaming* at the end of *Uncanny X-Men #522*, only to then be rocketed into *Second Coming* before we can get to answering them – but when something as amazing as *Second Coming* comes along, it's a pain worth enduring. It's a challenge, sure. But it keeps things from being boring. And, in my experience, all of these things are opt-in. I didn't write any *Iron Man* tie-ins for *Siege* or *Secret Invasion*, for example.

SPOTLIGHT: That's true. To the extent that the events have influenced Iron Man in a pretty game-changing way, though – for example the

Skrull Invasion disabling Extremis and taking Tony's job – did you get a lot of input into how they influenced the character? It sounds a bit like they pretty much fit with your initial plans for him.

MATT: It was the trajectory Tony – and the Marvel Universe – were already on when I came aboard and it locked into where I wanted to take the poor guy. I think the decision to *keep* Extremis deactivated might have been mine… Like, it was, as I recall, open-ended enough that if I wanted him to dose up again post-*Secret Invasion* I probably could've made my case for it. But very early on I knew where I wanted Tony, and the suit, to go, and why, and we're almost there. Sorry to be so cagey but hopefully there are still some surprises and twists coming that'll give your buck a couple more bangs.

SPOTLIGHT: Along similar lines, *Invincible Iron Man* began life as an accessible read for people who enjoyed the movie. Is there a pressure to make #25 another good jumping-on point for fans of the sequel?

MATT: Oh, no more than I normally feel. #25 is a perfect place for it all the same, but then again I'm always trying to make my stuff accessible.

SPOTLIGHT: Speaking of the films, not only is Iron Man one of the MU's major players, he is now one of the world's most famous action stars. We have to ask for your own personal thoughts on the movie *Iron Man*. Two thumbs up?

MATT: Yeah, I loved it. I thought he was the best, and most successful, Marvel hero on film to date. Better than Spidey, better than everything.

SPOTLIGHT: Since the movie went stratospheric, have you noticed a difference in how people react when you tell them you write Iron Man?

MATT: Yes! It's crazy. And when I tell 'em I consulted on the sequel, they give me stuff.

SPOTLIGHT: Some guys have all the luck! Any insider info you can give us?

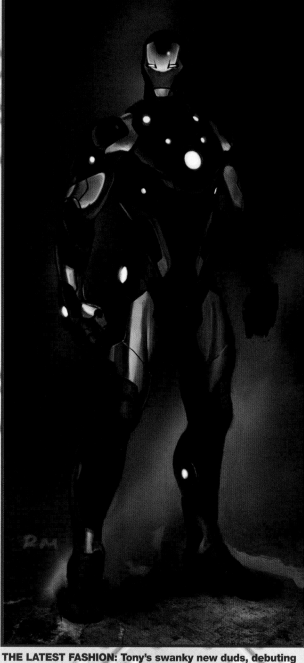

THE LATEST FASHION: Tony's swanky new duds, debuting in *Invincible Iron Man #25.* Art by Ryan Meinerding.

MATT: It is going to be very, very good.

SPOTLIGHT: C'mon, we won't tell anyone. At least spill a couple of insights into the Tinseltown process!

MATT: Marvel put me in the same hotel that TV On The Radio stayed in the night they played L.A. to kick off the *Dear Science* tour. I rode an elevator with TV On the Radio. *Only in Los Angeles, kids! Kaw Kaw!*

SPOTLIGHT: Nice. And these days, there's gotta be a threequel. What chance of Robert Downey having to disassemble himself in *Iron Man 3*?

MATT: Ha! That'd be amazing.

SPOTLIGHT: Lastly, you get the keys to any one suit of armor, from the comics or films, for a single day: Which one do you choose?

MATT: I started reading *Iron Man* with #198, so when the suit-change came in #200, I figured, man, this guy changes suits every three issues! Of course it doesn't work like that, but I remain inordinately fond of the Silver Centurion duds in the way that someone attaches to their first James Bond or Doctor. I suspect tooling around in it today would be like driving a DeLorean though – weird, supremely ironic, and dependent on shoulder-pads. So I'll go with the new one. You'll understand why at the end of #25. It's the best armor Tony Stark has ever had.

Speaking of being handed the keys, we're very glad it was Matt Fraction who is now behind the wheels of Iron Man. It's now one of Marvel's most invincible books, and we're not just talking about the title! Matt builds up the excitement as he continues to "disassemble" Tony Stark in the monthly INVINCIBLE IRON MAN, but also look for his writing in other flagship titles UNCANNY X-MEN and, starting in June, THOR! •

CLEAR!: The Big Three together again as Thor and Cap try to revive a disassembled Tony Stark. (Art from *IIM #21*.)

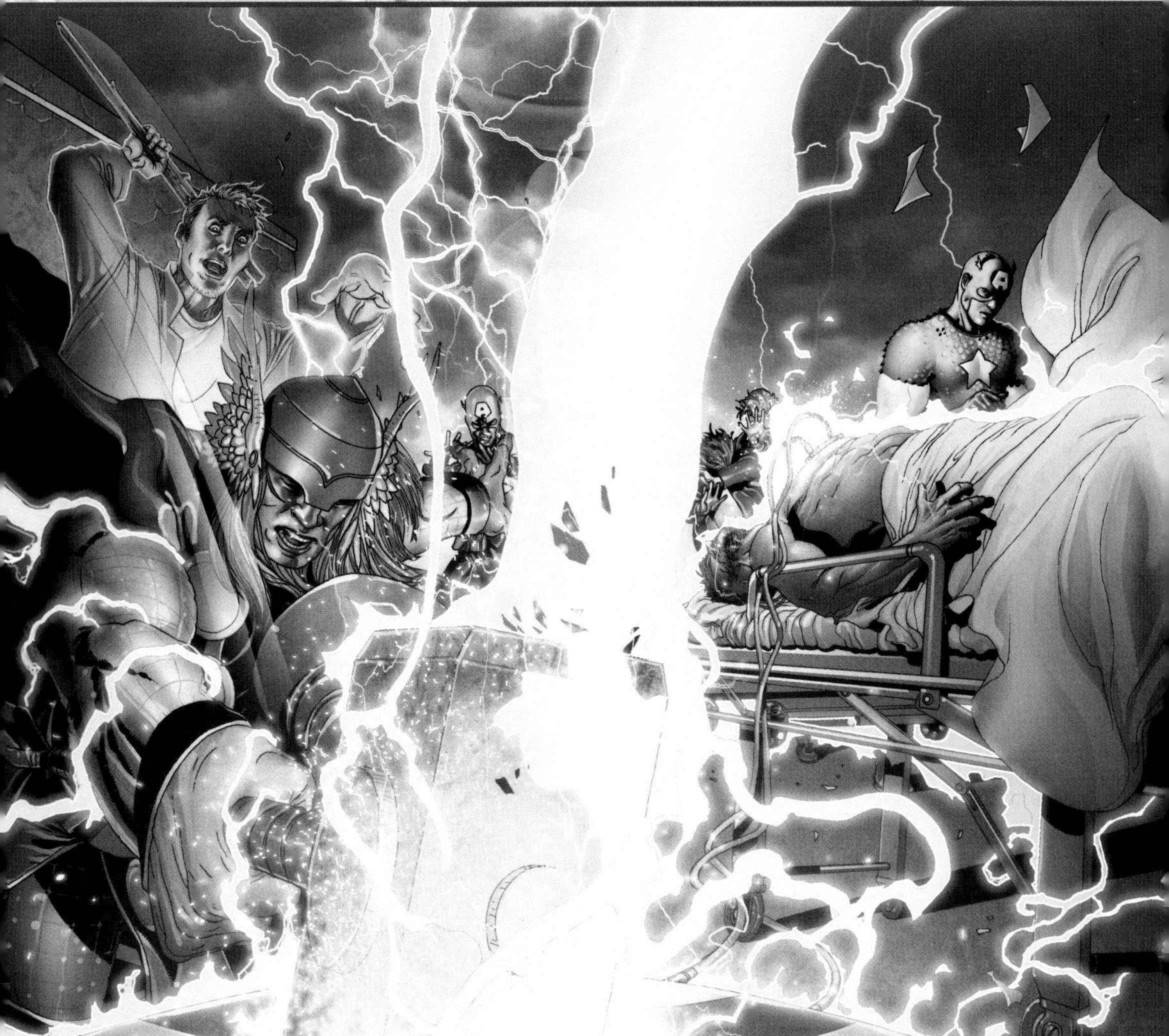

IRON MAN

KICKING OFF WITH A CLASSIC STORYLINE
AND BOB LAYTON SPARK A DECAD

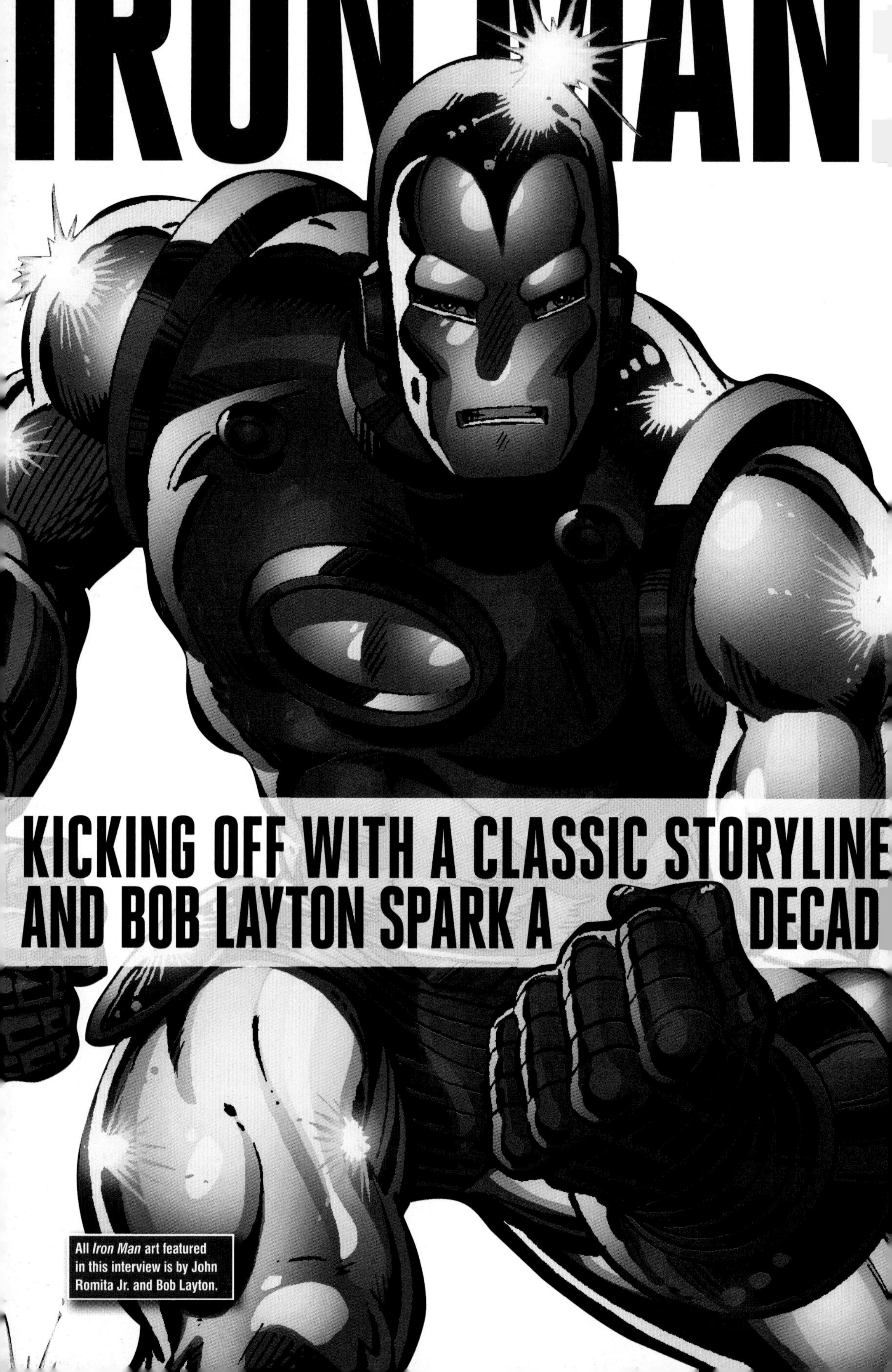

All *Iron Man* art featured in this interview is by John Romita Jr. and Bob Layton.

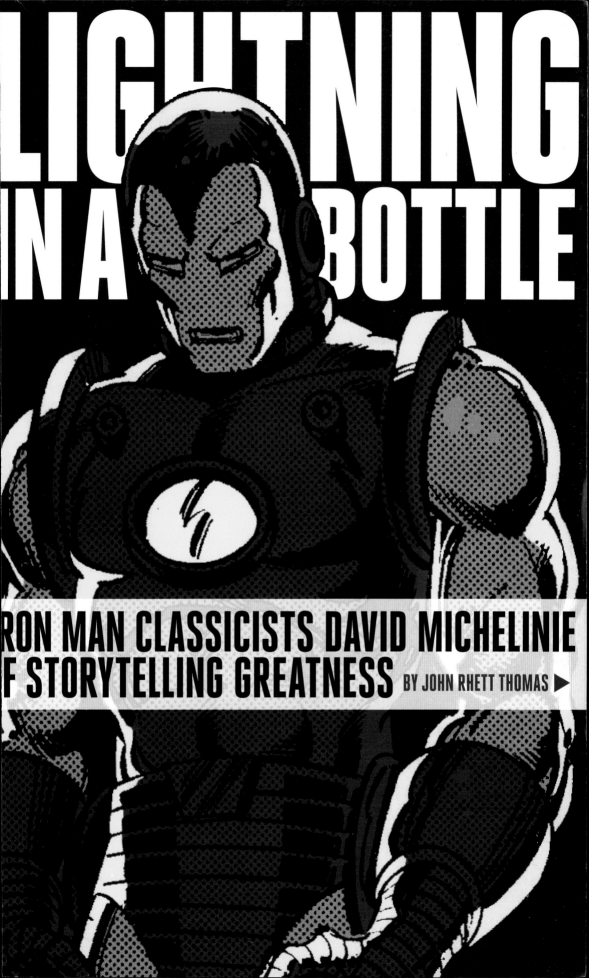

LIGHTNING
IN A
BOTTLE

RON MAN CLASSICISTS DAVID MICHELINIE
F STORYTELLING GREATNESS
BY JOHN RHETT THOMAS ▶

ONE THING this writer never saw coming was the way in which the masses have truly taken to Tony Stark and Iron Man, embracing the character and his armored alter ego so completely that it makes it seem like they've always been on the pop culture scene. Sure, the character has always been cutting edge in comics – first as the "cool exec with a heart of steel" in *Tales of Suspense*, then as a founding member of the Avengers alongside Captain America and Thor, all of which led to the start of the decades long run of his own solo title, the dynamism at the heart of Iron Man perfectly captured by Gene Colan on the cover to 1968's *Iron Man #1*. But now, *everyone* seems to love Iron Man, ever since his first movie became a trend-setting surprise smash hit at the box office, and its sequel serving as 2010's most anticipated movie release. • But at the end of the '70s, Iron Man was neither the white hot property he is today nor as state of the art as he was in the Swingin' '60s. The character had seen better days, his flagship title better matching the end of decade malaise seen in other corners of the comics industry – a (pardon the pun) stark contrast with the vibrant and fresh takes going on in books like Chris Claremont's *Uncanny X-Men* and Frank Miller's *Daredevil*. • So in any *Spotlight* celebrating the smash hit movie and its sequel, we ought to pay reverence to the two gentlemen who deserve renown more than any other for igniting the spark inside Iron Man that not only renewed the title's sales fortunes, but gave it the imprimatur of greatness. For much of the period from 1979 through the end of the '80s, the imprint of either writer David Michelinie or plotter/writer/artist Bob Layton – and often both in tandem – carried *Iron Man* to the upper echelon of Marvel's publishing strata. • And it all started with "Demon in a Bottle," the story arc that began almost as soon as the pair took on the title, with the classic *Iron Man #120*. It was a stunning tour de force of artistic synergy, with Michelinie, Layton, and young buck John Romita Jr. fusing action, humor, and the high-tech with a brutal assessment of Stark's worst demons getting the best of him. Spotlight had the honor of talking with both David and Bob about their groundbreaking work on the classic story that kicked off a new era of *Iron Man*.

SPOTLIGHT: One thing I think that's important to remember about "Demon in a Bottle" is that, running from issues #120-128, it's only a few months after you two climbed on board (along with John Romita, Jr. on pencils) to begin your run. Can you take us inside those early days on *Iron Man* and what it meant for you two to be on the title, plotting it together? And how did the gig come about in the first place?

BOB: Just before my contract expired at DC in the late '70s, David Michelinie and I (we had first formed our partnership at DC, working together on *Star Hunters* and *Claw the Unconquered*) had agreed to leave the company for greener pastures. We both sensed the impending "Implosion" and didn't want to be a casualty of it.

I WANT TO THANK YOU AGAIN, RHODEY, FOR CLEARING ME TO MEET TONY'S SHUTTLE FROM JFK.
NO PROBLEM, MS. CABE. I'VE BEEN WITH THE MAN EVER SINCE 'NAM, AND I THINK I KNOW HIM AS WELL AS ANY-ONE.
SI
AND RIGHT ABOUT NOW, A FRIEND LIKE YOU IS JUST WHAT HE NEE-- EH?
SI
WHAT'S UP, MRS. ARBOGAST?
WE'VE GOT TROUBLE, RHODES!

FRIENDS: A crucial part of Michelinie and Layton's *Iron Man* are Tony Stark's loyal friends Jim Rhodes, Bethany Cabe and Bambi Arbogast. (Art from *IM #120*.)

Together, we went to Marvel and interviewed to work as a team there. We were given a choice of lower-end books to work on and I jumped out of my seat when I realized that *Iron Man* was one of those choices. That was the one book in the entire industry that I wanted to do more than any other. Dave was not as familiar with the character as I was but he immediately seized on my unbridled passion for the series. Together, David and I retooled the series into the way I had always imaged it could be. David's unfamiliarity with Iron Man continuity proved to be a tremendous asset, translating into his fresh approach to the character. So every month, David and I would sit down and plot out the events of each story together. And annually, we would do an overview of the series to plot out where we intended to take the character over the next twelve issues.

SPOTLIGHT: Were the underpinnings of the story (Stark's alcoholism) part of the reason you wanted the gig?

BOB: When we initially accepted the assignment, we had no idea that the direction we were heading in would lead us to "Demon in a Bottle." As David has said before, it seemed to be a natural progression towards the direction we were taking the series.

SPOTLIGHT: What did it mean for you to bring this edge of reality to comic book fiction at that time, and was there any personal reason for either of you to tell this kind of a story?

DAVID: Marvel had always been the more reality-based of the "Big Two" comics publishers, so it wasn't really that much of a stretch to bring real problems into characters' lives. And looking at Tony Stark's situation when we took over plotting *Iron Man*, it just seemed logical that he'd seek an escape from the immense pressures he was facing. In that time period, alcohol was the obvious answer. But, no, there was no particularly personal meaning for me in the story; it just seemed like a good, strong storyline that would allow us to make some statements about the human condition.

SPOTLIGHT: Rereading the story, I was impressed by the amount of "laugh out loud" humor spread throughout the

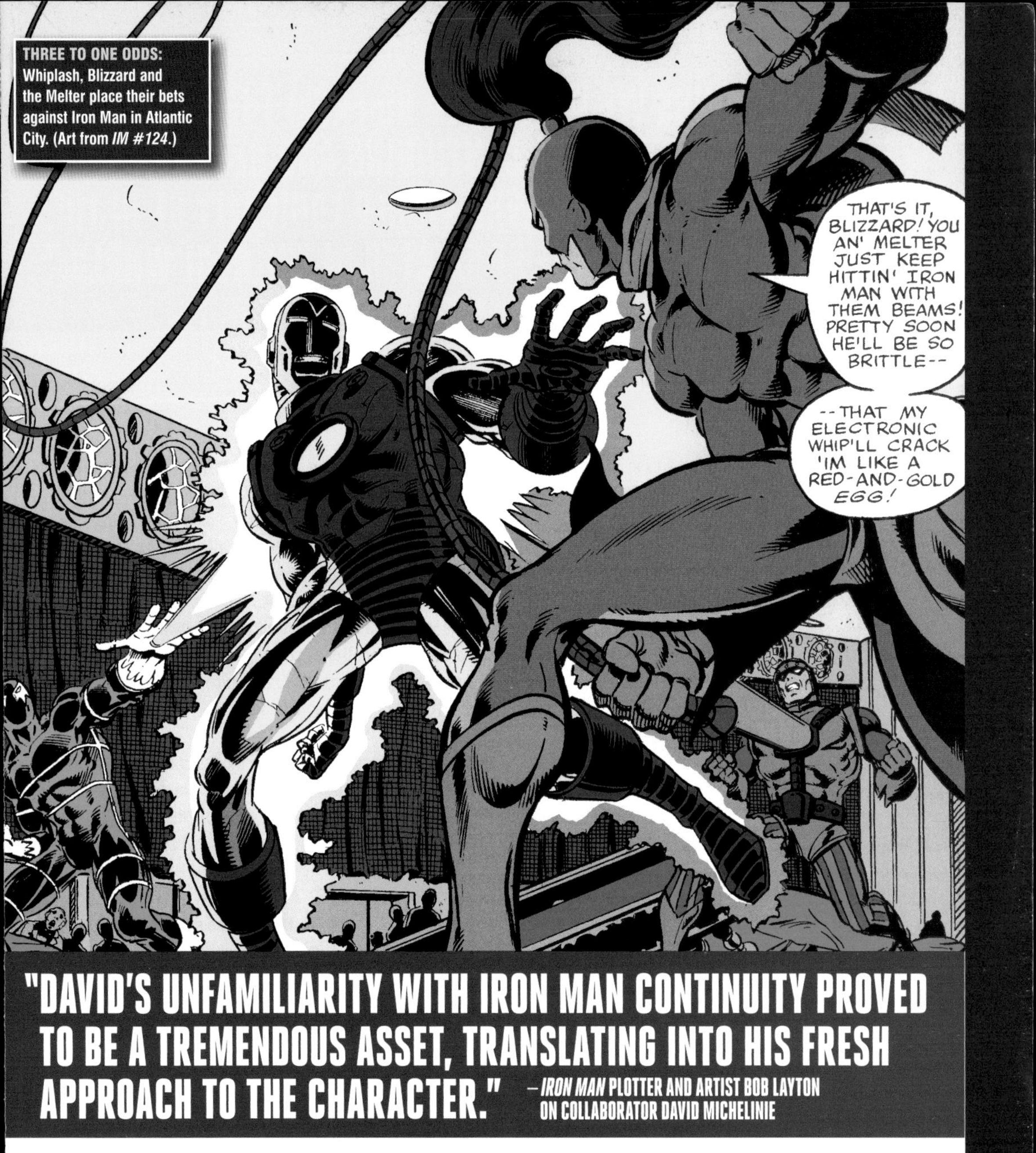
THREE TO ONE ODDS: Whiplash, Blizzard and the Melter place their bets against Iron Man in Atlantic City. (Art from IM #124.)
THAT'S IT, BLIZZARD! YOU AN' MELTER JUST KEEP HITTIN' IRON MAN WITH THEM BEAMS! PRETTY SOON HE'LL BE SO BRITTLE--
--THAT MY ELECTRONIC WHIP'LL CRACK 'IM LIKE A RED-AND-GOLD EGG!

"DAVID'S UNFAMILIARITY WITH IRON MAN CONTINUITY PROVED TO BE A TREMENDOUS ASSET, TRANSLATING INTO HIS FRESH APPROACH TO THE CHARACTER." —*IRON MAN* PLOTTER AND ARTIST BOB LAYTON ON COLLABORATOR DAVID MICHELINIE

book. Which of you guys was most responsible for "bringing the funny?" Is one of you funnier than the other and, thus, the go-to guy for writing the gags and humor?

BOB: I don't believe either one of us is funnier than the other. As I've told people candidly, if you can read David's emails to me, or some of the comments he makes in his written plots, you'd drop down on the floor, laughing out loud. David is an incredibly clever guy and has a unique way of delivering a punchline, especially in print. I mean it, his emails are freaking hilarious. Obviously, I have written my fair share of gags during my career in comics: *Hercules*, in particular, was known for that. When David and I see a moment where some humor can be injected, we both jump on that opportunity almost simultaneously. I can't speak for David, but I know he shares my philosophy that all good adventure stories are a roller-coaster ride, with extreme highs and tragic lows. I think the humor works because it's necessary to give balance to a good adventure story. I've been fortunate to have someone as clever as David to work with over the years. You want to hear something funny, you should hear the two of us on the phone ranting about the NFL. It's R-rated, but hilarious.

DAVID: I think a similar, if twisted, sense of humor is one of the things that has made our collaborations click for so many decades. We just think the same things are funny. I remember going to see the movie *Phantasm* back when Bob and I were living in the same small college town, shortly after we'd started doing *Iron Man*. There's a bit where a flying sphere embeds itself in a guy's forehead and pumps out about thirty gallons of blood. It was so over-the-top sick that Bob and I were rolling in our seats with laughter. Everyone else in the audience was appalled, and I think a few actually got up and moved farther away from us. But we thought it was the funniest thing in the universe. Now that's friendship!

SPOTLIGHT: A lot of the humor you put in Iron Man, specifically "Demon in a Bottle", was zany, particularly the

"ONE OF THE THINGS WE WANTED TO DO FROM THE OUTSET WAS TO GIVE TONY STARK A CONTINUING AND RECOGNIZABLE SUPPORTING CAST, PEOPLE WHO WOULD LOGICALLY BE IN THE LIFE OF A MAN LIKE TONY IF HE EXISTED IN THE REAL WORLD."

– WRITER MICHELINIE ON DEVELOPING A CAST THAT INCLUDED JIM RHODES AND BETHANY CABE

recurring character of the old lady who was always bumping into Tony at the worst possible moments. Was there any inspiration for this character?

DAVID: I don't remember any specific inspiration. Bob and I tended to crack each other up while plotting, and one way was to toss in bits with this cranky old lady shaking her fist at Tony and calling him "&*@$#!" Of course, I had to modify the language somewhat in the scripting stage, but basically that was just us amusing ourselves.

--IF I CAN JUST ;UNG; PUSH MY ARMOR'S MUSCLE AMPLIFICATION TO THE MAXIMUM... COMBINE IT WITH THE ;UNF; THRUST OF MY BOOT JETS--
--MAYBE I CAN SET THIS THING DOWN... WITHOUT SPLATTERING IT...

...OR ME!
AND THUS, HIS MASKED FEATURES ETCHED WITH LINES OF DETERMINATION, THE ARMORED AVENGER STRAINS--
KWISH!
--AND STRIVES--
SPASH!
--AND, ALMOST SURPRISING HIMSELF, SUCCEEDS!
CHOOSH!

SPOTLIGHT: And finally, another interesting thing about your use of humor is that much of it was in the service of setting up Tony's later fall into alcoholism. Some of the quips, one-liners, and visual humor in those earliest issues are related to his drinking problem. Was this to soften the reader up only to later lower the emotional boom on us, perhaps to drive home the fact that often, we view people who drink too much and get out of control as somehow charming or amusing, when there's really not that much funny about it at all. Or am I putting too much thought into this?

DAVID: Maybe, maybe not. I think most of the humor was pretty spontaneous and specific to the situations in a particular story. I don't recall that we used humor to set up things several issues down the road. But then, I don't remember what I had for breakfast this morning either, so I could be wrong.

SPOTLIGHT: Another character you set up very well in these stories was Bethany Cabe. What were your ultimate goals with her inception? Obviously in those initial issues, she was a rock for Tony.

DAVID: One of the things we wanted to do from the outset was to give Tony Stark a continuing and recognizable supporting cast, people who would logically be in the life of a man like Tony if he existed in the real world. That's why we introduced Jim Rhodes to be his buddy, why we populated his company with various employees like Mrs. Arbogast, Mr. Pithins, Vic Martinelli and such. Beth was added to give Tony a realistic relationship, a woman who was strong without having to prove herself or spout feminist slogans.

GET THOSE OTHER RAFTS OUT HERE, BLAST IT! I DON'T KNOW HOW MUCH LONGER THE FUSILAGE CAN STAY--

THE ORIGINAL CAPTAIN SULLY: Michelinie, Layton and Iron Man envisage a safe water landing for a jumbo jet in an action-packed *Iron Man #120.*

SPOTLIGHT: A legendary character you created was James Rhodes, aka Rhodey, who debuted in *Iron Man #118*, only a couple issues before the stories reprinted in *Iron Man: Demon In A Bottle*. In these early tales, we first see Jim in action as a supporting character. What were your intentions early on regarding this character? At that time, did you foresee his later development as Iron Man and then War Machine?

BOB: We had no idea that Jim Rhodes would be such a mainstay when David and I created him. He evolved from a small supporting role into a large role in our storylines. I don't think Dave or I knew at the time how big he would become in the series. Remember, there weren't a lot of strong African-American characters in the Marvel Universe at that time and David and I wanted to give Tony a foil with a dissimilar background from his own.

One of the biggest problems with comics in general these days is that few are couched in the real world. Everyone is a mutant or alien or cyborg. The supporting characters exist to ground the reader in a sense of reality, fulfilling a need in the series for the lead character to have normal human foils for him to bounce ideas and conflicts off of. Through their eyes, we witness the fantastic and react in a believable manner. Rhodey was created by David and me to ground Tony Stark's fantastic exploits in some degree of reality...David and I had nothing to do with the storyline that turned James Rhodes into Iron Man or War Machine.

DAVID: A lot of writers seem to have trouble figuring out how to make characters interesting if they don't wear a flashy costume and have super powers. (I'm not including Len Kaminsky here; he's a good writer and I'm sure he created War Machine with the idea of expanding the established characterization, rather than just to create another super-powered guy.) I remember something that happened shortly after I created Scott Lang to be the (then-) new Ant-Man [*way back in Avengers #181, Ed.*]. I'd given Scott a 10-year-old daughter, picturing him as an Everyman who had to juggle saving the world with being a single father. It also added the interesting dynamic of having a little kid who knew her dad was a super hero, but couldn't tell anyone. I remember another writer asking the editor in charge if he could borrow Cassie Lang for a story, but when he explained his idea it turned out that he wanted to give her super powers. Talk about missing the whole point! Fortunately, the editor agreed and turned down the request. [*Of course, thirty years later, Cassie Lang is a card-carrying member of the fan-favorite Young Avengers! – Ed.*]

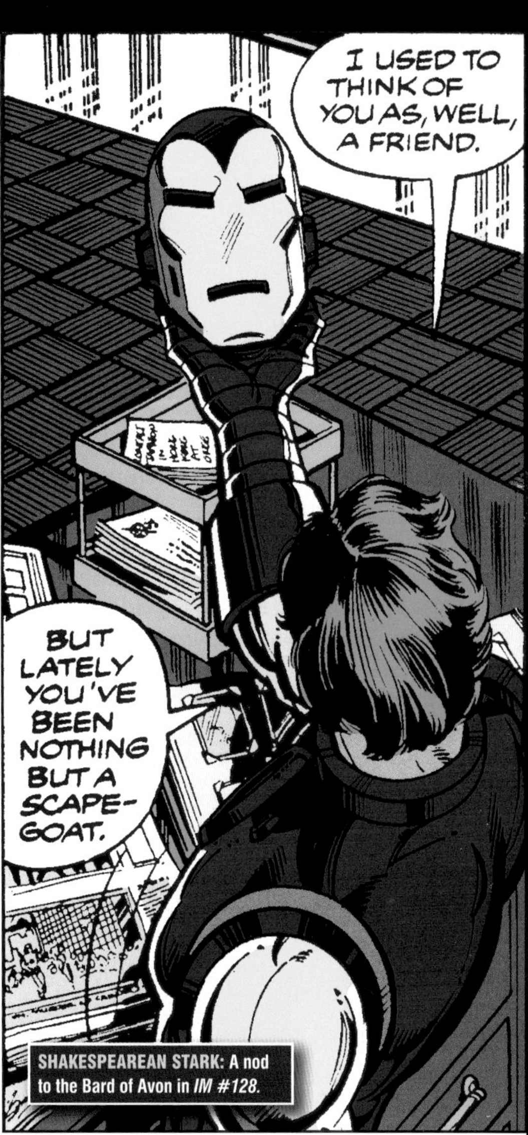
I USED TO THINK OF YOU AS, WELL, A FRIEND.
BUT LATELY YOU'VE BEEN NOTHING BUT A SCAPE-GOAT.
SHAKESPEAREAN STARK: A nod to the Bard of Avon in *IM #128.*

SPOTLIGHT: One of the things we learn about Tony is that he's a Poco fan. Songs from their then new album, *Legend*, in particular. OK, fess up, which one of you guys was the Poco fan?

DAVID: Ya got me. I've always liked folk-rock and country-rock, and when Walt Simonson introduced me to Poco (and Pure Prairie League) back in the '80s I was hooked. And, like a fondness for Dr. Pepper and Zagnut bars, personal preferences tend to crop up in the characters one writes.

SPOTLIGHT: What do you think of the way some of the novel concepts you and David came up with in the comics showing up in the Iron Man films?

BOB: As far as I'm concerned, as long as they make good movies, they are free to use any plot threads that we created in the *Iron Man* series with my blessing. More than anything, I want to see the spirit of my favorite character up there on the silver screen and done properly.

SPOTLIGHT: Can you describe what it was like working with John Romita Jr. at the time? He was really young, but not merely a chip off the old block, either. What did you think about his style then, his demeanor as a new kid on the scene, and also about how he developed over the years?

BOB: Every penciler presents different challenges to an inker. The good news is that we were all young at the time and we've all since progressed way beyond the aesthetic problems. John Romita Jr. has been one of my all-time favorite people to ink when I reflect back over my career. He and I were learning our craft during those early days on *Iron Man* and I think you can see the progression and confidence improve from issue to issue. JRJR did breakdowns for me and left the finished look generally to my discretion. Johnny was one of the strongest natural storytellers that I've ever worked with and we rarely had to do anything to alter his work. I am troubled that JRJR and I lost touch over the years. I'm still a huge fan of JR's work and I think he's one of the all-time greats. Johnny has certainly done well for himself.

SPOTLIGHT: Way back in the day, the classic "Demon In A Bottle" storyline was one of the very first Marvel collected editions, back before they were omnipresent on the market. How did you feel then when your story entered the canon of Marvel classics and how does it feel now to see it represented in Marvel's Premiere Edition Classic hardcover line?

IN MODERN TIMES, ADDICTION WITHDRAWAL HAS COME TO BE THOUGHT OF IN ANIMAL TERMS: "MONKEY ON MY BACK," "COLD TURKEY," ETC. AND BETHANY CABE SOON LEARNS WHY, AS SHE LISTENS TO A MATURE, SOPHISTICATED PLAYBOY'S DOGLIKE WHIMPERS, HIS PLEAS FOR "JUST ONE DRINK"-- AND THEN SUFFERS HIS FERAL ANGER AND ABUSE WHEN SHE REFUSES.
FOR DAYS, THE STALEMATE RAGES--
--UNTIL AT LONG, LONG LAST, EMOTIONAL BLOCKS BEGIN TO CRACK, THEN CRUMBLE--

DESCENT INTO MADNESS: Iron Man fights back as his worst enemy takes hold. (Art from *IM #128.*)

DAVID: Of course, it's flattering to have one's work reissued in any form. That means the company expects to make money on it because they expect it to sell a lot of copies because people like it, which must mean we did something right. Smiles all around. And since I became a diehard Marvel fan back in the 1960s, knowing that some of the stories I've written have been accepted as an enduring part of the Marvel Universe is very gratifying indeed. And having those stories collected into a hardback edition is just icing on the cake.

SPOTLIGHT: Before we wrap up, the two of you recently reunited for *Iron Man: Legacy of Doom*. Can you give us a sneak preview about what that will entail?

DAVID: *Legacy of Doom* is a four-issue miniseries that wraps up what we call "The Camelot Trilogy." It's a saga pitting Iron Man against Dr. Doom in a struggle that began in *Iron Man #149-150* (in the old numbering), and was followed-up in issues #249-250 (all reprinted in the *Iron Man: Doomquest* trade editions). The new miniseries concludes that conflict, but is a totally accessible stand-alone story if people haven't read the previous tales. It basically features Dr. Doom recruiting Iron Man to thwart Mephisto's plan to bring about the End Of Days – essentially the end to all life on Earth. But there are secret agendas and private machinations going on behind the scenes, and each issue features twists that (hopefully) the reader won't see coming.

Well, hopefully by now you've seen that nifty little sidebar showcasing all of the Michelinie/Layton Iron Man comics in print – including DOOMQUEST, LEGACY OF DOOM and (what else?) DEMON IN A BOTTLE! Available at all of the finer comic shops and bookstores around the corner or on the internet!

STABILIZING GYROS SEEM TO BE WORKING FINE NOW.
FRIK FRIK FRIK FRIK
NO PROBLEM WITH MY MUSCLE AM-PLIFICATION CIRCUITS, EITHER!
FRIK
FRIK
PERFECT! THE SUCTION DISCS IN MY BOOTS AND GLOVES WOULD DO EVEN A CERTAIN WALL-CRAWLER PROUD!
KRAKARRUNK
I'LL SET THE FLEXICOIL FOR TWO TONS AND TRY IT AGAIN!
SHRRAAKK
AND THIS JET-SKATE/REPULSOR COMBO IS STILL MY BEST ONE-TWO ACE IN THE HOLE!

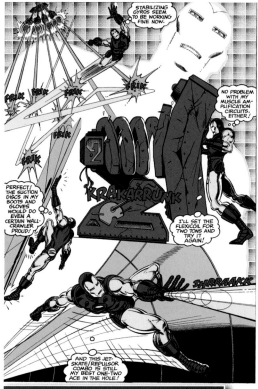

LAYTON UNLEASHED: Nobody knows better than Bob Layton how to run Iron Man's armor through its paces. In collaboration with artist JRJR, this fun splash page sequence charts an Iron Man training session. (Art from *IM #123.*)

IRON MAN CLASSICS IN COLLECTED EDITIONS: MICHELINIE AND LAYTON

It started with "Demon in a Bottle" but it did not end there! Iron Man legends David Michelinie and Bob Layton's tenure on *Iron Man* is second to none, and well-represented in several fine trade paperbacks and hardcovers. Take your pick!

IRON MAN
DEMON IN A BOTTLE

1. Iron Man: Demon in a Bottle HC/TP
Collects *Iron Man #120-128*
By David Michelinie, Bob Layton and John Romita Jr.
All-time classic tale by all- time classic team!

THE INVINCIBLE
IRON MAN

2. Iron Man: The Many Armors of Iron Man TP
Collects *Iron Man #47, 142-144, 152-153, 200 and 218*
By David Michelinie, Bob Layton, John Romita Jr., Barry Windsor-Smith and more!
Every armor tells a story!

3. Iron Man: Armor Wars Prologue TP
Collects *Iron Man #215-224*
By David Michelinie, Bob Layton, and Mark Bright
Setting the stage for fan-favorite Armor Wars!

IRON MAN
ARMOR WARS

4. Iron Man: Armor Wars HC
Collects *Iron Man #225-232*
By David Michelinie, Bob Layton, Mark Bright and Barry Windsor-Smith
Gripping drama and high adve nture make for an Iron Man classic!

IRON MAN
DOOMQUEST
MICHELINIE·LAYTON·ROMITA JR

5. Iron Man: Doomquest HC
Collects *Iron Man #149-150 and 249-250*
By David Michelinie, Bob Layton and John Romita Jr.
Part 1 and 2 of the Camelot Trilogy!

6. Iron Man: Legacy of Doom HC/TP
Collects *Iron Man: Legacy of Doom #1-4*
By David Michelinie, Bob Layton and Ron Lim
The Camelot Trilogy is completed by its original storytellers!

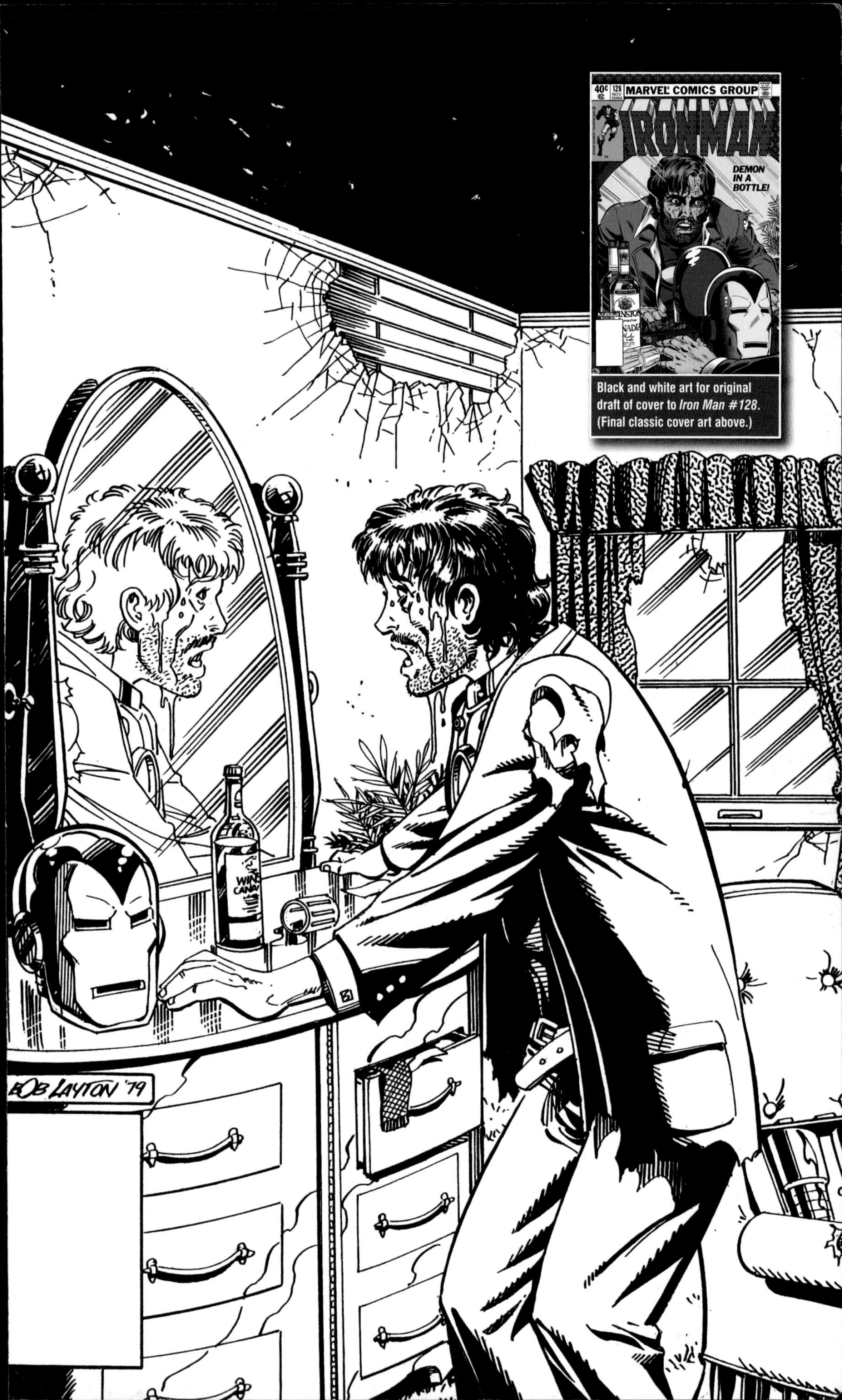
40¢
128
NOV
02464
MARVEL COMICS GROUP
IRON MAN
DEMON IN A BOTTLE!
BOB LAYTON '79

Black and white art for original draft of cover to *Iron Man #128*. (Final classic cover art above.)

ARMOR W

Warren Ellis Looks To The Ultimate Future Of Iron Man

By Chris Arrant

Technology. It's all around us. From the super-powered devices in most of our pockets and purses to even this magazine you hold in your hands. You may not know it, but this *Marvel Spotlight* was written, designed, edited and printed by people spread out all over the world – working hand-in-hand with only a computer and some phones tying them together.

No comics character has taken more to this high-tech modern age than Iron Man. Originally created in 1963 by a powerhouse quartet of Stan Lee, Larry Lieber, Don Heck and Jack Kirby, a character that what was once conceived as a Cold War-era weapons manufacturer has transitioned today into a tech-geek with a playboy vibe, a hero with a devil-may-care attitude but with the skills to back it up. Considered one of the key heroes in Marvel's character library, Iron Man broke out to the mainstream public with the 2008 film *Iron Man*.

In recent years, famed comics writer Warren Ellis has written stories about Tony Stark on several occasions. His first stint was on the "*Extremis*" arc of the *Iron Man* title, which realigned Stark and his tech toys in a modern – and even near-future – setting. Ellis' take on the Armored Avenger was well received by fans as well as movie folk, as elements from that story arc appeared in the 2008 *Iron Man* film. In Marvel's Ultimate line of books, Ellis has taken on Shellhead on three occasions – in a supporting role in the *Ultimate Galactus Trilogy* and as central figure in *Ultimate Hulk vs. Iron Man* and the recent *Ultimate Comics Armor Wars* miniseries. In the latter, Ellis took one of the integral story arcs from Tony Stark's rich history and brought it up to speed – technologically and creatively – with the modern times of the Ultimate Universe.

We spoke to Ellis about his work on that miniseries, as well as the broader aspects of Tony Stark and Iron Man that Ellis has developed over the years.

SPOTLIGHT: It's good to talk to you again, Warren. You've had the opportunity to write Iron Man on several occasions, the next being the upcoming *Iron Man* anime. With such a diverse array of titles you've undoubtedly exposed many different facets in Iron Man; but between them all, what would you say are the core tenets of Tony Stark?

WARREN: Well, I'm working with three different iterations of Tony Stark there. The Tony Stark of "Extremis" is sober (or, at very least, a dry drunk), haunted and driven. The Tony Stark of the Ultimate comics is an apparent extrovert who's trying to fit in as much as possible before a tumor in his head kills him *and* self-medicates with alcohol against chronic pain. The Tony Stark of the *Iron Man*

Marvel anime throws himself into any situation assuming he can think a technological way out of it. I suspect the only tenet they share is the drive: that the key to a better future is a technological one, that he can take the weight of the world and get it done, and that it needs to be done fast.

SPOTLIGHT: And you're one to know about drive, Warren, with all the various projects you have going on – not just at Marvel. [*Like how about a revival of* Fell *at Image and his WildStorm miniseries* Red *being adapted into a feature film starring Bruce Willis? – Ed.*] In your writings about Iron Man, you've done a lot about bringing the bells and whistles of the Iron Man technology up-to-date and even into the near future. How do you bring it all together – this

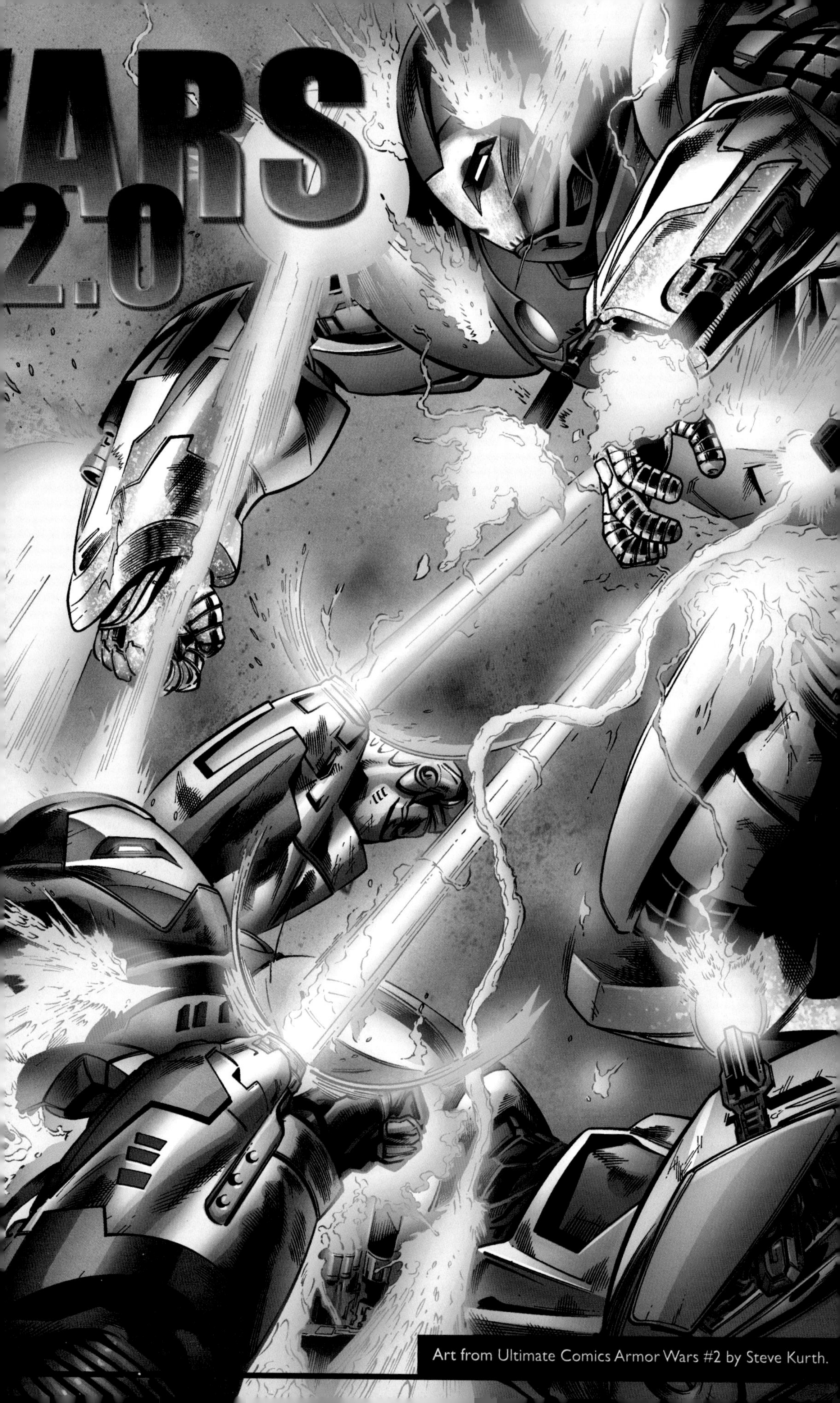

ARS
2.0

Art from Ultimate Comics Armor Wars #2 by Steve Kurth.

THE FUTURE SUITS HIM: Warren Ellis fits Ultimate Tony Stark with the latest in Iron Man armor chic. (Art from *UCAW* #2.)

WHAT IS IT?
iMAN. STEVE JOBS HASN'T COPYRIGHTED THAT ONE YET.
A LIGHT, FAIRLY LIMITED ENHANCEMENT KIT.
ELECTRICALLY-ACTIVATED NANO-STRUCTURED POLYMERIC-GEL EXOMUSCLES.
BUCKYTUBE SHEETING. WEIGHTLESS, FLEXIBLE, TWO ORDERS OF MAGNITUDE STRONGER THAN STEEL, ABLE TO SOAK UP ABOUT A HUNDRED GIGAPASCALS OF PRESSURE.

technology such as Extremis doesn't exist, but the way you describe it, it sounds like it could. How do you go about compiling this research and making these ideas seem realistic while not becoming too dense for a casual person to read?

WARREN: I dunno if there's a special trick to it. It's probably tools from journalism: how to get a handle on any notional object in the fewest words and the clearest way. With something like Extremis... obviously, it doesn't exist, and is highly unlikely to ever exist. But many of the pieces of it do. And, sometimes, if I can convince you of the details of the trees, maybe I can fool you into not seeing the forest.

> "...there are worse ways to spend four months than listening to Tony Stark be crazy."
> – **Writer Warren Ellis**, on electing to write *Ultimate Comics Armor Wars.*

As far as compiling the research goes, it's just a question of tuning your information-gathering devices. I have the headlines from several sci/tech news services piped directly on to my desktop and phone screens all day. I eat a lot of data. (It goes straight to my thighs, you know.)

SPOTLIGHT: We see a lot of that tech news show up on your website [Visit www.WarrenEllis.com – Ed], but I don't know about the thighs part. (*Laughter.*) Your interest in technology – I remember you talking once in an interview about one of your earliest memories: watching an Apollo space launch. What do you think pushed you into your sci-fi leanings?

WARREN: Probably the fact that the first comic I ever saw was an issue of a sci-fi comic called *Countdown* that my dad brought home for me one night. He liked to tell people I caught the SF bug off him. I think it was more of a deliberate infection, like making me wear a smallpox-ridden blanket.

SPOTLIGHT: However you caught the bug, it's become part of you; your writing in comics has put you up as one of the leading writers on futurology, which seems to dovetail straight into the concept of Iron Man. Iron Man was originally little more than a weapons manufacturer who built his own tank armor – how do you see that concept developing into what is has become today?

WARREN: I don't think I'm any kind of leading writer on futurology. I'm pretty sure I was hired by *Wired UK* solely for my excellence in swearing.

SPOTLIGHT: (*Laughter.*)

WARREN: You're missing something important about the original Iron Man: transistors. Read that old stuff, and it's all about miniature transistors. Transistors were the microchip of their day. Old Stan was invoking the future by imagining a powered exo-skeletal shell with transistor relays. And building the original out of spare parts and his own munitions? Pure William Gibson. I honestly don't think the concept's moved: It's about a mechanical genius under pressure constructing a networked exoshell out of scrap and his own poisoned legacy.

Only the details change.

SPOTLIGHT: You've got me there. Let's talk about your recently finished Iron Man miniseries, *Ultimate Comics Armor Wars*. First of all, what made this a story you wanted to do?

WARREN: I think I was offered money?

SPOTLIGHT: And good money at that, I hope.

WARREN: Joe (Quesada, Marvel Editor-In-Chief) just called me up and said they needed an Ultimate Iron Man book for a 2010 collection and could I help them out. And, honestly, Ultimate Tony Stark (heh) is such a fun character to write that I agreed right away – there are worse ways to spend four months than listening to Tony Stark be crazy. Of course, then I had to cast around for the plot. The Ultimate line is all about retelling/reinventing old Marvel comics in manners accessible to a new audience, and "*Armor Wars*" is a very well remembered *Iron Man* arc. It wasn't hard to settle. And it let me both put a new kind of window on the Ultimate world, and have a bit of fun with showing how other people would purpose that kind of technology.

SPOTLIGHT: Playing right alongside Tony in this miniseries is a new character, Justine Hammer. Iron Man fans tingle at that last name, as Justin Hammer is one of Iron Man's most classic foes. The idea of bringing in a progeny of Justin Hammer – and having her on the same side as Iron Man, is a new

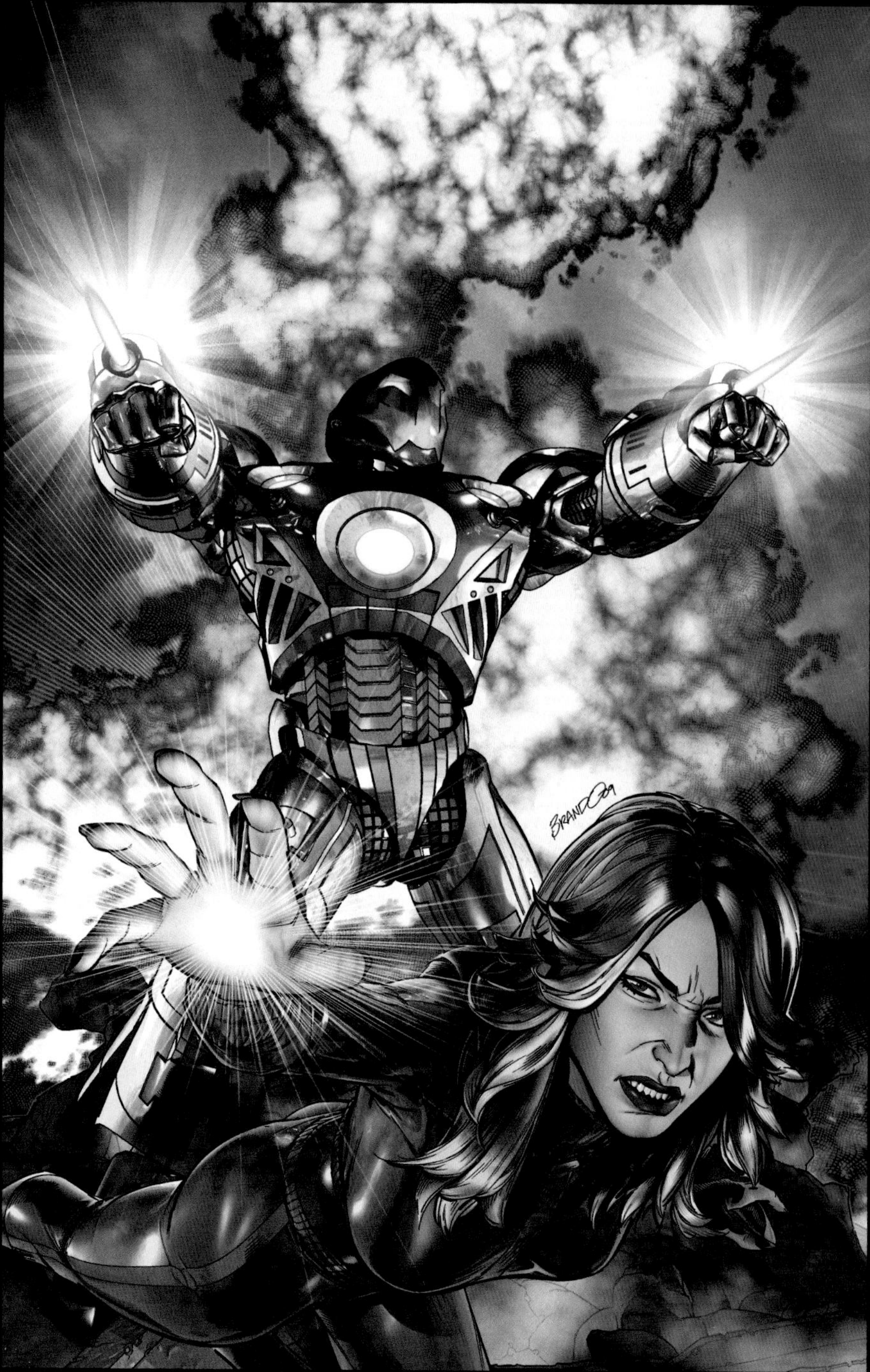

LAYING DOWN THE HAMMER: Stark and his unexpected fellow Armor warrior, Justine Hammer. (Cover to *UCAW* #2.)

EXTREMIS: Warren Ellis and Adi Granov's milestone Extremis arc will hit stands in oversized hardcover in May. (Art from Iron Man #6 by Adi Granov.)

When you're in the bookstore looking at Iron Man collected editions, one of the guys you want to look for on the spine is Warren Ellis! ULTIMATE COMICS ARMOR WARS, in collaboration with artist Steve Kurth, is just now finishing up its four-issue run so look for a trade paperback collection in May!

one – was it something you worked up or inspired by a talk with Marvel editors?

WARREN: No, that was me. Without giving anything away for those who haven't read it yet: Tony needed a foil, a guide to the underworld of the Ultimate milieu, and a look at how other people in Tony's tax bracket have been dealing with the new opportunities of a world with these kinds of high technology in it.

Also, James Bond needs a James Bond girl.

SPOTLIGHT: I like that analogy – but before I let you go, let's spin it to the real world. What would you say the closest real-world comparison to Tony Stark and his company? Bill Gates on a case of Red Bull?

WARREN: There's no one even close to Tony Stark's league. Maybe Elon Musk counts, since he did finance and launch his own space rocket?

I would, however, draw your attention to, if you haven't heard of him, Doctor Steven Mann out of the University of Toronto. He's one of the pioneers of wearable computing: constantly wearing a rig of computers, cams and sensors, with data flowing in and out of him every second. I mean, to the point where, when in 2002 he was forcibly stripped of his gear by airport security, he couldn't function properly as a human anymore and ended up having to board the plane in a wheelchair. That's the guy you want to look at. •

IRON MAN BY ELLIS

Enjoy the sublime combination of Warren Ellis, Tony Stark and Marvel Futurism in these Iron Man collected edition

Iron Man: Extremis HC/TPB
Collects *Iron Man (2005) #1-6*
By Warren Ellis and Adi Granov
The contemporary classic that inspired Iron Man moviemakers! Look for a new, oversized hardcover edition in April!

Ultimate Galactus Trilog TP
Collects *Ultimate Nightmare #1-5, Ultimate Secret #1-4, Ultimate Extinction #1-5* and more!
By Warren Ellis, Steve McNiven Brandon Peterson, Trevor Hairs and more
The ominous Gah Lak Tus has come to Earth — but for wha purpose?

Ultimate Human HC/TP
Collects *Ultimate Human #1-4*
By Warren Ellis and Cary Nord

Iron Man vs. Hulk in a primal battle between technology and monstrosity!

THE ARMORED AVENGER

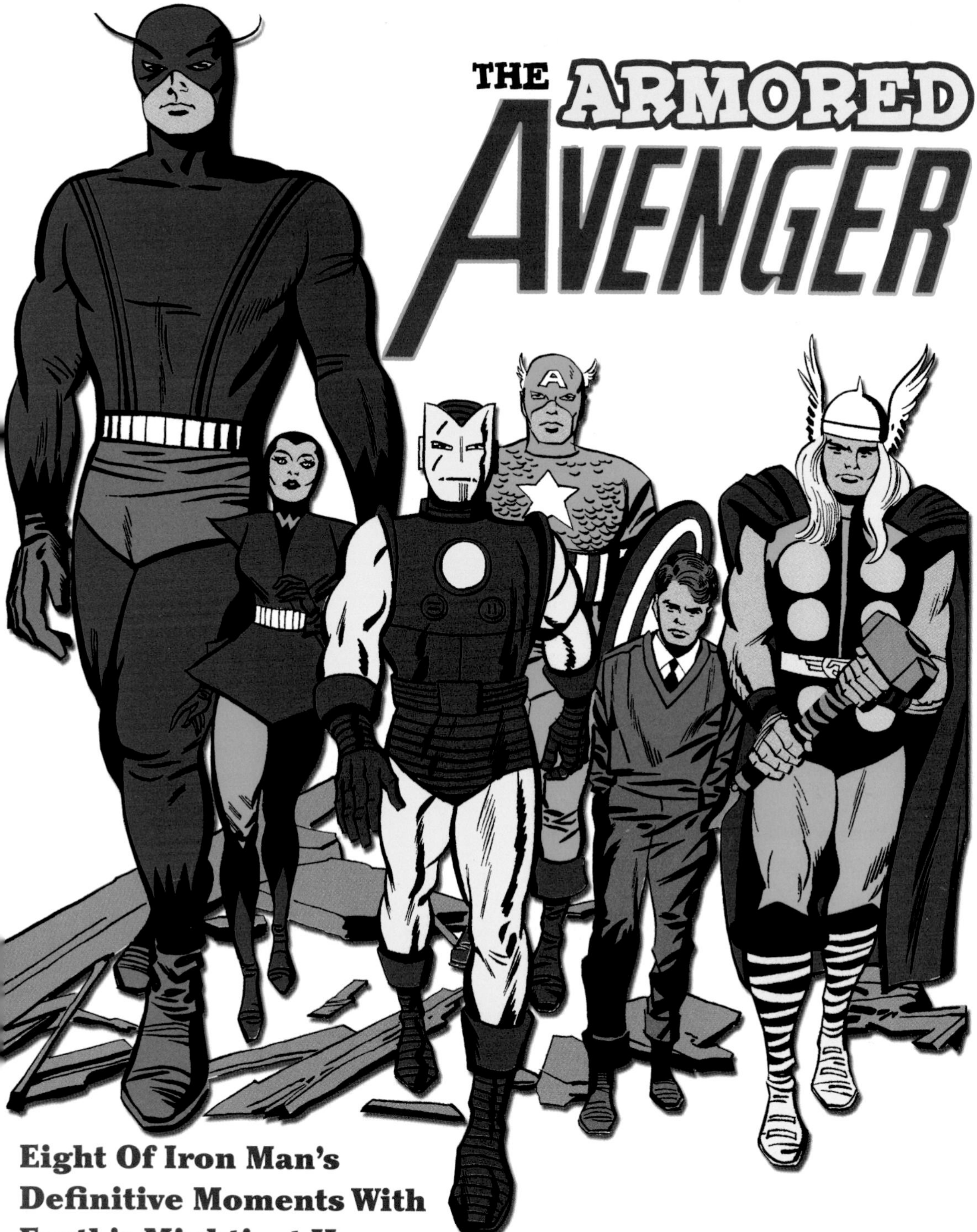

Eight Of Iron Man's Definitive Moments With Earth's Mightiest Heroes

By Dugan Trodglen

Iron Man is one of the three characters – along with Captain America and Thor – most associated with the Avengers. They are called the "Big Three" with good reason. You might say Cap is the heart and Thor the soul of the team. In any case, Iron Man is definitely the brain. His money has helped support the team and his intellect has held the team together during many seemingly impossible challenges. He has served as team leader on several occasions and was around from the very beginning (three different beginnings, actually: the original team, the "New Avengers" and the "Mighty Avengers"). While loaded with raw power as Iron Man, it is usually his big Tony Stark brain that has provided his definitive moments with the team. Let's take a look at some of them.

AVENGERS, INC.

***Avengers: Earth's Mightiest Heroes* #1-8**

Reprinted in *Avengers: Earth's Mightiest Heroes HC*

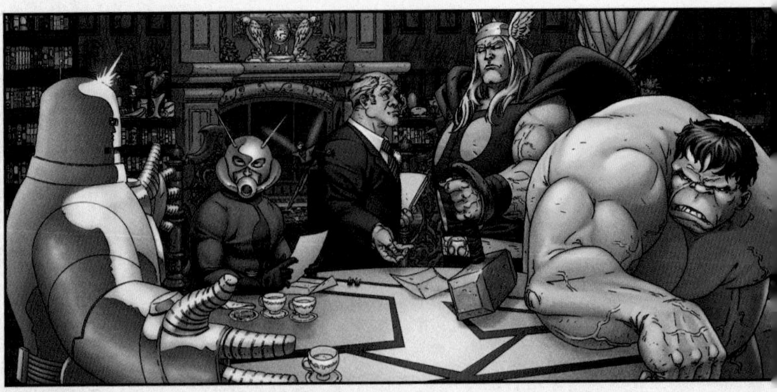

Earth's Mightiest Heroes art by Scott Kolins.

"And there came a day, a day unlike any other, when Earth's Mightiest Heroes found themselves united against a common threat. On that day the Avengers were born." So goes the famous Avengers prologue. But it really wasn't that simple, as this limited series from 2004 illustrates. The series, by Joe Casey and Scott Kolins, gives us a behind-the-scenes look at the Avengers' formative months and shows how precarious this gathering of heroes was, and how it was the sheer will (and corporate know-how) of Tony Stark that held the group together during its infancy.

From drawing up the team's charter to negotiating A1 Priority Clearance with the National Security Council to adapting PR strategies surrounding the departure of the Hulk and arrival of Captain America, Tony Stark shines thanks to his executive experience running a major corporation, particularly one that has had prior dealings with the Department of Defense. In particular, Stark knew how to play hardball when it came to the government's need for an alliance with the Avengers and vice versa. When offered full A1 Priority Clearance in exchange for working for the Pentagon, Stark turned them down flat, only to gain clearance later after the Avengers defeat of Kang showed how valuable to national security this team was. *Earth's Mightiest Heroes* is especially interesting in light of everything that has happened with the Avengers' status post-Civil War.

ON THE OTHER HAND

What If?...#3

Reprinted in *What If? Classic Vol. 1 TP*

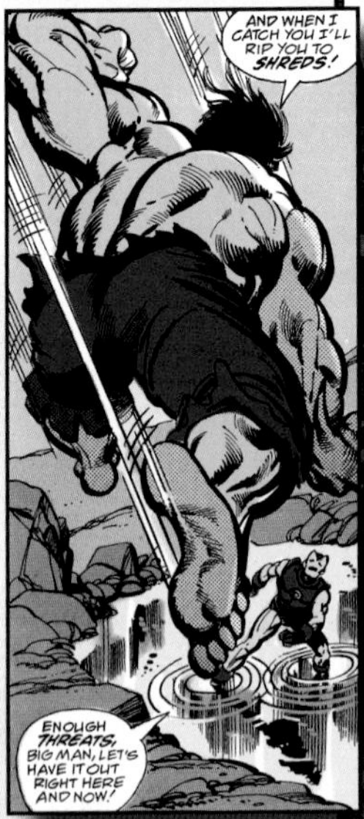
AND WHEN I CATCH YOU I'LL RIP YOU TO SHREDS!
ENOUGH THREATS, BIG MAN, LET'S HAVE IT OUT RIGHT HERE AND NOW!

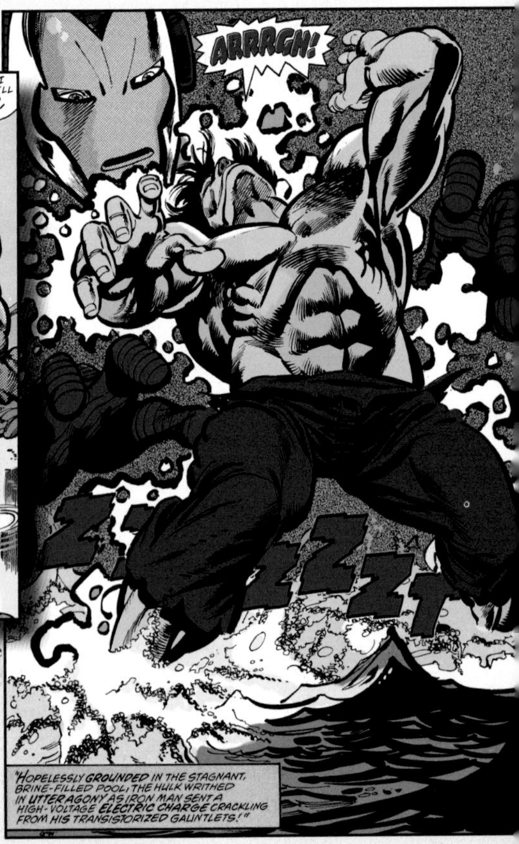
ARRRGH!
"HOPELESSLY GROUNDED IN THE STAGNANT, BRINE-FILLED POOL, THE HULK WRITHED IN UTTER AGONY AS IRON MAN SENT A HIGH-VOLTAGE ELECTRIC CHARGE CRACKLING FROM HIS TRANSISTORIZED GAUNTLETS!"

***What If? #3* art by Gil Kane and Klaus Janson.**

Okay, so this one didn't *really* happen, but as a flipside to the previous entry it's fascinating, and Tony Stark's heroism shines in this Jim Shooter/ Gil Kane classic, alternate reality or no. The key question presented in this comics classic was, "What if the Avengers had never been?" In this take on the Avengers' early days, the characters' fragile egos drove the team apart almost instantly, Stark's will is not enough to hold the team together. The problem was, there was still an active threat no single hero could withstand: the rampaging Hulk, now allied with Namor the Sub-Mariner (as seen originally in *Avengers #3*). Desperate to handle this threat, Stark recruits Rick Jones and a retired Giant-Man and Wasp to don specially designed armor to go after the two titans. Things don't work out and Iron Man is forced to handle it on his own. After overloading his armor, and a last-minute save from his fellow armored Avengers (eventually Hulk and Namor turn on each other), Tony Stark dies a hero, his heart giving out from the strain of his overloaded armor.

FATHER'S LEGACY

engers Annual #9

engers Annual #9 was one of those great
ne-in-one annuals the '70s produced, pitting
e Avengers against the terrifyingly powerful
nd mysterious) android named Arsenal.
rough the course of the issue we uncover
senal's backstory: a WWII–era doomsday
apon the Allies had developed. Arsenal and its
ntient control unit codenamed Mistress were
epers, to be awakened only in the event of
Nazi victory. Well, as it turned out they were
cidentally awakened (in *Iron Man #114*) and
sumed it was time to carry out the mission.
eir bunker was in a cavern well below
engers Mansion; as a result, the first people
encounter Arsenal were the Avengers, whom Arsenal
lieved to be the enemy.

AND, AS THE GOD OF THUNDER DIVES INTO THE DARKNESS AFTER HIS FALLEN COMRADE...
THAT THE CAPTAIN AMERICA OF THIS AGE SHOULD SERVE THE AXIS POWERS! THE MASTER WOULD BE APPALLED!
LORD! MY FATHER'S ROBOT IS STILL FIGHTING WORLD WAR TWO! HOWARD STARK'S CREATION MAY JUST SLAY HIS SON AND THE REST OF THE AVENGERS AS WELL!
I HOPE I DID THE RIGHT THING IN SENDING THOR AFTER WONDER MAN. IF NOT, I MAY HAVE--

***Avengers Annual #9* art by Don Newton and Joe Rubinstein.**

ny was the bunker below Avengers Mansion? In a
illing moment, we discover that it was none other
an Howard Stark – Tony's father – that was director
the Arsenal project. To make matters worse for Iron
an, his mother Maria Stark's brain patterns were the
basis for Mistress' sentience. When Tony went down to confront Mistress, he found himself in the position of not only telling Mistress that the Allies won the war and the Avengers were not an enemy, but that Maria's husband – not to mention Maria herself – were dead. Mistress self-destructed (ending the threat of Arsenal) as an emotionally stunned Iron Man walked away unable to bear the death of his mother a second time, virtual or not.

I KNOW THIS SEEMS A BIT SILLY, BUT ON THE SPUR OF THE MOMENT--!
NO NEED FOR APOLOGIES, IRON MAN. YOUR DECISION WAS TACTICALLY SOUND.
SURE. LIKE HOW MANY TIMES HAVE WE GONE OUT TO SAVE THE WORLD-- COURTESY OF THE M.T.A.?
ER, ANYBODY GOT A SPARE TOKEN...
EXCUSE ME, SIR? SIR?
HUH? WH-WHAT IS THIS?
WE HAVE AN EMERGENCY SITUATION, DRIVER, AND I'M AFRAID I HAVE TO COMMANDEER THIS BUS! NOW, IF YOU'LL JUST HAVE YOUR PASSENGERS GET OFF...?
LOOK, PAL YOU GOT YOUR JOB-- AN' I GOT MINE! MAYBE I CAN GET YOU AN' YOUR BUDDIES A GROUP RATE, BUT--
I SAID NOW, MISTER!

***engers #176* art by David Wenzel and Pablo Marcos.**

A LEADER TESTED

Avengers #168-191

Reprinted in *Avengers: Korvac Saga HC and Avengers: Nights of Wundagore TP*

The Avengers' dealings with the government were again a factor during the late-'70s run by writers Jim Shooter and David Michelinie. It all started in *Avengers #168* when the team first encountered Henry Peter Gyrich of the National Security Council, peaked in issue #181, when Gyrich seized control of the team's membership, and culminated in the restoration of A1 Priority status in issue #191. Throughout, Iron Man was Avengers chairman and chiefly responsible for dealing with Gyrich. This led to several moments for Iron Man to shine in his attempts to balance the need of the team to remain as autonomous as possible while still working with the approval of the U.S. government.

Tensions were very high at this time and Iron Man's leadership was constantly put to the test, with none other than Captain America calling Iron Man out (even taking a punch at him in issue #168). Another (humiliating) low point: a revoked Priority status forced the Avengers to take the bus to confront Korvac.

PULLING RANK

Avengers #347

Reprinted in *Avengers: Galactic Storm Vol. 1-2 TP*

The sprawling "Operation: Galactic Storm" epic took a lot out of Iron Man. Tough battles with Shatterax and Ronan the Accuser had taken their toll on his armor, his power was all but tapped out, and he was reflexively taking his frustration out on Hawkeye. So when the opportunity arose to put an end to the battle between the Kree and the Shi'Ar by killing the Supreme Intelligence, Iron Man was in no mood for debate. While Captain America was appealing to the Avengers to avoid killing, Iron Man interrupted and announced that as the only original Avenger present, it was his call to make. He, the Black Knight, and other agreeable Avengers then went and did the deed they thought needed doing. When they returned from their deadly mission, Iron Man, with nothing left in the tank physically or emotionally, brushed Cap and his concerns aside.

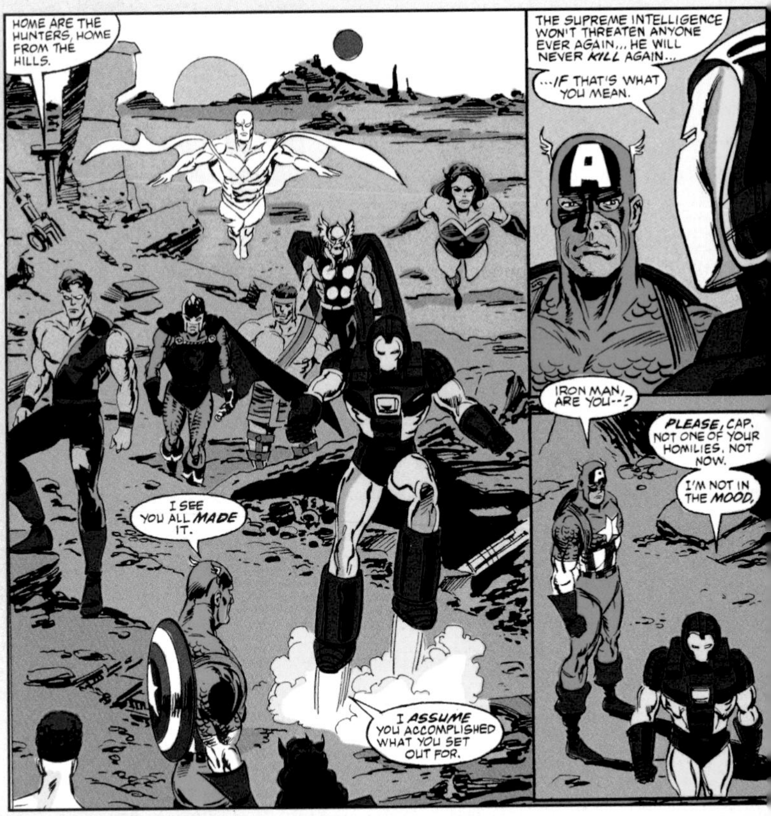

HOME ARE THE HUNTERS, HOME FROM THE HILLS.
I SEE YOU ALL MADE IT.
I ASSUME YOU ACCOMPLISHED WHAT YOU SET OUT FOR.
THE SUPREME INTELLIGENCE WON'T THREATEN ANYONE EVER AGAIN... HE WILL NEVER KILL AGAIN...
...IF THAT'S WHAT YOU MEAN.
IRON MAN, ARE YOU--?
PLEASE, CAP. NOT ONE OF YOUR HOMILIES. NOT NOW.
I'M NOT IN THE MOOD.

***Avengers #347* art by Steve Epting and Tom Palmer.**

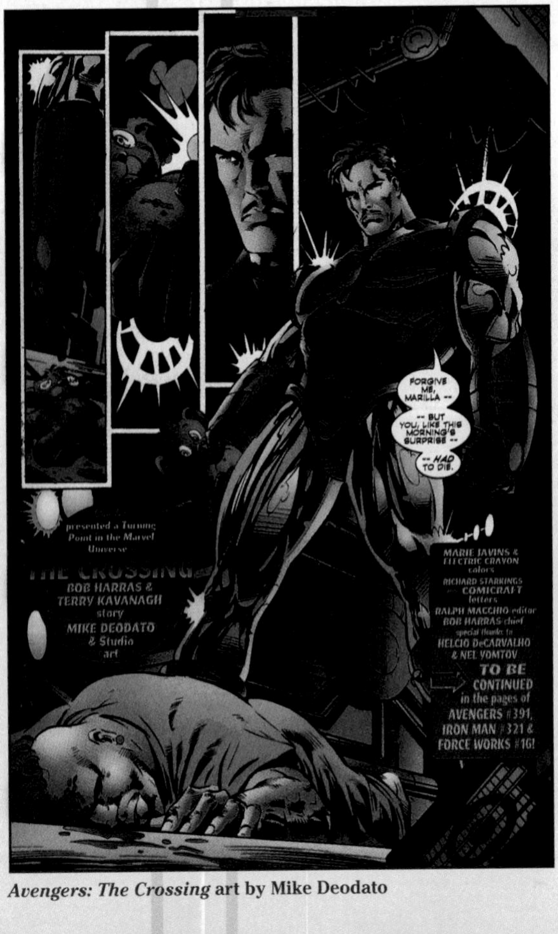

FORGIVE ME, MARILLA --
-- BUT YOU, LIKE THIS MORNING'S SURPRISE --
-- HAD TO DIE.
presented a Turning Point in the Marvel Universe
BOB HARRAS & TERRY KAVANAGH story
MIKE DEODATO & Studio art
MARIE JAVINS & ELECTRIC CRAYON colors
RICHARD STARKINGS COMICRAFT letters
RALPH MACCHIO editor
BOB HARRAS chief
special thanks to HELCIO DeCARVALHO & NEL YOMTOV
TO BE CONTINUED in the pages of AVENGERS #391, IRON MAN #321 & FORCE WORKS #16!

***Avengers: The Crossing* art by Mike Deodato**

BY IRON MAN BETRAYED!

Avengers: The Crossing* one-shot, *Avengers #390-395* and more in *The Crossing crossover saga

Okay, maybe not Iron Man's best moment as an Avenger. Okay, maybe his worst. But, it certainly qualifies as a significant turn of events. This story revealed Tony Stark to be a sleeper agent on behalf of Kang (for years!), culminating in a plot to destroy the Avengers put in motion by Mantis (or was it the Space Phantom?). Iron Man killed Yellowjacket II and framed Hawkeye for it, then ruined Janet Van Dyne's fortune. The Avengers took the unorthodox approach of traveling back in time to find a young Tony Stark to deal with their out of control Iron Man, one reason being that Iron Man's armor was tied to Tony Stark's DNA. The older Stark ended up dying and for a while it was "Teen Tony" who wore the armor (This was all more of less "fixed" when the "Heroes Return" event brought the classic Avengers, including the "real" Tony, back to the Marvel Universe.)

'HE BIG THREE AT EVEN
3IGGER ODDS!

***ɔengers (1998) #62-64, Thor (1998) #58* and**
ɔn Man (1998) #64

ːprinted in *Avengers: Standoff HC*

ɒn Man. Captain America. Thor. These three
ıaracters will always be at the core of the Avengers
eal...but that doesn't mean they always get along. In
tandoff," the goings-on in their individual titles led
an Avengers-size conflict. A mortal sect of Thor
ɔrshippers were being slain by the government of
ɔkovia, inspiring Thor to launch a rescue mission
th his fellow Asgardians; a clear provocation with
ıternational incident" written all over it. Enter
ɒn Man, the newly minted Secretary of Defense of
e United States. Iron Man wants Thor to back off
ıd let the U.N. handle the situation but Thor will
ıve none of it. Iron Man, with the help of Dr. Doom,
ɒns a "Thor-Buster" armor and the two allies go at
much to the dismay of a Captain America caught
tween loyalties to his two friends. Eventually,
ıor relents and quits the Avengers. An excellent
ɔk at the dynamic between these characters,
e Big Three have never been the same since
tandoff."

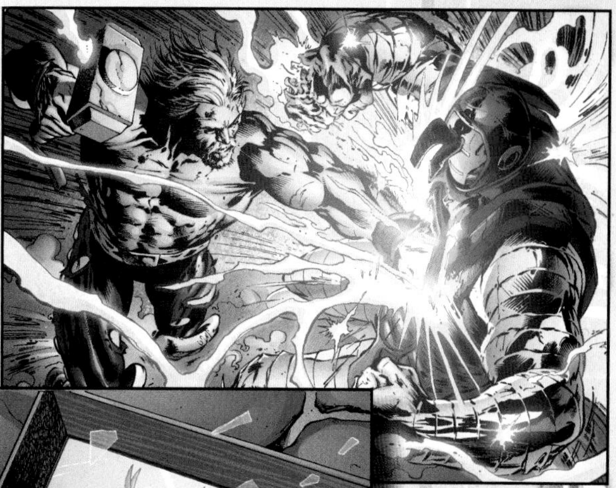

Avengers #63 **art by Alan Davis**

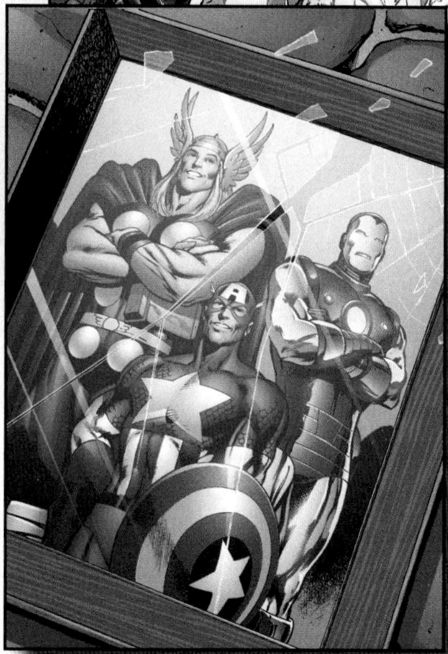

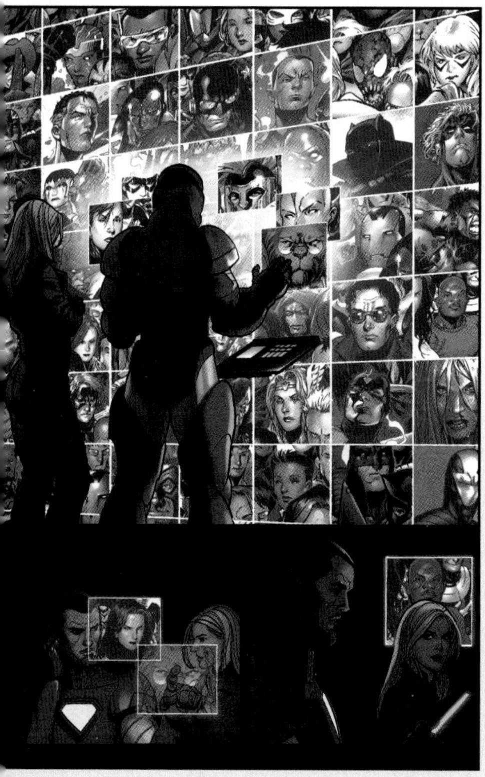

***ghty Avengers* art by Frank Cho**

MIGHTY AVENGERS ASSEMBLE!

Mighty Avengers #1

Reprinted in *Mighty Avengers Vol. 1 HC*

Iron Man may have "won" the super hero Civil War and he may have been made head of S.H.I.E.L.D. and thus the de facto leader of the entire super hero community, but that doesn't mean everything was coming up roses for ol' Shellhead. He lost his good friend Captain America to an assassin's bullet, and his beloved Avengers were no more. One of the first items on his agenda had to be rebuilding the super team. This time he had a chance to remake the Avengers from scratch. No chance gathering of heroes; instead, the brilliant engineer could, with a clear sense of purpose, construct his greatest weapon yet. First step: he wisely decided that due to his other responsibilities he is not the best choice for leader. Instead that role went to Carol Danvers, Ms. Marvel. Together they assembld a truly "mighty" team consisting of the Wasp, Black Widow, Wonder Man, and the powerhouse of powerhouses, Sentry.

But something was missing. Iron Man liked having Wolverine around in the "New Avengers." He was someone who could do the dirty work the more traditionally heroic Avengers couldn't. Ms. Marvel knew just the person, and this guy could even fill the "god" role on the team! Enter: Ares, an instant classic Avenger. Iron Man (in the hands of Brian Michael Bendis and Frank Cho) had put together a brilliant team, ready to take on all comers. Or so it seemed. If only the Skrulls hadn't shown up... •

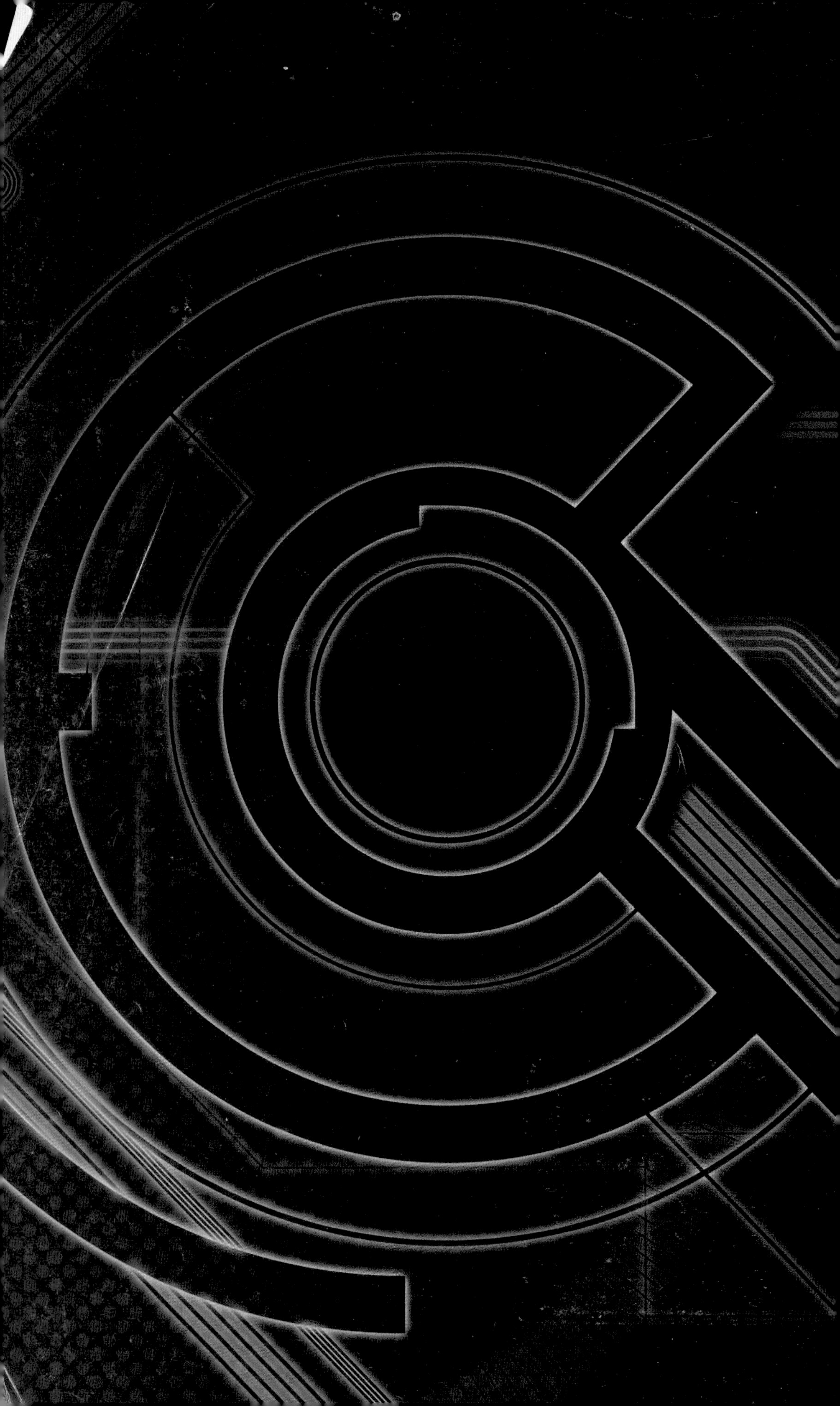